New Perspectives
on Ben Jonson

New Perspectives on Ben Jonson

Edited by
James Hirsh

Madison ● Teaneck
Fairleigh Dickinson University Press
London: Associated University Presses

Associated University Presses
440 Forsgate Drive
Cranbury, NJ 08512

Associated University Presses
16 Barter Street
London WC1A 2AH, England

Associated University Presses
P.O. Box 338, Port Credit
Mississauga, Ontario
Canada L5G 4L8

The paper used in this publication meets the requirements
of the American National Standard for Permanence of Paper
for Printed Library Materials Z39.48–1984.

Library of Congress Cataloging-in-Publication Data

New perspectives on Ben Jonson / edited by James Hirsh.
   p.   cm.
Includes bibliographical references and index.
ISBN 0-8386-3687-X (alk. paper)
   1. Jonson, Ben, 1573?–1637—Criticism and interpretation.
I. Hirsh, James E., 1946– .
PR2638.N48   1997
822'.3—dc20   96-30907
                                         CIP

PRINTED IN THE UNITED STATES OF AMERICA

For Matthew and Elizabeth

Contents

New Perspectives
on Ben Jonson

Introduction: Jonsonian Voices

James Hirsh

COLLECTIONS of essays on major literary figures fall into several distinct categories. Some attempt to serve as comprehensive introductions to the current state of scholarship—an example would be *The Cambridge Companion to Shakespeare Studies,* edited by Stanley Wells. Some collections focus on a particular topic or bring together contributors who share a common methodology or ideology—notable examples include *Ben Jonson's 1616 Folio* (edited by Jennifer Brady and W. H. Herendeen) and *Political Shakespeare: New Essays in Cultural Materialism* (edited by Jonathan Dollimore and Alan Sinfield). A few, such as *Shakespeare Left and Right* (edited by Ivo Kamps), take the form of a debate in print by bringing together contributors with diametrically opposed points of view.[1] Each type of collection serves valuable functions.

The current collection occupies yet another category. It brings together essays written from a variety of points of view and using a variety of methodologies in order to provide readers with some sense of the diversity of current scholarly approaches to Jonson. In a way, the function of the collection resembles that of novelistic discourse as described by Mikhail Bakhtin. According to Bakhtin, a novel presents a medley of distinctive voices that interact in complex ways and represent the varied languages that interact in society.[2] Instead of presenting a series of essays that would provide an authoritative summary of current knowledge or that would speak with a single voice, this collection is intentionally polyphonic. A debate format can be quite useful in revealing the direct contrasts between intellectual positions; the strength of such a format is also its weakness, however, because it reduces what may be a complex field of intellectual positions to a polarity. The present collection attempts to reflect the more complex interplay of current scholarly languages.

Among such languages are those that concern the relationships between literature and cultural contexts. Several essays in the present collection—particularly those by Carol P. Marsh-Lockett, George A. E. Parfitt, Bruce Thomas Boehrer, and myself—explore the ways

11

in which Jonson's works reflect or confront political, religious, moral, or social issues of his day. Other critical languages are concerned with performance and dramatic technique. The essays by Kate D. Levin and Alexander Leggatt disclose important aspects of Jonson's dramaturgy. Still other languages concern the dynamics of literary influence and audience response. Jennifer Brady, Anne Lake Prescott, and Robert C. Evans explore Jonson's attitudes about literary influence in general and his use of particular sources. Frances Teague and Ian Donaldson examine the history of Jonson's reception and reputation. But even these categorizations are somewhat misleading. Each contributor has raised a precise intriguing question and has used whatever methods were required in seeking an answer.

In the opening essay, Jennifer Brady explores the complex position on literary influence that Jonson reached in his late prose work *Discoveries*. Asserting his differences from other writers even while trumpeting his debts to them, Jonson presents his readers, especially those who would emulate himself, with a model of responsible engagement. Having witnessed the early stages of bardolatry and having acquired his own band of would-be followers, the Sons of Ben, Jonson recognized the unfortunate results when writers feel so intimidated by earlier writers that they react with subservience or with self-conscious rebelliousness. Anne Lake Prescott has applied her scholarship and wit not only to Jonson's use of Rabelais in his own works but to Jonson's handwritten annotations in a copy of Rabelais's 1599 *Oeuvres*. She has discovered that Jonson's Rabelais is not simply "Rabelaisian" in the usual modern sense. In his marginal glosses, Jonson tried to give the linguistic riot of *Gargantua* a marble fixity that Pantagruel would approve but that Rabelais himself enjoyed undoing. Finding holiday transgression as much a problem as a delight, Jonson's Rabelais is not Bakhtin's festive materialist. (Neither was Rabelais, according to some recent scholars.) Instead, Jonson found most useful those passages of Rabelais that satirize intellectual pretension, the misdirections of ingenuity, and despotic religious illusion. Robert C. Evans demonstrates Jonson's debt to the Flemish humanist Justus Lipsius, who published a compilation of quotations taken from classical authorities to support Lipsius's "neo-Stoic" political, ethical, and religious arguments. Jonson's markings in a copy of Lipsius's work provide us with new information about his access to classical sources and about the complex ways in which classical influence was mediated by such works of humanist scholarship.

Utilizing a variety of methods, several essays in the collection analyze aspects of Jonson's pessimism. George A. E. Parfitt argues that, although Jonson's career was dominated by the effort to find, maintain, and persuasively articulate enduring moral positives, those positives are constantly tested and threatened, in his work, by Jonson's acute awareness of human frailty. Jonson's art shows surprisingly little engagement with the great mysteries of the Christian religion. Although not an atheist, he seems to have seen ethics, rather than metaphysics, as the only means of salvation for the individual and society. Yet evidence from throughout his work in various genres suggests that Jonson doubted the efficacy even of ethics. Alexander Leggatt revisits the issue of the double plot in *Volpone* and argues that an emphasis on simple thematic parallels between the two plots distorts the dramatic significance of their relationship. The contrasts between Sir Pol and Volpone are more striking than the similarities. Each presents an extreme: Volpone is antisocial man, Sir Pol social man. Neither is tolerable but, disturbingly, no other possibility is offered in the play. In my own essay, I argue that *Volpone* confirms and even deepens the cynical views expressed by the knaves in the play that everyone is either a knave or a fool and that language itself is an instrument by which knaves manipulate fools. Although each knave eventually exposes his or her own foolishness, this eventuality merely refines the knavish viewpoint: every character in the world of *Volpone* is either a naive fool or a knavish fool. The play suggests that, because foolishness is universal and incurable, it would be futile to seek a cure and that therefore any artist who claims to be able to cure foolishness is a con artist, a mountebank selling a phony elixir.

Having herself directed a production of *Epicoene*, Kate D. Levin conducts a meticulous analysis of certain features of Jonson's dramaturgy. As Levin shows, the conventional critical discussion of Jonson's plays apart from his masques has obscured certain structural peculiarities that his plays share with his masques. And the usual critical focus on the literary qualities of Jonson's plays as opposed to their theatricality has obscured Jonson's occasional disregard of playhouse pragmatism.

Carol P. Marsh-Lockett discusses aspects of Jacobean court politics that bear on Jonson's masque *Pleasure Reconcild to Vertue*. She explores the tension in the masque between praise of James and implicit criticism by focusing on the characters of Hercules, Atlas, and Daedalus as figures that illustrate the difficulty of preserving virtue. She also shows how the masque reflects the Eurocentrism and gender politics of Jonson's age. Bruce Thomas Boehrer places Jonson's long epigram "On the Famous Voyage" in the context of social history. Jonson's mock-epic account of a journey through the waste disposal system of London is a sustained exploration of alternative strategies for the treatment and disposal of literal and metaphorical excrement. Most of Jonson's epigrams are concerned with distinguishing virtue from vice, excellence from mediocrity—yet this sustained effort culminates in a poem that challenges any such activity by calling attention to the difficulty of eliminating the waste products of civilization.

Two essays focus on aspects of Jonson's reputation. Frances Teague challenges the common assumption that Jonson's later plays were failures. She notes the lack of evidence for this assumption and ascribes it to a set of narratives that have been constructed to make sense of Jonson's career. In particular, Jonson's failure makes a convenient contrast to Shakespeare's success. Ian Donaldson also explores the interrelationships between the reputations of Shakespeare and Jonson. He traces not only how Jonson's reputation fell as that of Shakespeare's rose but how Jonson's writings, in contrast to those of Shakespeare, have been valued and devalued on account of their supposed relationship to the age in which he lived. Donaldson examines the construction of the reputation that overtook Jonson so disablingly in the eighteenth century and that lingers to the present day: the reputation of a chronicler locked irretrievably within the confines of his age.

Although Jonson rarely inspires affection, he still demands attention. The present collection attends to some of his major works such as *Volpone* and *Epicoene* and also demonstrates the significance of some neglected works. Parfitt makes a case for the importance of "A Speech according to Horace," and Boehrer's essay should stir interest in "On the Famous Voyage." Teague's questioning of the assumption that Jonson's late plays were "dotages" invites readers to look at those works in a more receptive way. Evans and Prescott even unmarginalize Jonson's marginalia.

The medley of voices in the present collection, the range of topics and critical methods, not only reflects the current critical dialogue about Jonson but echoes the medley of voices in Jonson's own works. According to Peter Womack,

> Bakhtin maintains that the protean possibilities of internal dialogization are fully worked out only in the novel. . . . But the novel in this sense has a rich prehistory . . . in satire, travesty, antimasque, farce, burlesque, abuse. The type of writing, in fact, of which Jonson's theatrical output is, among other things, a vast and sophisticated compendium.[3]

Jonson's works not only supply such a compendium, but also contain Jonson's dialogue with himself. Reputed to be among the most authoritarian of writers, Jonson sometimes—perhaps in spite of himself—could be surprisingly dialogic. Several essays in the present collection note, in the words of Parfitt, the "struggle at the center of Jonson's art." That struggle gave his works an energy lacking in many writers with more genial personalities.

Notes

1. Stanley Wells, ed., *The Cambridge Companion to Shakespeare Studies* (Cambridge: Cambridge University Press, 1986); Jennifer Brady and W. H. Herendeen, eds., *Ben Jonson's 1616 Folio* (Newark: University of Delaware Press, 1991); Jonathan Dollimore and Alan Sinfield, eds., *Political Shakespeare: New Essays in Cultural Materialism* (Ithaca: Cornell University Press, 1985); and Ivo Kamps, ed., *Shakespeare Left and Right* (New York: Routledge, 1991).

2. See, for example, M. M. Bakhtin, *The Dialogic Imagination: Four Essays,* ed. Michael Holquist, trans. Caryl Emerson and Michael Holquist (Austin: University of Texas Press, 1981).

3. Peter Womack, *Ben Jonson* (Oxford: Blackwell, 1986), 8–9.

Progenitors and Other Sons in Ben Jonson's *Discoveries*

JENNIFER BRADY

> "For the mind, and memory are more sharpely exercis'd in comprehending an other mans things, then our owne; and such as accustome themselves, and are familiar with the best Authors, shall ever and anon find somewhat of them in themselves, and in the expression of their minds, even when they feele it not, be able to utter something like theirs, which hath an Authority above their owne. Nay, sometimes it is the reward of a mans study, the praise of quoting an other man fitly."
>
> —Ben Jonson, *Discoveries* (1640)

> "a text is never its own contemporary."
>
> —Barbara Johnson, *A World of Difference* (1987)

THE doubtful reception of Ben Jonson's *Discoveries* has been closely tied to the disrepute of the 1640 Folio in which it was first published. A late project in Jonson's career, the fragment reflects his growing absorption during his Caroline years with the legacies that poets, scholars, and other humanist founders leave their heirs. The notes and translations that make up *Discoveries* negotiate his fascinated compunction at discovering what it can mean to influence, whether Jonson takes his own case, or Aristotle's, or Shakespeare's, as his model. As Dryden and many of Jonson's contemporaries recognized, he had inscribed himself in the 1616 Folio as a "monopolist" of learning.[1] His posthumously published texts in the second folio mitigate and contest that carefully constructed authorial pose. In *Discoveries* a distinctive Jonson is emerging: a reader, teacher, and guide less invested in amassing intellectual riches for his own use than in examining the legacy he had inherited and was disseminating to his successors. The prose fragment charts its compiler's understanding of intense influence during the period, late in life, when Jonson considered his status as a progenitor of poets—not only the Tribe of Ben, but generations as yet unborn. Jonson provided for those

16

successors by documenting among his commonplaces the process of his own readerly immersion in pondering the responsibilities entailed in the transmission and reception of influence.

Until the reappraisal of Jonson's Caroline period launched in the mid-1980s by Anne Barton and Annabel Patterson, among others, *Discoveries'* comparative neglect has reflected the impact of the monumental Oxford edition, which persistently devalued Jonson's post- (or pre-) classical corpus.[2] The Oxford editors championed the 1616 *Workes* as their paradigm; for them, the first folio defined Jonson's unchanging principles of textual production.[3] The hallmark of Jonson's classical period had been exclusivity, the privileging of works whose consonant value reified the newly created author in him.[4] By comparison, the 1640 Folio seemed a travesty. Insofar as the volume produced by Jonson and Digby's collaboration departed from its revered Jacobean precursor—in its sloppy printing, its inclusion of unfinished projects, its apparently haphazard embrace of experimental texts that would have been (or had been) excluded from canonicity in 1616—Herford and the Simpsons disowned it. In repudiating the second folio, they disparaged much of Jonson's Caroline productivity.

Herford and the Simpsons invested deeply in the "Ben Jonson" they had constructed in their compelling account of the 1616 Folio's triumph. When, for instance, the Oxford editors depict Jonson as "mercifully spared the sight of his [second folio's] disorganized proofs," their remark projects an impulse to shield the editor of the classical *Workes*.[5] By the same token, they prefer that idealized Jonson over his successor, the disenfranchised writer exposed in *Underwood*'s begging poems or represented piecemeal in the fragments of *The English Grammar* and *Discoveries*. The 1640 Folio, which preserved all of these late texts, became the locus for the Oxford editors' abiding discomfort with Jonson's second act. Herford and the Simpsons' dismissal of *Discoveries* follows duly from their low estimation of the second folio's authority. In their view, the fragments of *Discoveries* collected "discoveries made by other men. He [Jonson] fuses, rearranges, and adapts his borrowed material; the weakness of the collection is that he seems to have thought out little or nothing for himself" (11.212–3). Since this judgment is based on, or rather justified by, their diligent tracking of Jonson's reading (volume 11 of the Oxford edition amasses more than eighty pages of sources), it has carried considerable weight with Jonsonians, who have typically absorbed the verdict with the scholarship.

As David Riggs has pointed out, modern readers have too often treated the Caroline fragment as a convenient "repository" of classical and neoclassical commonplaces that Jonson transcribed—and presumably subscribed to—over a lifetime of reading.[6] *Discoveries* warrants a more historicized account of its anomalous place in the enterprise of the 1640 Folio. In Jonson and Digby's volume, its heading reads "EXPLORATA: or, DISCOVERIES" (8.563). This provisional double title insists on the exploratory nature of the undertaking, the sense in which this prose fragment represented a departure, even a new mode of critical inquiry, for Jonson; to recast the point, neither heading implies that Jonson or Digby thought of *Discoveries* as a mere storehouse for neoclassical truisms.

Ben Jonson died in 1637, having entrusted to Sir Kenelm Digby a folio's worth of largely unpublished poems, plays, and prose works. Writing to Bryan Duppa shortly after Jonson's death, Digby registered his dismay that a number of the manuscripts in his possession were "alas, . . . but pieces!," adding in the next breath that he would safeguard even these "religiously . . . to yt end" (9.102). When he brought out the second folio three years later, Digby acted on his resolve to preserve all of Jonson's texts. Digby embraced a pluralistic inclusivity as his modus operandi for the folio. According to an informed source, the stationer Humphrey Moseley, Digby deemed Jonson's fragments "of too much value to be laid aside" (9.102). His editorial stance represented a significant and immediately influential departure from the ideal of magisterial self-containment promoted in the 1616 *Workes*.[7]

Early in 1641, *Discoveries* was added during the final hurried printing of the folio that was to have been released the previous year. The fragment was annexed to the section containing the *English Grammar* and the translation of Horace's *Ars poetica*. Published out of sequence—most of the fourth and final section was already in press—it may narrowly have missed being "laid aside." In fact, *Discoveries* was not registered by any stationer until 1658. The circumstances under which Jonson's prose fragment came to be printed in the 1640 Folio were hardly such as to dispel presumptions of its incoherence.

Discoveries would further have proved a slippery text for its first editor to classify. Its closest affinity was to a genre not customarily associated with seventeenth-century print culture: the commonplace book. These miscellanies, which typically collected Renaissance readers' transcriptions of or excerpts from other writers' works, were compiled for private study or circulated among an intimate group—an aristocratic household, for example, or a court clique—but they were not in themselves recognized as suitable texts for publication.[8] By choosing to publish other fragments of Jonson's, Digby had already challenged his Caroline contemporaries' ideas of Jonsonian authorship. Readers of the second folio would nevertheless readily grasp the logic behind preserving the three extant acts of Jonson's pastoral play *The Sad Shepherd* or the utility of having even an incomplete *English Grammar*. Recognizing the value of *Discoveries'* mode of engagement with other writers' texts or granting the appropriateness of claiming for print a kind of work so strongly associated with the rival manuscript culture placed larger demands on readers. If Digby wavered about asking his contemporaries to share with him in appreciating the sheer diversity of Jonson's late projects, he had prudent reasons for hesitating about including *Discoveries* in the folio.

Jonson's preface to his *English Grammar* bears on this point: "Yet we must remember, that the most excellent creatures are not ever borne perfect; to leave Beares, and Whelps, and other failings of Nature" (8.465). Unlike its imposing precursor, the 1640 Folio was the offspring of a collaboration between a devoted but unfussy novice editor and a writer backing away from the pose of authorship that had garnered him his authoritarian reputation with Jacobean readers. When measured against the classical standards realized in the 1616 *Workes,* the second folio could be characterized as a failing of "Nature"; but like other beings born comparatively shapeless, that volume had its own worth for readers willing to forgo perfection. *Discoveries* imagines such a receptive readership for its fragments.

1

Jonson often speaks out of dual allegiances in his prose entries. Any firm demarcation of the roles of writer and reader, or progenitor and son, tends to blur in *Discoveries*. The humanist inhabits both (or all) places, either by turns or at once. Despite their asymmetry, no position is understood to be inherently privileged, since Jonson assumes their necessary complementarity: for him, an author is only as good as his emulators, a copy very conceivably as valuable as the original. Mature poets are also readers, and founders remain some precursors' sons. Throughout *Discoveries,* Jonson meets his readers in the guise of a writer who remembers being—because he still is— a professed emulator. He exhibits a capacious recall for his own history of imitating other classic writers; in fact he continues to engage (most conspicuously in this text) *as* a reader with other classical and neoclassical theorists, quoting, translating, and actively responding to works he has found intellectually clarifying. His commentary for the most part suspends authorial privilege in favor of transmitting other writers' insights. That this is a conscious strategy, rather than an intellectual abdication, is made clear in a passage openly borrowed from Quintilian: "the mind, and memory are more sharply exercis'd in comprehending an other mans things, then our owne . . . Nay, sometimes it is the reward of a mans study, the praise of quoting an other man fitly" (8.616-7).

A prime beneficiary of his culture's dominant model of influence, Jonson remains sensitive to the rewards and hazards of imitation. He can identify with the heirs' position and affirm their need to achieve individuation. In *Discoveries* he sets out to demystify the sway powerful founders like himself have exerted over their followers, at the same time as he protests the ways in which followers choose to perpetuate a writer's authority submissively. The critical question for Jonson is not whether to endorse humanist pedagogic ideals—he is their committed proponent—but rather, how best to equip his readers with a constructive model of responsive and responsible humanism.

In Jonson's Caroline notebook, poets and their imitators enter into a complementary relation. The progenitor must grapple with the fact of his own influence and with his successors' need to be mentored. He does so, in part, by summoning up his own experiences with the formative figures in his intellectual and artistic development and using that knowledge to foster his heirs' growth. The heirs themselves must learn to "convert the substance, or Riches" of their precursors' work to their "owne use" (8.638). Both parties to this transaction are held accountable by Jonson. An author who colludes with the founding of sects or "parties" in his name has abdicated the care he should take for his followers' well-being. The misconstructions of an author's intentions by his followers form another threat to the transmission of ideas and humanist values across the generations. In *Discoveries'* representation of this process, a damaging asymmetry prevails when any party reneges on the trust placed in him. The system of humanist instruction then founders. Aristotle's interpreters, and Shakespeare's misguided enthusiasts, the players, provide Jonson with two case studies in emulation gone awry. Nor does he sound much more sanguine about his own influence on his followers.

Early on in *Discoveries,* Jonson adapts a passage from Vives's *In Libros de Disciplinis Praefatio* into an autobiographical reflection. He begins by citing *In Libros* to characterize his own relation as a humanist reader to the classical tradition. (In Vives's text, the influential precursors are identified as Plato and Aristotle.) Jonson presents himself as a poet-son whose gratitude to these thinkers does not hamper him from discriminating what is of durable value to him in their writings. He embodies the successor who is able to assimilate his precursors—and just as capable of dissenting from them without fear of rupturing the affiliation:

> I know *Nothing* can conduce more to letters, then to examine the writings of the *Ancients,* and not to rest in their sole Authority, or take all upon trust from them; provided the plagues of *Judging,* and *Pronouncing* against them, be away; . . . For to all the observations of the *Ancients,* wee have our owne experience: which, if wee will use, and apply, wee have better meanes to pronounce. It is true they open'd the gates, and made the way, that went before us; but as Guides, not Commanders . . . Truth lyes open to all; it is no mans *severall* [exclusive property]. . . .
>
> If in some things I dissent from others, whose *Wit, Industry, Diligence,* and *Judgement* I looke up at, and admire: let me not therefore heare presently of Ingratitude, and Rashnesse. For I thanke those, that have taught me, and will ever: but yet dare not thinke the *scope* of their labour, and enquiry, was to envy their posterity, what they also could adde, and find out. (8.567)

The analogy Jonson discovers for his readers is calculated to benefit them: as he reads the Ancients, so he wishes to be read by later generations. His adaptation of Vives culminates in a fervent clarification of Jonson's stance: "I am neither *Author,* or *Fautor* [partisan] of any sect. I will have no man addict himselfe to mee" (8.568). Jonson's edicts underscore his recoil from authoritarian models of influence, even as he resorts, under some implied pressure, to an authoritarian grammar. He likens the follower's self-abnegating reliance on an author's "sole Authority" to a state of unreasoning dependence. (In *Discoveries,* the verb "to addict" is used on three occasions, in each instance to intensify a claim Jonson is making.) His pejorative term *sects* represents blindly devoted followers as nothing less than cultists. Jonson sets out to forestall any such tendencies in his own Sons—or, failing that, to distinguish his will from the misconstructions others may place on it. His rebuke is aimed at those who would credit him with subscribing to oppressive and autocratic values: "I am neither . . . I will have no man. . . ." But such correctives are rarely issued in a vacuum. Underlying Jonson's painstaking defense of his own assimilation of the Ancients moments earlier in the text or his pointed disclaimer here is his anxiety that his own first-generation Sons have become "addicted" to him. For many of these followers, *Discoveries* came too late to have any ameliorative impact.

Later in his entries, Jonson speculates on the transmission of influence across the generations. His Oxford editors were unable to locate any prior source for this somber passage, which interrupts two translations of Seneca's *Controversiae* on unrelated topics. Its subtext reminds us that *Timber* was one of the alternative headings to *Discoveries:*

> *Greatnesse* of name, in the Father, oft-times helpes not forth, but o'rewhelmes the Sonne: they stand too neere one another. The shadow kils the growth; so much, that wee see the Grand-child come more, and oftner, to be the heire of the *first*, then doth the *second:* He dies betweene; the Possession is the *thirds.* (8.576)

During the 1620s and 1630s, when he was recording his *Discoveries*, Jonson seems to have worried that he was inadvertently overpowering his Sons, casting too long a shadow for the undergrowth to thrive. He consoles himself with the prospect of a next generation, even as he mourns the first. The progenitor who would "helpe . . . forth" all his sons may not be able to offset the daunting effects of his own reputation on his immediate successors. His name exacts a dire price, stunting and for a time eclipsing their growth; "The shadow kils," in Jonson's melancholy phrase. He stops short of fashioning this perception into a universal—"oft-times" and "oftner" admit exceptions, which is to say, wish for exceptions—but the fragment's close moves toward a validation of the proposition. The short clause ": He dies betweene;" precisely bisects the long clause that moves from the progenitor ("the *first*") to the heir who eventually takes possession of his estate ("the *third*"). The enclosing colon and semicolon and the canny mirroring placement of the predictive sentence inevitably reinforce Jonson's conviction that this fate is already in the process of being accomplished.[9] The shabby eulogies published in 1638 in Bryan Duppa's collection, *Jonsonus Virbius*, fulfill Jonson's reluctant prophecy.[10]

2

In *Discoveries*, humanist writers ideally serve as exemplary teachers who form their readers' judgments. The truths they inculcate belong to the "common good" (8.568) rather than to any faction or individual. Jonson has maturely examined the Ancients' writings. He advises his Caroline readers to examine "my reason . . . with theirs," not to "rest in [his or] their sole Authority" (8.567).

Elsewhere, following Francis Bacon, Jonson argues that "Nothing is more ridiculous, then to make an Author a *Dictator,* as the schooles have done *Aristotle.* The dammage is infinite, knowledge receives by it" (8.627). The ceding of responsible judgment to the revered precursor proves one of the more dubious dividends of imitation. In Aristotle's case, his followers have, over the generations, constructed him into a tyrant. Jonson raises the awkward question of authorial collusion in this process when he suggests gingerly that he "dare[s] not thinke the *scope* [or end] of their [the Ancients'] labour, and enquiry" (8.567) was to pre-empt their successors' initiatives; by contrast, he is resolved to be unambiguous about his own motives. Jonson disengages from his followers' adulation, challenges them to adopt constructive forms of dissent that would counteract the impact of his own dominant character. His late prose aspires to depersonalizing influence: his, Aristotle's, Shakespeare's. By offering himself up to his Sons as a confessed imitator who makes informed choices among his own progenitors' truths, as a writer who is comfortable both with asserting his differences from and with trumpeting his debts to other humanist thinkers, Jonson presents his readers with a model of responsible engagement.

According to *Discoveries* no author has a monopoly on the truth, which "lyes open to all; it is no mans *severall* [or exclusive property]" (8.567). Jonson explicitly authorizes his own readers to "dissent" from him "in some things," as he has done in assimilating his classical precursors. Within a cultural system of transmission premised on the assumed value of emulation, the option of dissent becomes vital since it allows artistic and intellectual advances to flourish together with the preservation of a continuity to the past. Such dissent further enables a form of resistance that does not rupture the link forged to the precursor. Jonson rejects the thought that the follower's contesting impulse should always be read—or interiorized by him—as a sign of ingratitude. Drawing on Francis Bacon's *Of the Advancement of Learning,* he observes:

> For to many things a man should owe but a temporary beliefe, and a suspension of his owne Judgement, not an absolute resignation of himselfe, or a perpetuall captivity. Let *Aristotle,* and others have their dues; but if wee can make farther Discoveries of truth and fitnesse then they, why are we envied? (8.627)

Jonson is, however, careful to distinguish between acknowledging one's necessary indebtedness to others (the margins of his text credit Bacon with this distinction) and the son's right to dispute his forefathers' discoveries.

The son's "perpetuall captivity" can take two inverse shapes in *Discoveries*. The first is submission, entailing the renunciation of his need, right, and responsibility to achieve individuation. A second, more masked, form of dependency enters in with the denial of influence. Jonson is characteristically precise about the forms that unresolved negative transferences take. In his criticism they are labeled as *"envy, bitternesse, precipitation, impudence,* and *scurrile scoffing"* (8.567). Each of these ways of relating to the precursors locks the neophyte poet-reader into an unwinnable conflict with the figure of the father: unwinnable because the son has lost *conscious* access to the knowledge that his father was once beloved; unwinnable because his affixing of himself to one expression only of his own ambivalence inevitably accomplishes an end quite other than that he envisages— the son perpetuates the progenitor's aura of hegemony.[11] As Freud remarks in a cryptic passage centering on "the primordial ambivalence of feeling towards the father" in his *Civilization and its Discontents,* "His sons hated him, but they loved him, too."[12] It is then also the case that the father who is hated, yet loved still in the inaccessible unconscious, remains always a father, as immovably fixed in that role as his progeny is in his. The precursor is thus ironically kept alive (by envy, bitterness, and other mechanisms of negative transferences) as a potent threat in the heir's imagination. The illusion of repudiating the father is that the son is freed, that he escapes the form of captivity he fears most. But, as Jonson intuits, *"scurrile scoffing"* begs a response; it requires the father's pained acknowledgment of repeated affronts to his authority. That the precursors were, and are, beloved is not at issue in *Discoveries.* For Jonson, that fact has a primacy that at times supersedes the counterbalancing desire to gain a measure of separateness. And because that is so, Jonson can never envision the wholesale repudiation of his influential precursors as a viable response: "I thanke those, that have taught me, and will ever" (8.567), he writes. His gratitude can co-exist with maturely considered dissent, where envy cannot. The son who resolves on a course of denying his precursors' influence only affirms their power and control over him. He remains as inexorably bound to them as the follower who turns his fathers into charismatic demigods.

During his later career, Jonson had witnessed both of these reactive transferential extremes in his readers.[13] In *Discoveries* he alludes with sardonic chagrin to the plight of writers who "have out-liv'd the peoples palats. They have beene too much, or too long a feast" (8.576). Or elsewhere in the fragment, adapting J. C. Scaliger on the subject of envy, Jonson wonders:

Is it a crime in me that I know that, which others had not yet knowne, but from me? or that I am the Author of many things, which never would have come in thy thought, but that I taught them? . . .

Indeed, nothing is of more credit, or request now, then a petulant paper, or scoffing verses; and it is but convenient to the times and manners wee live with, to have then the worst writings, and studies flourish, when the best begin to be despis'd. (8.571–2)

These laments have considerable resonance for Jonson in his last years. His reputation, based in large part on his classic *Workes,* was unassailable, but he was at the same time the target of ad hominem attacks on his "dotages," circulated by enemies he identifies in *Discoveries* as willing "prentises to slander" (8.571).

The author enshrined in the 1616 Folio had been essentially an authoritarian whose primary means of gaining "*Greatnesse* of name" had involved the judicious intimidation of his readers.[14] By the time he was compiling *Discoveries,* Jonson was disengaging from such tactics, perhaps because he had begun to realize the consequences for his Sons of what he had won for himself. They had divided into partisan camps, into sects who praised or scoffed. "It profits not me to have any man fence, or fight for me, to flourish, or take a side. Stand for *Truth,* and 'tis enough" (8.568), Jonson writes, in what amounts to a gesture at undoing his Sons' personalizing of the issues at stake, but during his lifetime Jonson would continue to inspire partisanship in his followers and tirades from his antagonists.

In his Caroline notes, Jonson locates a common denominator to this phenomenon in the persistent overvaluing of the progenitor. When fathers can only be fathers for their sons, they are transmuted into objects to be worshipped and hated. When they are also human, capable, that is, of more fluid self-definitions, they may protest their monumentalizing, as Jonson does in this text. His *Discoveries* in this respect contests the achievement of his first folio, in particular its bold claim that the *Workes* are the sole property of their author-editor. *Discoveries* reassigns these humanist texts to the collective, preferring the "common good" over any individual's claim to exclusive ownership. By tacitly democratizing his own literary estate, which now belongs in theory to any reader capable of assimilating its truths, Jonson disinvests the author he had invented in his first folio of his (recently) assumed hegemony. If he loses his exclusive proprietary claims to his own works in this redistribution of rights, Jonson regains access to the humanist tradition he had inherited— as a reader, he reclaims his sonship in *Discoveries.*

In this late fragment Jonson seems to revel in the parade of his indebtedness to those intellectual precursors whose work he is appropriating, adapting, rediscovering, and learning from. Like them, he is a link in the transmission of literary history across the generations. "If I have any thing right, defend it as Truth's, not mine (save as it conduceth to a common good)" (8.568), he counsels. The poets capable of absorbing that truth will now, it is implied, inherit Jonson's estate: they will know *how* to value their possession because they will know *what* to value in the transmission.

3

In *Discoveries'* most infamous passage, Jonson returns to the constructions first-generation readers place on a charismatic author's work. His discussion of Shakespeare's reception by the players has often been decontextualized, excerpted from the text, and held up as a presumptive proof of bard envy. According to this view, Jonson is engaging in an individious detraction of a far greater writer whose genius he fails to appreciate.[15] The presumption of an acute rivalry on Jonson's part (Shakespeare is exempted from the charge) has encrusted his remarks for centuries, and Jonson's irritability with the actors' posture of adulation has only fueled the attribution of envy. Jonson is, I think, responding to a phenomenon that worried him as well when he reflected on his own career, the effects of idolatry on his followers. His caustic disengagement from their worshipful stance, captured in "I will have no man addict himselfe to mee" (8.568), carries over to his critique of Shakespeare's enthusiasts. Shakespeare, too, had become the object of an evolving cult worship, praised for a facility that might well inspire his imitators to emulate his faults. The passage, then, needs to be situated in relation to *Discoveries'* anxious preoccupation with the transmission of poetic legacies. Jonson's beleaguered corrective is pointedly addressed to posterity, who are asked to adjudicate the quarrel because he assumes (wrongly, as it happens) that later generations will be less invested in celebrification than his contemporaries:

> *I remember,* the Players have often mentioned it as an honour to *Shakespeare,* that in his writing, (whatsoever he penn'd) hee never blotted out line. My answer hath beene, Would he had blotted a thousand. Which they thought a malevolent speech. I had not told posterity this, but for their ignorance, who choose that circumstance to commend their friend by, wherein he most faulted. And to justifie mine owne candor, (for I lov'd the man, and doe honour his memory (on this side Idolatry) as

much as any.) Hee was (indeed) honest, and of an open, and free nature: had an excellent *Phantsie;* brave notions, and gentle expressions: wherein hee flow'd with that facility, that sometime[s] it was necessary he should be stop'd: *Sufflaminandus erat;* as *Augustus* said of *Haterius.* His wit was in his owne power; would the rule of it had beene so too. . . . But hee redeemed his vices, with his vertues. There was ever more in him to be praysed, then to be pardoned. (8.583–84)

Jonson's opening salvo recalls the pugnacious writer recorded in Drummond of Hawthornden's notes of 1619; despite his disclaimer, Jonson seems very much determined to preserve his riposte for posterity. "Would he had blotted a thousand" is a remembered vanity the speaker does not regret. He has punctured the actors' preposterously naive expression of their admiration; the major-domo has spoken, chastising those too ignorant to recognize how essential revision is to achieving excellence. His implication of Shakespeare in his quarrel with the actors may be, at first, incidental. The players are Jonson's designated targets because he is absorbed by the issue of responsible reception—until, that is, he turns to a vindication of his own candor. In justifying his "malevolent speech," Jonson's tone alters; he moves from an exhibition of his trenchant wit toward a by-now-awkward but felt encomium to Shakespeare the man and Shakespeare the author. He is willing to make amends to both and to clarify what his answer to the actors had left ambiguous: that the "fault" is less Shakespeare's than that of his disciples, who have promulgated the mistaken view that fair manuscripts translate into a record of unblemished artistry.

The section of *Discoveries* that contains Jonson's remarks on Shakespeare's reception argues this position at more length. It would be more accurate to represent "Would he had blotted a thousand" as a culminating instance of Jonson's overarching pedagogic agenda in these notes. "*Nothing* in our Age, I have observ'd, is more preposterous, then the *running Judgements* upon *Poetry,* and *Poets*" (8.581), he begins, vexed from the outset at the dubious grounds proposed for commending contemporary writing. He shortly gives an example of what he is protesting: the utterly disposable productions the public cries up and which, on closer inspection, "a man would scarce vouchsafe, to wrap any wholsome drug in; hee would never light his *Tobacco* with them" (8.582). The writers of such ephemera are fashioned by their readers into celebrities, miracles of the hour. But if their writing is examined by a mature poet, "hee must make all they have done, . . . but one blot. . . . A Sponge dipt in Inke will doe all" (8.582). Jonson later identifies two of the culprits as John

Heath, whose *Epigrams* in his view represented the nadir of the genre, and John Taylor, the Water Poet, who is invoked as the epitome of the kind of poetaster the public is certain to prefer to a Spenser. These favorites are consigned by Jonson's satiric sponge to a not terribly premature oblivion: in *Discoveries,* the aggregate of bad writing makes "but one blot." By comparison, he recommends modest red-pencilling in Shakespeare's case: it might bear noting that, translated over some thirty-seven plays, the excision of a thousand lines would hardly constitute radical revision.

Even writers whose inventiveness approached Shakespeare's would, however, Jonson argues, benefit from the ingrained discipline of revision. There are good reasons to be skeptical of the actors' claims that Shakespeare "never blotted out line." But Jonson is primarily disturbed by the likelihood that their mystification of Shakespeare's facility will be construed by his successors as a model to emulate; as an interiorized idea of excellence, such a model would inspire only negligence. Later in *Discoveries* Jonson restates his objection, this time without the distracting causticity or the ad hominem application of his earlier remarks:

> For all that wee invent doth please us in the conception, or birth; else we would never set it downe. But the safest is to return to our Judgement, and handle over again those things, the easinesse of which might make them justly suspected. So did the best Writers in their beginnings; they impos'd upon themselves care, and industry. They did nothing rashly. They obtain'd first to write well, and then custome made it easie, and a habit. (8.616)

The principles being enunciated here are unexceptionable, and felt. They underscore the pedagogic dimension of Jonson's notes and advocate a stance identical to the one he takes in appealing to posterity to settle his dispute with the players.

While his tribute to Shakespeare self-consciously positions itself "(on this side Idolatry)," an attitude consistent with Jonson's posture toward his classical forebears in *Discoveries,* he offers a generous appraisal of Shakespeare's worth. He sums up the man he knew succinctly: "Hee was (indeed) honest, and of an open, and free nature." It would be just possible to interpret these remarks as chary praise were it not for Drummond of Hawthornden's notes on his conversations with Jonson in Scotland. Under the heading "Miscellanies" Drummond jotted down that "of all stiles he [Jonson] loved most to be named honest, and hath of that ane hundreth letters so naming him" (1.150). Jonson's reported preservation of those letters suggests the extraordinary freight the attribute *honest* had for him.

It is what he values first in remembering Shakespeare, and his "(indeed)" underlines the emphasis already implied by the hierarchical positioning of *honest* in his sentence. Jonson praises Shakespeare by associating him reflexively with the self-image he cherished most; in naming this trait as preeminent he has sealed his friend's reputation for openness, candor, and a generosity of spirit.

In writing to the question of Shakespeare's artistic accomplishment, Jonson acknowledges its otherness. Shakespeare was preeminently for him the possessor of an "excellent *Phantsie*," a quality exhibited in his "brave notions, and gentle expressions." So far, Jonson confirms the actors' praise and grants Shakespeare an excellence quite unlike his own. Contemporaries would hardly characterize Jonson's talent in these terms and nearly all would give precedence to Shakespeare, or Fletcher, in the realm of imagination. The central fault Jonson designates—that Shakespeare's "wit was in his owne power; would the rule of it had beene so too"—would be repeated incisively by Samuel Johnson in his edition of Shakespeare.[16] Jonson dissents here from the actors' accolades. He cedes the virtues of an expansive imagination but, as he argues throughout *Discoveries,* "There is difference betweene a liberall, and a prodigall hand" (8.623). Even so, Jonson concedes a good deal. Generally mistrustful as he is of such profuse wit, he finds more to praise than to censure. His own preference lies elsewhere, with poets like Virgil, who "brought forth his verses like a Beare, and after form'd them with licking" (8.638), a model Jonson emulated in the revision of his quartos into the *Workes* of his classical period. But his own preferences are not turned into absolutes to be legislated to subsequent generations in *Discoveries.* In his Caroline commonplaces, Jonson largely affirms diverse kinds of talents, the value of differential blends of fancy and self-regulation.

If his tone is more admiring when he lauds "the incomparable *Virgil*" (8.638), his estimation of Shakespeare seems balanced, fair at once to his competitor and colleague and to Jonson's own criteria of excellence. He is constrained by having to compete with unalloyed adulation, and, one suspects, affronted by the imputations that had dogged his earlier deflation of a pernicious myth about creativity. Having long survived Shakespeare, Jonson had witnessed bardolatry in its infancy, in the actors' nostalgic transfiguration of a major playwright into an object of cult worship, a dramatist whose facility was such that he could dispense with revision. Jonson's dissenting voice protested the public's unquestioning adulation of any writer—himself included, together with Shakespeare—and, more specifically, contradicted the players' professed reasons for lauding Shakespeare's achievement. Given these various constraints, Jonson acquits himself well.

4

In watching and vigorously protesting bardolatry in its nascent stages, or in thinking through his own shadowing greatness and its impact on his first-generation followers, Jonson explored the transmission of influence from an unusual position: that of the progenitor who is capable of identifying with his heirs' need to convert humanist legacies to their own use. *Discoveries* encourages its readers to assimilate, to emulate, and to dissent. As Jonson had anticipated, the major beneficiaries of his ministering counsel would be later generations of writers: "wee see the Grand-child come more, and oftner, to be the heire" (8.576) who takes possession of his precursor's estate. John Dryden, separated from "Father Ben" not only by the intervening generations but by the cataclysm of civil war, was—unlike the Caroline sons, who stood "too neere"—the ideal legatee. His essays of the 1660s and 1670s are irradiated by his scrupulous attention to Jonson's *Discoveries,* including its account of Jonson's assimilation of his classical precursors and his warnings against adopting a self-defeating stance of adulation toward any influential progenitor. Like Jonson, Dryden emerges as a forceful advocate of the balanced critical appraisal that steers a middle course between taking the humanist legacy "upon trust" (8.567) and a resistant, envious denigration of one's forefathers. Jonson's fragment of humanist criticism had a durable worth for his Restoration readers. Unlike the cowed contributors to *Jonsonus Virbius,* Dryden responds to Jonson as a guide, a formative and ultimately an assimilated mentor to his own criticism, rather than as the founder of a sect he has joined. When Dryden applies *Discoveries'* model of imitation and dissent to Jonson's own writings, he not only confirms but conforms to the Caroline fragment's professed values.

Three of the four speakers in *An Essay of Dramatick Poesie* refer their listeners to *Discoveries,* which functions as a kind of communal handbook to be invoked in adjudicating their debates and which all concur in admiring.[17] Yet there are subtler dividends, passages formed after the example of *Discoveries* in which Dryden recasts Jonson's *explorata* into a dissenting critique of his Renaissance precursor, in an arc of divergence that bespeaks a vast debt to the hand guiding his successor's criticism. The close of his "Defence of the Epilogue" is one such passage, written in the idiom of late Jonson. After reminding his readers that "the Poets . . . work is imitation," Dryden sums up his generation's self-consciously skeptical attitude toward their great forebears:

> Let us therefore admire the beauties and the heights of *Shakespear*, without falling after him into a carelessness and (as I may call it) a Lethargy of thought, for whole Scenes together. Let us imitate, as we are able, the quickness and easiness of *Fletcher*, without proposing him as a pattern to us, either in the redundancy of his matter, or the incorrectness of his language. . . . Let us ascribe to *Jonson* the height and accuracy of Judgment, in the ordering of his Plots, his choice of characters, and maintaining what he had chosen, to the end: but let us not think him a perfect pattern of imitation . . .
>
> To conclude all, let us render to our Predecessors what is their due, without confineing our selves to a servile imitation of all they writ: and, without assuming to our selves the Title of better poets.[18]

As Dryden acknowledges, and this passage enacts, the Restoration writer's work involves him in a discerning, selective emulation of his precursors. One of the pleasures of this ostensibly contestatory essay is its shrewd conversion of *Discoveries'* precepts on the reception of influence to the heir's own use. Here, as elsewhere in his criticism, Dryden is provided with the "perfect pattern" of dissent through his intensive study of Jonson's Caroline notebook. But his debt extended to include at least one other principal in the transmission of this fragment to posterity. It was Sir Kenelm Digby's fortunate judgment that Jonson's "pieces" were "of too much value to be laid aside" that preserved this particular humanist legacy for his heirs.[19]

Notes

1. In his *Discourse concerning the Original and Progress of Satire* (1693), John Dryden writes that Jonson "who by studying *Horace,* had been acquainted with the Rules, yet seem'd to envy to Posterity that Knowledge, and like an Inventer of some useful Art, to make a Monopoly of his Learning." See Dryden, *The Works of John Dryden,* ed. Edward Niles Hooker, et al., 20 vols. (Berkeley: University of California Press, 1955–), 4:4; hereafter cited as *Works.* See also, for their extensive historicist documentation of Jonson's reception in the seventeenth century, G. E. Bentley, *Shakespeare and Jonson: Their Reputations in the Seventeenth Century Compared* (Chicago: University of Chicago Press, 1945), and a particularly valuable resource that supplements Bentley's researches, D. H. Craig, *Ben Jonson: The Critical Heritage, 1599–1798* (London: Routledge, 1990). I am indebted to Robert L. Entzminger, Timothy Murray, and Sara van den Berg for their considered, helpful

comments on this essay. I want also to thank Sandra McEntire, Judith Rutschman, and Gail Stroud.

2. See Anne Barton, *Ben Jonson, Dramatist* (Cambridge: Cambridge University Press, 1984), 258–351, for an influential account of Jonson's nostalgia for the Elizabethanism being revived in Caroline England, as also her quarrel with the Oxford edition's dating of Jonson's last plays; Annabel Patterson, *Censorship and Interpretation: The Conditions of Writing and Reading in Early Modern England* (Madison: University of Wisconsin Press, 1984), esp. 120–44, on the hermeneutics of censorship in *The Under-wood;* Timothy Murray, *Theatrical Legitimation: Allegories of Genius in Seventeenth-Century England and France* (New York: Oxford University Press, 1987), 47–49, who rightly emphasizes the originality of Jonson's project in *Discoveries;* Martin Elsky, *Authorizing Words: Speech, Writing, and Print in the English Renaissance* (Ithaca: Cornell University Press, 1989), 81–88, on Jonson's complex humanism; Richard Burt, *Licensed by Authority: Ben Jonson and the Discourses of Censorship* (Ithaca: Cornell University Press, 1993), 61, on Jonson's use of the body to characterize his poetics of assimilation; and Thomas M. Greene, *The Light in Troy: Imitation and Discovery in Renaissance Poetry* (New Haven: Yale University Press, 1982), passim, on Jonsonian imitation. Greene writes provocatively of "the intensification of resemblance into fusion" in Jonson's model of imitation, which, he argues, entails the "total assimilation of the other" and simultaneous "total self-surrender to the other"; Greene concludes that, for Jonson, "In imitation one becomes a very Another" (275–77). Also valuable are earlier studies of *Discoveries* that diverge from Herford and the Simpsons' dismissal of the fragment, most notably Ralph S. Walker's idiosyncratic edition of *Ben Jonson's Timber or Discoveries* (Syracuse: Syracuse University Press, 1953) and George Parfitt, *Ben Jonson: Public Poet and Private Man* (London: J. M. Dent, 1976), 14–35, which explores the dichotomous views of Jonson offered in *Discoveries* and the *Conversations* with Drummond of Hawthornden.

3. For a more detailed critique of the Oxford edition, see Kevin J. Donovan, "Jonson's Texts in the First Folio," in *Ben Jonson's 1616 Folio*, ed. Jennifer Brady and W. H. Herendeen (Newark: University of Delaware Press, 1991), 23–37, who argues that "Herford and Simpson overestimated the authority of the Folio in comparison with some of the quarto editions of plays and masques that preceded it and made greater claims than are warranted for Jonson's involvement at the press. In this sense the Oxford edition represents the apex of the Folio's textual authority and reputation" (34).

4. On Jonson's invention of authorship, see the classic studies of Richard C. Newton, "Jonson and the (Re-) Invention of the Book," in *Classic and Cavalier: Essays on Jonson and the Sons of Ben*, ed. Claude J. Summers and Ted-Larry Pebworth (Pittsburgh: University of Pittsburgh Press, 1982), 31–58; Richard Helgerson, *Self-Crowned Laureates: Spenser, Jonson, Milton, and the Literary System* (Berkeley: University of California Press, 1983); Joseph Loewenstein, "The Script in the Marketplace," *Representations* 12 (1985): 101–14; Murray, *Theatrical Legitimation*, esp. 23–93; and Sara van den Berg, "Ben Jonson and the Ideology of Authorship," in *Ben Jonson's 1616 Folio*, 111–37.

5. *Ben Jonson*, ed. C. H. Herford, Percy Simpson, and Evelyn Simpson, 11 vols. (Oxford: Clarendon, 1925–52), 9:107. I have normalized i/j and u/v. All subsequent references to Herford and the Simpsons' commentary and to Jonson's works will be to the Oxford edition, cited by volume and page number.

6. Riggs, *Ben Jonson: A Life* (Cambridge, Mass.: Harvard University Press, 1989), 346.

7. Digby's break with Jonsonian classicism would establish an acknowledged precedent for other seventeenth-century poets and editors. Digby's inclusion in the 1640 Folio of the unfinished *Sad Shepherd* and *Mortimer His Fall* is cited by Moseley as a "sufficient President in works of this nature" (9:102) when he in turn chose to include Suckling's fragment *The Sad One* in his edition of the *Last Remains*. Milton may have been another beneficiary; in his *Poems*, published in 1645, he showcased an unfinished lyric, "The Passion," thus claiming, however obliquely, his warrant from Jonson's recently published second folio.

8. For a sound historical account of the commonplace book, see Ruth Mohl, *John Milton and His Commonplace Book* (New York: Frederick Ungar, 1969). As Timothy Murray has argued in *Theatrical Legitimation*, "*Discoveries* differs significantly in style and form from other extant English commonplace books of its period. It is not arranged according to readily identifiable commonplaces whose order is determined by alphabetization or theme. . . . Indeed the recognizable sources . . . are often paraphrased and intermixed in the book with Jonson's own prose musings" (48).

9. For a persuasive, rigorous study of Jonson's use of punctuation to discriminate meaning in his poetry, see Michael McCanles, *Jonsonian Discriminations: The Humanist Poet and the Praise of True Nobility* (Toronto: University of Toronto Press, 1992), esp. 3–45.

10. On *Jonsonus Virbius*, interpreted as an "embattled, contentious book, which simply continues Jonson's own enterprise of self-assertion and self-defense," see Robert C. Evans, *Ben Jonson and the Poetics of Patronage* (Lewisburg: Bucknell University Press, 1989), who adds that many of the elegists "claim the unfitness of their own art in the face of Jonson's achievement" (189–90); Jennifer Brady, "'Beware the Poet': Authority and Judgment in Jonson's *Epigrammes*," *SEL* 23 (1983): 95–112, esp. 95–99, which treats the elegists' abjection before their intimidating subject; and Earl Miner, *The Cavalier Mode from Jonson to Cotton* (Princeton: Princeton University Press, 1971).

11. I owe this insight to Robert Byer. An exemplary text in this mode would be Harold Bloom's *The Anxiety of Influence: A Theory of Poetry* (New York: Oxford University Press, 1973), in which the ephebe's strategies for denying influence, predicated on the oedipal model of contestation, include the repression of his necessary ambivalence; the poet-son resists acknowledging his prior attachment to his strong father. For a perceptive critique of Bloom's model of influence, see Thomas McFarland, *Originality and Imagination* (Baltmore: Johns Hopkins University Press, 1985).

12. Sigmund Freud, *Civilization and its Discontents,* in the *Standard Edition of the Complete Psychological Works of Sigmund Freud,* ed. James Strachey, et al., 24 vols. (London: Hogarth Press, 1953–74), 21:132.

13. I have explored these poles of reaction to Jonson at greater length in "'Noe fault, but Life': Jonson's Folio as Monument and Barrier," in *Ben Jonson's 1616 Folio*, 192–216.

14. See further Brady, "Authority and Judgment," on Jonson's pressuring of his readers in the *Epigrammes*.

15. For representative arguments emphasizing Jonson's rivalry with Shakespeare as revealed in "To the Memory of my Beloved, the Author, Mr. William Shakespeare, and What he hath Left us," the poem that headed the 1623 Folio, see Lawrence Lipking, *The Life of the Poet: Beginning and Ending Poetic Careers* (Chicago: University of Chicago Press, 1981), 138–46; and Roger B. Rollin, "The Anxiety of Identification: Jonson and the Rival Poets," in *Classic and Cavalier*, 139–54. Schol-

ars who regard Jonson's poem as generous and sincere, rather than as a vehicle for insinuating negative strictures, include Gerald Hammond, *Fleeting Things: English Poets and Poems, 1603–1660* (Cambridge, Mass.: Harvard University Press, 1990), 141–53; Sara van den Berg, *The Action of Jonson's Poetry* (Newark: University of Delaware Press, 1987), 143–54; Barton, *Ben Jonson, Dramatist,* 258; and Barbara L. DeStefano, "Ben Jonson's Eulogy on Shakespeare: Native Maker and the Triumph of English," *Studies in Philology* 90 (1993): 231–45. DeStefano claims that "Jonson intends to praise convincingly Shakespeare as a national hero, who in fixing immortal truth in the English vernacular . . . immortalizes English and therein celebrates his country" (233).

16. "Shakespeare with his excellencies has likewise faults . . . sufficient to obscure and overwhelm any other merit," Johnson writes, before entering, as an illustration of Shakespeare's faults, the famous passage on quibbling: "A quibble is to Shakespeare, what luminous vapours are to the traveller; . . . it is sure to lead him out of his way, and sure to engulf him in the mire. It has some malignant power over his mind, and its fascinations are irresistible." See Samuel Johnson, *Johnson on Shakespeare,* ed. Arthur Sherbo (New Haven: Yale University Press, 1968), 7:71–74.

17. Neander's character of Jonson in Dryden's *Essay of Dramatick Poesie* (1668) ends on this note: "To conclude of him, as he has given us the most correct Playes, so in the precepts which he has laid down in his *Discoveries,* we have as many and profitable Rules for perfecting the Stage as any wherewith the *French* can furnish us" (*Works* 17:58). Neander and Crites openly acknowledge their intellectual debts to *Discoveries;* Lisideius, who advocates the superiority of French drama over English, refers on several occasions to Jonson's plays but makes no explicit allusion to *Discoveries,* but Eugenius borrows its phrasing and adapts its precepts in his defense of modern dramatists (*Works* 17:21–22). On Dryden's reception of Jonson, see Jennifer Brady, "Collaborating with the Forebear: Dryden's Reception of Ben Jonson," *Modern Language Quarterly: A Journal of Literary History* 54 (1993): 345–69, and "Dryden and Negotiations of Literary Succession and Precession," in *Literary Transmission and Authority: Dryden and Other Writers,* ed. Earl Miner and Jennifer Brady (Cambridge: Cambridge University Press, 1993), 27–54.

18. Dryden, *Works,* 11:217–18.

19. See further on Digby's patronage of Jonson, Robert C. Evans, *Jonson and the Contexts of His Time* (Lewisburg: Bucknell University Press, 1994), 147–77.

Jonson's Rabelais

Anne Lake Prescott

F IFTY years ago Huntington Brown laid out the evidence for Jonson's knowledge of Rabelais;[1] some of it is unconvincing, but there
can be no doubt that by 1616 and probably earlier Jonson had read
around in *Gargantua et Pantagruel.* Critical times change, though,
as witness Brown's comparison of the two writers: "Jonson was a
hearty animal, honest, convivial, and frank to the point of bear-
ishness, and his excess of spirits frequently found vent in the grotesque vein that distinguishes so much of Rabelais's work" (93).
These days Jonson looks less hearty, if still bearish: attracted to the
material world, he was also disturbed by it, even his own eventually
mountainous body an embarrassment, whatever the comic roles he
found for his obesity (using it, says one critic, like a personal antimasque).[2] Recent work on Jonson has scrutinized the connection
between his bulk and his writings and how this plays out in terms
of his sense of authorship, stance toward his audience, and suspicion
of an economy relying on an increasing consumption of matter and
words.[3] As Katharine Maus puts it, far from taking materiality for
granted, he "struggles with the problem of *whether* material life,
however it may be defined, really possesses this priority."[4]

It has been useful, in rethinking Jonson, to imagine what he is
unlike. Although staging Bartholomew Fair, he finds holiday transgression as much a problem as a delight; he does not quite celebrate
the lower body, for his recurrent scatology is more anally clenched
than hang-loose indulgent; and, at the other end of the alimentary
tract, the mouth as he imagines it is the often grotesque hole from
which too many silly words come out and too much fattening or
unmanning matter goes in. He is, in sum, unlike Rabelais. In *Volpone*, writes Joseph Loewenstein, "Jonsonian gourmandise catches
the physiology of hoarding at a profoundly ambivalent moment, a
moment at which Rabelaisian gusto is on the verge of collapsing into
an antisocial, indeed repulsive, miserliness of the body," while the
"hungry flesh of Jonson's experience" is unlike what "Bakhtin discovers in Rabelais."[5]

To be sure, what has happened to Jonson has also happened, to a lesser degree, to Rabelais. Bakhtin's festive materialist, never the only Rabelais around, has been revised as recent work has found in him a divided view of the popular and the corporeal, especially in the later books.[6] Still, compared to Jonson, Rabelais seems more at ease with appetite (or more willing to appear so), happier—in books—to pass around the cakes and ale, more pleased by the grotesque, more obscene, and more concerned with disputes over sex and marriage. Perhaps what the two writers share most is a fascination with language, notably language part way to being matter and matter that behaves like words.

Many who write on Jonson mention Rabelais, either to cite or deny an affinity or because several of Jonson's works allude to him. It is not widely known, though, that he owned and annotated a copy of Rabelais's 1599 *Oeuvres* now at the British Library; in the lamentably cropped margins of *Gargantua*'s first twenty-one chapters are many lexical glosses in English or Latin.[7] In this article I will suggest what may be deduced from them and then look at some Rabelaisian echoes in Jonson's drama. Larger comparisons of the two writers deserve a long study; here I will confine myself to a few words, names, what used to be called "borrowings," and overt intertextual gestures. They show, I think, that Jonson's Rabelais is not simply "Rabelaisian" in the current modern sense; nor is he fully accountable for by the playwright's fascination with festivity and the body. Looking at him might redefine the terms in which to compare the two writers.

Jonson's copy of Rabelais is inscribed "The Gift of Beniamin Johnson the Poet to Thos Skynner. 1628." The hand is probably not that of Jonson, who dropped the "h" from his name's usual spelling— perhaps as a gesture differentiating himself from the other, lesser, Johnsons in England.[8] Whoever wrote the inscription ignored the author's preference in this regard, as did many others. I have not been able to identify the recipient, although several Thomas Skinners appear in the *Calendar of State Papers,* including a son of Sir Thomas Skinner of Lannam Park, Suffolk, examined in early 1616 upon suspicion of recusancy for trying (after being driven out of the house by his mother) to join his father in Paris without a passport.[9] I cannot connect Jonson to these or any other Thomas Ski/ynners. The significance of Jonson's gift is also unclear, as is the presence of glosses only in *Gargantua.* Had he tired of Rabelais? Did his stroke in 1628 interrupt his glossing? Now that he was older, did he want to simplify his shelves? Did this copy replace one burned in his 1623 fire? Did Skynner or a friend beg persuasively? It is puzzling that the words marked for attention by underlining include such easy ones as "gros" and "gras," defined in the margin as "thicke" and "fat."

It is no wonder that Jonson needed—or thought someone would need—such glosses, for Rabelais's prose is daunting. One can sympathize with anyone who opened a volume and read:

> —Voulez-vous (dist Her Trippa) en sçavoir plus amplement la verité par pyromantie, par aëromantie, celebrée par Aristophanes en ses *Nuées,* par hydromantie, par lecanomantie, tant jadis celebrée entre les Assyriens et exprovée par Hermolaus Barbarus? Dedans un bassin plein d'eaue je te monstreray ta femme future brimballant avecques deux rustres.
> —Quand (dist Panurge) tu mettras ton nez en mon cul, sois recors de deschausser tes lunettes.[10]

Those with minimal French can deduce that this is comic, and the indecent parts are easy; but many English readers would have welcomed Randle Cotgrave's *Dictionarie of the French and English Tongues* (1611), one of the funniest works in the history of lexicography. As I will show, Jonson himself had the pleasure of using it. It would have told him a lot about Rabelais.

The dictionary's verve is due in part to hundreds of words taken from Rabelais and flagged by a "¶Rab."[11] Cotgrave mentions Chaucer and Du Bartas a few times, but Rabelais is the only writer regularly identified as a source, sometimes very precisely: "commenial" is defined as "(¶Rabelais l.4.chap.44.) A barbarous jeasting repetition of the word comme going some two lines before, and used by Frier John." Some words that Cotgrave adopts, in fact, have no practical use except for reading Rabelais. Why else explain that "cope gorgée" is "in stead of, Gorge coupée"? This dictionary, in other words, is precisely what Jonson needed to make sense of *Gargantua.* Consulting it, he would soon have acquired a sense of ¶Rab's personality. ¶Rab knows the body and its needs: definitions like "Nephrocartaticon" ("physicke that purgeth the reines") imply an authority on anatomy, while words for the genitalia are often his, not always defined soberly. Under "comment" ("how, in what sort") we also find "Le comment a nom de sa femme," defined as "his wives how-should-I-call-it," while "Cuscoamy" is "well hanged, well stoned" and "desmorché" is "without powder in his touch-hole."

Jonson might also have liked the mild scatology: here are "habeliné," meaning "distempered; or (as some have understood it) all-to-bepissed"; "scybale," translated as "a hard or hardened, turd"; "syparathe" as "the dung of a Goat, or Sheepe"; "tyrepet" ("a great farter"); and others. Far more frequent are words from ¶Rab that relate to food and drink. From "alloyandier" ("a roster of short ribbes of beefe") to "ventripotent" ("big-paunch, bellie-able, huge-guts"), many summon up a world of laden tables for the hungry and of brimming cups for any "mouille-vent" ("a tipler, quaffer, bibber; one that often wets his windpipe"). The impression is not, I think, of carnival reversal but of material comfort, even of pigging out ("morpiaille": "greedie eating; ill favoured or hastie devouring"). Other entries suggest humanist wit or satirical skepticism, such as the running gag of including words for methods of prognostication from "axionomantie" ("divination by a hatchet") to "solistisme" ("a falling on the ground of bread given unto chickens").[12]

I cannot tell when Jonson made his glosses, although he must have done so at different times: no one could do them all at one sitting. That some underlined words have no gloss suggests that he first marked words for translation and then went back over the chapters. It seems clear that he consulted Cotgrave, which would mean that some or all glosses date from 1611 or later (with the Latin definitions it is harder to tell). The number of English glosses is small but enough to work with. Jonson's method seems to have been to read Cotgrave, perhaps together with some other dictionaries, and to pick out or devise a definition he liked. That is to say, his translations are on occasion the same as Cotgrave's first definition but are just as likely to parallel a word or phrase toward the end of an entry in the *Dictionarie*. In a few cases, the gloss shows that Jonson was pondering and considering which English word or phrase might do best. It is this picking and choosing that makes Jonson's marginal translations seem so thoughtful, if brief.

The evidence for Jonson's use of Cotgrave is sparse but compelling. Several words or phrases for which he gives English glosses are not in Claudius Holyband's 1593 French dictionary (the best alternative) but are there in Cotgrave. Thus the latter's entry for "monochordiser" is "to quaver with the fingers, to wag or play with them, as if he touched a Manicordion"; Jonson's margin has "playing." Jonson writes "whippers (or whip pots)" next to "fessepinte," which Cotgrave defines as "A tipler, bibber, quaffer, can-killer, pot-whipper, faithfull drunkard." Jonson's definition, in fact, better captures the order of the word's elements, and, since Cotgrave gives "whipper" for "fesseur," he would have no doubt as to which syllable means what. A "pinte" is a "pint," but Jonson sticks with Cotgrave's "pot." Another example: Holyband defines "poulain" only as "a colt," which hardly exhausts its meaning and would not have helped Jonson understand the answer to the question (in Chapter 5, "Les propos des Beuveurs") "what is a synonym for ham?" Ham is "un compulsoire de beuveurs [i.e., goad for drinkers]: c'est un poulain."

Cotgrave helps us understand this reply: "A fole, or coult; also, the rope wherewith wine is let downe into a seller; a pullie rope; also, a botch in the groine, a Winchester Goose" (this last a slang term for "whore"). Jonson underlines "poulain" and, in the margin, calls it a device with which "they let wine downe into ye cellar." Next to "huchant," part of the phrase "huchant en paume," Jonson writes "whistle." Holyband defines "hucher" as "to call," and Cotgrave's entry reads "To whoope, or hallow for; to call unto"; but under "huchant," fascinated as always by phrases and idioms, the latter adds "huchant en paume. Whistling for, or calling unto by whistling in the fist." And only in Cotgrave, under "frimas," would Jonson have found the entire phrase "avalleurs de frimats." His gloss reads "swallowers of mists," a brief and literal version of Cotgrave's "cousening knaves, idle companions, loytering rogues; also, a nickname for Judges; who using to rise, and goe abroad early, swallow a great deal of mist in their dayes."

Jonson was willing not only to weigh Cotgrave's synonyms ("vigilant" for "veillant" is Cotgrave's fourth definition, and "covertly" for "en tapinois" his seventh) but to deduce a more precise one. For "trongne" ("a face or countenance" in Holyband), Cotgrave gives "the face, aspect, looke, visage, countenance." Jonson has "chappes," specifying the area that includes the mouth. He does so, I suspect, because Cotgrave's subsidiary phrases concern drinking: "à la trongne cognoist on l'yvrongne" means "Two things a drunkard doe disclose, a fierie face, and crimson nose" and "bonne bouche bonne trongne" signifies that "a temperate mouth breedeth a fresh complexion; or, a well-shap'd mouth makes all the face shew faire; or, a silent mouth settles the countenance." Fully to consider "trongne," in other words, is to think not just of the face in general but of that consuming and talking part so relevant to *Gargantua* and to Jonson.

Jonson's glosses are as thoughtful, then, as one would expect from the man who wrote them. They are too localized and thickly clustered to reveal much about what in Rabelais most interested Jonson. He is, after all, beginning at the beginning, not choosing passages to work with, although it seems fitting that the pages he glossed include the notorious episode in which young Gargantua describes the joy of wiping oneself with a goose and the deliciously awful oration by a Parisian scholastic begging the giant to return Notre Dame's bells. It may be significant that so many glosses are in Latin, as if Jonson tended to think in it when considering words as words, or as if, whatever his views on the social nature of language, he ascribed to it a material *gravitas* and breadth allowing other languages to meet and negotiate on its solid ground. Precisely because classical Latin was dead, fixed, monologic, and canonical, argues Peter Womack, Jonson could further dehistoricize it in a vernacular context and then set it against modern words' proliferation, opacity, and decay. Removed from a living culture, that is, classical Latin splinters into words with the paradoxical stability of lexical isolation, occupying an unpressured linguistic space where other languages can steady themselves.[13]

If so, it is piquant to see Jonson giving the linguistic riot of *Gargantua* a marble fixity, a steadiness that Pantagruel would approve but that Rabelais himself enjoyed undoing. And yet Jonson was also willing to use Cotgrave (and to gloss the margins of Martial's epigrams on food in English). Perhaps we can see in his turn both to the jostle of Cotgrave's expansive English and to the sobriety of a French-Latin dictionary something of his divided imagination.[14] In any case, his desire to define and the intelligence with which he does so suit the preoccupations that led him to write a tract on English grammar and to comment frequently on speech in his *Discoveries*. Thinking that how words are used indicates the user's inward reality, they were for him intimately if ambiguously connected with the self that concerned him and the authorship he claimed.[15] His marginal glosses, at times heavy with Latin, suggest a mind imagining a similar weightiness within itself, yet they also prove he spent time with the pleasures of *Gargantua*. As he turned Cotgrave's pages, he perhaps recognized in ¶Rab a fellow spirit—even a fellow author. And Jonson was, of all people, well equipped by interests, habits, and assertions to appreciate Cotgrave's affectionate joke on Rabelais and authorship: next to "Alcofribas" (with no ¶Rab) we read "A greedie glutton; a great devourer." Alcofribas is, of course, "Alcofribas Nasier," the anagram under which Rabelais published before later emerging as a named and licensed author.

※　※　※

Rabelais's words are nowhere more impressively located than in his disconcerting trickster, Panurge, master of a dozen or so languages including Pantagruel's native Utopian (see *Pantagruel* 9). Had Jonson heard of him by 1597 when he wrote *The Case is Altered*? The evidence is uncertain. The play's aptly named and miserly Jaques, it will be recalled, has hidden his stolen gold in his "back side" [i.e., back yard] under a load of horsedung. When he is safely offstage, the cobbler Juniper asks his friend Onion, who has been watching, "What's the old panurgo gone? departed? cosmografied, ha?"[16] Juniper perhaps means "transmogrified," but why a "panurgo"? Herford and the Simpsons cite a lost English chapbook about a folklore giant named Gargantua, but its French original has no Panurge. Something else must be going on. Since Juniper often muddles his words it is unclear what he means by this one, but applied to Jaques it makes sense. This "panurgo" need not descend from Pantagruel's Panurge; he certainly emerges from the same dramatic and lexical material.

Panurge, as Jonson would have recognized at once, had begun life as a noun: *panourgos*.[17] Pagan Greek writers had used it for the fox and his games, the *rhetor* and his shifts, even the Olympians' deceits. In the Septuagint, *panourgia* indicates astuteness or wisdom, but St. Paul uses it for craftiness that lies in wait (Eph 4.14), subtlety that beguiles simplicity (2 Cor 11.3), worldly cunning that is foolishness with God (1 Cor 3.19; the margin of the Geneva Bible adds, "When they them selves are entangled in the same snares, which thei laid for others"). As a trickster, Panurge recalls Hermes, god of lies, magic, rhetoric, and merchants. There is much of him in Volpone, yet he is also the busy-body courtier: Jonson's Sir Politick Wouldbe but smarter.[18] Cooper's *Thesaurus* (1565) calls "panurgus" a "craftie, deceitfull, or wily person: an old beaten foxe" (1584 ed.); Cotgrave defines him as "A slye, craftie, deceitfull companion; an old beaten fox; one that hath experience, or hath been tampering, in most things; also, one that will meddle with, or have a flirt at, anything." And although in fact Plautus never uses the word, Ambrosius Calepinus's great dictionary quotes him as saying "panurgia te in pistrinum dabit," a "pistrinum" being a mill and also a place of punishment for slaves.[19]

Jonson would also have found "panourgia" in Aristophanes. The word stars in *Knights* (424 B.C.). Demos (the Athenian people) has acquired a slave, Paphlagon (Cleon, the tanner's son now leader of Athens).[20] Paphlagon is a rascally ("panourgotata," l. 56) cheater who plays tricks ("panourgia," l. 331) but, undone by a bigger rascality ("poly panourgiais"), is condemned to sell sausages at the city gates. As he is beaten with tripe, a crowd of knights repeatedly shouts, "smite the panurge, smite the panurge" (ll. 247–50). Nor was Rabelais's Panurge the first man with that name. Cicero's *Pro Quinto Roscio Comoedo* defends the actor, Roscius, who had contracted to train a slave named—or, more likely, nicknamed—Panurgus. Panurgus would go on stage and the tutor and owner would divide his earnings. Panurgus is soon murdered, but Roscius has already invested some profits in a now valuable farm and the dead slave's master is suing for half its worth.[21] "Panurge" is thus an ominous name to carry in a play. As Michel Coignet warns in *Politique discourses*, "wisedom and eloquence, without truth and justice, are a Panurgie, that is to say a guyle or sleight, such as we reade the slaves to use in Comedies, which still turneth to their owne domage and confusion."[22] This does indeed sound like Jonson's Jaques, a fox (the title puns on "case," a legal term and a pelt) who comes to lament that "I have no starting hols! . . . I plaid the thiefe, and now am robd my selfe" (5.12.88–91).

Rabelais's aging and cowardly Panurge is more notoriously a spendthrift than skinflint, but when in the *Tiers livre* he gives up his doublet and sword for a plain robe and pair of slippers he is dressing like a miser; even his outstanding codpiece disappears, as though retracted in a sort of sexual hoarding. Compared to Pantagruel's friend, though, Jaques makes a sour and less polyvalent *panourgos*, being suspicious, grasping, and shifty behind his walls (so unlike those that Panurge famously hopes to build of genitalia), with an anal-retentive obsession with gold. The love with which he addresses his treasure, even thinking it smells good in its dungy hole, gives his lines a proto-Volponean force suggesting Jonson's own imaginative engagement if not the perhaps foolish energy that drives Panurge to seek the Oracle of the Bottle and learn his marital future.[23]

*   *   *

It has long been known that many English references to Gargantua are not to Rabelais's giant but to a chapbook hero. The matter is more complex than is sometimes thought, though, for Rabelais may have had a hand in one or more of the semi-parodic chronicles describing the giant's adventures. Since he and the chapbooks' compilers borrowed from each other, moreover, and since the lost English translation was apparently based on a text with material from *Pantagruel*, it is a nice question "whose" Gargantua the English were recalling.[24] For all we know Jonson thought the *History of Garagantua* (its likely title) was by Rabelais; nor would he have been quite wrong.

Gargantua was among the biggest giants ever known: his shape and size, even his clothes and club, provided a handy way of thinking seriocomically about perspective or proportion as they relate to language. It is in these terms that Jonson mentions the giant's breeches, doing so in the context of belligerent speech, as though the loose anus within the clothing represented the mouth at its angriest. Bobadilla, the *miles gloriosus* of *Everyman in His Humor* (performed 1598), calls Giulliano, another ill-tempered gentleman, a "scavenger" (a cleaner of privies and streets). Giulliano is furious: "by this good day (God forgive me I should sweare) if I put it up so, say I am the rankest——[the 1616 folio has "cow"] that ever pist. S'blood and I swallowe this, Ile neere drawe my sworde in the sight of man againe while I live . . . Scavenger? 'Hart and Ile goe neere to fill that huge tumbrell slop of yours with somewhat and I have good lucke, your Garagantua breech cannot carry it away so" (1.4.123–30).

Whatever Jonson has read (the extra "a" is usually found in "popular" contexts), this Gargantua, like the pissing————(or cow), conveys the inflated choleric "humor" that will later lead Giulliano to thrash Bobadilla. We know he is big, for his brother calls him "tall" (4.3.12), while his speech shows his vulgarity, even if he himself scorns those who read "Ballads and Rogery, and Trash" (3.4.172–73). Something has happened to the scatology that the chapbook shares with Rabelais, though, for as usual Jonson's imagination is both drawn to and dismayed by what hides beneath civilization's breeches. Gargantua and the imagined excrement associated with him express explosive wrath, not comic exuberance or reversal. The chapbook Gargantua's colonic looseness is a sign of a fluent vitality serving both comedy and King Arthur's military needs; here the threatened filth is an index of the speaker's own wrath, a fecal humiliation projected onto an enemy in response to a socially degrading and dirty insult. The comic focus is on words, on inventive jibes and distended language. The implication is that an angry mouth can move another's bowels, that speech can cause excrement. Yet it matters that there is no "real" shit in the fiction, only a whiff of it in the invective; it betokens the discourse, but only the discourse, of the lower body. It has been well said that "Jonson's constant ridicule of jargon, cant, affected speech, rhetoric, and swearing of oaths is structurally transformed into food and its byproducts, feces, farts, and vomit."[25] He can also proceed in an opposite way, however, generating a body of words alluding to but through its very excess eliding a material reality spoken of but, perhaps understandably in this case, not staged.

Rabelais himself is more audible in *Volpone* (printed 1607). Playing the mountebank, Volpone claims he can cure teeth so loose they dance like virginal jacks (2.2.246–47), just as Rabelais proffers the pseudomedical advice in his prologue to *Pantagruel* that teeth leaping like virginal keys have been helped by the application of dung and a chapbook about Gargantua. And, in *The Alchemist* (printed 1612), the opening scene's abortive reference to licking figs from something evidently disgraceful recalls a story in *Quart livre* 45 about Milanese prisoners forced upon pain of death to remove figs from a mule's rear—with their teeth. None of this is proof (teeth do look like a keyboard and the fig story was going around).[26] Yet the probability is there. More significant is the nature of what struck Jonson. Rabelais's scatology is obvious. But the contexts of both sets of loose teeth also share a marketplace "step right up, folks" rhetoric as seductively energetic as it is untrustworthy,[27] for although Volpone is a villain and Alcofribas a boon companion, each has a compelling ambiguity, a panurgic uncanniness. Even more intriguingly, the figs appear in a chapter telling how a once happy land of Pope-scorners has been laid waste by Pope-worshipers. One would like to know what Jonson thought of this. It was in the year of *Alchemist's* first performance, 1610, that he rejoined the Church of England, impelled in part, thinks David Riggs, by worried anger at Catholic militants who threatened the Stuart establishment.[28]

The Devil is an Ass (1616) gains resonance from just these concerns, its instance of feigned possession an echo of the fuss over exorcisms that the government had accused Catholics of faking; Shakespeare, of course, had given this some attention in *King Lear*. Brown thinks that Panurge's multilingual first meeting with Pantagruel lies behind Fitz-dottrell's mock polyglot fit in *Devil* 5.8 (Justice Eitherside, in fact, believes the man truly possessed: "It is the divell, by his severall languages," he says, a reminder of *panourgia's* linguistic prowess and brimstone smell).[29] Jonson most clearly remembers Rabelais, though, in an indirect allusion to the monopolistic "projects" that concern him.[30] (The two activities—staging possession and imagining clever procedures or inventions—are related, for both appeal to mere opinion.) When the young demon Pug begs to go home, outclassed by London's city slickers, he asks Satan for easier work:

> O, Call me home againe, deare Chiefe, and put me
> To yoaking foxes, milking of Hee-goates,
> Pounding of water in a morter, laving
> The sea dry with a nut-shell, gathering all
> The leaves are falne this Autumne, drawing farts
> Out of dead bodies, making ropes of sand,
> Catching the windes together in a net,
> Mustring of ants, and numbring atomes; all
> That hell, and you thought exquisite torments, rather
> Then stay me here, a thought more: I would sooner
> Keepe fleas within a circle, and be accomptant
> A thousand yeere, which of 'hem and how far
> Out-leap'd the other . . .

(5.2.1–13)

Pug's prayer suits a tangle of concerns that the drama of those years often mocks or explores: projection, fantasy, devils (real or sham), and Catholic deceit. Of the eleven tasks, six are those at which Queen Entelechie's servants also work in the land of Quintessence, where Pantagruel's company is wined and dined (*Cinquième livre* 21). Along with enterprises that Jonson ignores, the queen's "abstracteurs" yoke foxes, milk billygoats, pound water in a mortar, keep fleas in a circle and measure their leaps, catch wind in nets, and pull farts from a dead ass.[31] These unlikely jobs may hint at the vanity of works and what the author thinks the illusive project of transubstantiation, for this book, whose ascription to Rabelais many doubt, is more decidedly Protestant than the first four. Like the scatological figs, the text Jonson remembers, even if he is not evoking it for his audience, mocks a faith he had now given up.

Performed on Twelfth Night, 1618, *Pleasure Reconcild to Vertue* opens with the entry of a "bouncing belly" named Comus but modeled on Rabelais's Gaster [the stomach]. Pantagruel and his shipmates come upon the latter several chapters after leaving the Pope-worshipers (*Quart livre* 57–62). Like Comus, Gaster lives near a hill, identified by Pantagruel as the Mount of Virtue and thus related to the mountain into which *Pleasure*'s Atlas has mutated. Both stomachs are premier masters of art, ride in triumph, fart a lot, tell time, teach birds to talk, invent technologies, lack ears, keep Poverty nearby (Comus has Hunger), and are associated with tripe and carnival. Pantagruel does not censure Gaster (as a doctor, Rabelais respected the stomach), but he detests the abject Gastrolatres. Nor does he admire Gaster's other followers, the Ventriloques, who speak from the *venter* in counterfeit divinations; with his interest in sham magic and possession, Jonson must have enjoyed reading about them.

Pantagruel's noble scorn anticipates that of *Pleasure*'s Hercules, in one tradition also a giant, who enters when the first antimasque is over. But Rabelais *starts* with heroic distaste and his giant spends time observing the natives, their piles of food, and their god. In other words, whereas Rabelais juxtaposes his hero and fools, *Pleasure* follows the typical masque structure by dividing folly from reason discursively and temporally. Jonson's antimasques derive power from the sense that what they dramatize is somehow basic to humanity yet must finally be let go: virtue cannot embrace any pleasure with swollen belly and sodden brain. Dr. Rabelais might agree, but he lets his giant linger for six chapters before getting him back on course. As he sails away, Pantagruel also leaves behind deceptive prophecy and technological ingenuity, for Jonson's eye has again lit on "projections": Gaster has invented farming—hardly progress, if we may believe Hesiod and Ovid—and also war engines, elaborate defense systems, and the gunpowder that Rabelais, like others, calls diabolical. Once more, Jonson focuses on a passage concerning the material world, certainly, but also the dark or sottish uses to which human-kind, driven by deaf desire, has put its imagination.

A decade later Jonson remembered Rabelais when writing his splendid unperformed masque, *Neptune's Triumph* (1624), intended to put a patriotic anti-Spanish spin on Prince Charles's failed and unpopular attempt to woo the Infanta.[32] In the opening scene a cook argues that "the Art of Poetry was learnd" first in the kitchen, and there discovered "the same day, with the Art of Cookery." When a poet says, "I should have giv'n it rather to the Cellar, if my suffrage had bin askt," the cook replies, "O, you are for the Oracle of the Bottle, I see; Hogshead Trismegistus: He is your Pegasus." In the printed text, a note says "Vid. Rabl.lib.5" (*Cinquième livre* 33–47)— Rabelais is now author enough to join Lucian, Strabo, Homer, and others in these learned margins.[33] Drink was notoriously important to Jonson, so there must be self-mockery here. But the connotations go further, and we are invited to hear them when Jonson identifies the source of his imported bottle. After their long sea voyage past many marvels, Pantagruel and his friends have finally reached Bacbuc (Hebrew for *bottle*), the sybil who, they hope, can advise Panurge on marriage. Jonson would have noticed several significant elements in this conclusion to the journey: the issue, as in the geopolitical events lying behind the masque, is whether marrying is worth the risk of being beaten, robbed, and betrayed. After drinking a book-shaped bottle, Panurge decides that it is (with regard to the Spanish marriage, also the object of a royal trip across water, the English disagreed, and in this sense Jonson's allusion has a touch of irony).

Drink also drives Panurge to a frenzy of rhyme, and no wonder, for the oracular bottle itself appears in chapter 44 both as a shaped poem and an illustration: in the text the bottle has wine, but in the picture it has text. The bottle says it has mysteries, being the liquor of Bacchus, vanquisher of India. In it is all truth and no "tromperie" (no *panourgia*, in effect, although one should not always trust self-referential bottles). If Jonson's poet is "for" this bottle, then, his claim is to Bacchic rapture, to insights beyond the architectural arts and mere *mimesis* of Renaissance haute cuisine—beyond Inigo Jones, perhaps.[34] Finally, the end of Book V, for all its quasi-parody, may make a serious religious point. Bacbuc's bookish liquor has a scriptural as well as Hermetic taste and her architecture (by way of Francesco Colonna) a mystically Vitruvian harmony. More important, after a first sip that tastes of mere water, each drinker delightedly perceives a different but familiar wine in the temple's mystical fountain, seemingly a comment on biblical hermeneutics and Holy Communion. Each drinker's mind, that is, undirected by

O Bouteille   Pleine toute
De mysteres.   D'vne aureille
Ie t'escoute, Ne differes,
Et le mot proferes,
Auquel pend mon cœur
En la tant diuine liqueur.
Bach° qui fut d'Inde vaïqueur,
Tient toute verité enclose.
Vin tant diuin, loin de toy est forclose
                          (perie
Toute mensonge, & toute tró
En ioye soit l'Aire de Noé close
Leq̃! de toy nous fit la têperie,
Sonne le beau mot ie t'en prie,
Qui me doit oster de misere.
Ainsi ne se perde vne goutte
De toy, soit blanche, ou soit vermeille.
O Bouteille   Pleine toute
De mysteres,   D'vne aureille
Ie t'escoute, Ne differes.

Ceste chanson paracheuée, Bacbuc, ietta ie
ne sçay quoy dedans la fontaine : & soudain
commença l'eau bouillir à force, comme fait
                    Q iiij

The Bottle of the Oracle from the edition of *Rabelais*
that Ben Jonson owned. Courtesy of The Bancroft Library, University of California at Berkeley.

outside authority, makes of the liquid what it will and according to what it knows and remembers.[35] In sum, Jonson's remarkably (inter)textured allusion recalls a scene germane to the joys of wine and the claims of poetry, but also to the risks of marriage—or those other commitments marriage can symbolize—and to how spiritual truth relates to the inward self and its perceptions of the world.

Jonson recycled this passage in *The Staple of News* (1626; 4.2.7–10), for good measure having his cook call the poet a "heretic" and the oracle "vain." The printed text has no marginal note to direct the reader, and in its new context the reference to the bottle has a different tone. *Staple* satirizes gossip and the press, but it is structured by tensions between youth and age, prodigality and stinginess, Carnival and Lent (this last a battle found in several Renaissance works including the *Quart livre*).[36] The dispute between cook and poetaster mocks poetry's airier claims, yet any winebottle must be Lickfinger's ally in Feast's war on Fast. Those who recognized the allusion may also have remembered Panurge's ecstatic anticipation of his wedding night—a pleasure denied in Lent—and the opposing verses by the tosspot monk, Frère Jean, resolving *not* to be a husband. The issue of who will marry Lady Pecunia, Infanta of the Mines, has a general political significance; still, marriage here seems less immediately topical (although the king had recently taken the plunge), more closely related to the play's interest in containment and release, hoarding and circulation.

Another reminiscence of Rabelais shows, again, that even when the passages Jonson remembers are festive or scatological they bear political and religious meaning. The cook, wanting news to "strew" at dinner, asks for the latest on Gondomar, the recent Spanish Ambassador who suffered from an anal sore and had been further humiliated by Middleton's anti-Spanish *A Game at Chess*, a play he supposedly helped get closed. We hear he has used the printed text as toilet paper with painful results (maybe he should have tried a goose): "A second Fistula, / Or an excoriation (at the least) / For putting the poore English-play, was writ of him, / To such a sordid use, as (is said) he did, / Of cleansing his posterior's." The cook cries "Justice! Justice!" (3.2.207–12). The joke repeats one in an episode near the scene from which Jonson probably took *Alchemist*'s scatological figs. Pantagruel's ship has reached the land of the Papimanes, who disgust the giant by idolizing the Pope and his edicts. In a set of anecdotes about the punishments attending the profane use of such edicts, each followed by papimanic exclamations at divine justice, Frère Jean recalls how when he wiped himself with one he got terrible hemorrhoids (*Quart livre* 52)—God's vengeance, he is told. Derision like this, which Rabelais may have thought Gallican but others could find anti-Catholic, suits a slap at Gondomar; like the figs and Entelechie's projects, it must have resounded complexly in Jonson's now Protestant mind.

Jonson recalled Rabelais twice in *The New Inn*, performed in 1629 before an apparently unimpressed audience of sparks and scholars at the Blackfriars. The host is a gentleman in disguise, and the inn's charwoman, a nurse who claims to be Irish, is his unrecognized wife, driven to her own disguise by "melancholy" over marital neglect and the lack of a son. When the host asks the whereabouts of her charge and the nurse replies "Gra chreest!" ["for the love of Christ!"], she is scornfully told to "Goe aske th'oracle / O'the bottle, at your girdle, there you lost it: / You are a sober setter of the watch" (4.4.343–45). This comment on careless insobriety may have invited the urbane audience to remember Bacbuc's bottle and its encouragement of a worried older man's nuptial plans. Although the insult seems primarily a passing sarcasm, it has psychosexual implications, not least of which is the fact of Jonson's fastening to an injured wife's waist the bottle he so often wielded himself.

Inn has one other Rabelaisian moment. Lovel, described in the printed play's list of characters as "A compleat Gentleman, a Souldier, and a Scholer," was once page to Lord Beaufort and later "companion of his studies." Beaufort had classy taste:

> He had no Arthurs, nor no Rosicleer's,
> No Knights o'the Sunne, nor Amadis de Gaule's,
> Primalions, and Pantagruel's, publique Nothings;
> Abortives of the fabulous, darke cloyster,
> Sent out to poison courts, and infest manners . . .
>
> (1.6.124–28)

A note in the Revels edition follows Herford and Simpson in saying confidently that Lovel alludes to "the sixteenth century English Gargantuan chapbooks."[37] But in the late 1620s, before this smart London audience, it would have been hard to say "Pantagruel" without evoking "Rabelais." The chapbook's probable model, moreover, owed its pages on Gargantua's son to Rabelais's *Pantagruel*: this giant, before Rabelais refashioned him, had been a little thirst-making devil, not a romance or chapbook figure. With effort, one can find other mentions of Pantagruel in such contexts,[38] but Jonson must have made a mental connection to Rabelais and known that many in his audience would have done so, too. Nor was the chapbook, let alone *Pantagruel*, a monkish fable; both texts, especially the latter, are send-ups of such literature. I have, then, no explanation for the reference aside from Jonson's use of a humanist (and sometimes Puritan) *topos* common since the mid-sixteenth century, a common tendency to associate parody with what is parodied (some such lists included *Don Quixote*), or perhaps an effort to make Lovel look a little snobbish and narrowly "classical" in a play that is itself a romance advocating hospitality and forgiveness.

* * *

Who was Jonson's Rabelais? At first a name, presumably, possibly linked to the lost *History of Garagantua*. And we know that at some point after 1599, if not before, he was the author of *Oeuvres* that Jonson handled. He also became, certainly by the mid–1620s, an author to be cited—and in Latin. He was comically scatological, entertaining on bottles, and useful as a satirist of the fancy's problematic contortions.[39] Although there must have been many passages that Jonson relished without wanting to adapt, in their original context most of those to which we know he gave particular attention do more than make ambiguous comedy of bodily materiality. They satirize intellectual pretension, the misdirections of ingenuity, or, more dangerously, what Rabelais and the author(s) of the fifth book took to be despotic religious illusion. The figs, the inventions of Gaster, the sore-making edicts, the odd jobs in the service of Quintessence, the Oracle of the Bottle, are relevant to religious and geopolitical issues that had not dissipated since the mid-sixteenth century.

Jonson could have found a different Rabelais—the logorrheic maker of lists and fantasy libraries, the humanist scholar and doctor, the expert on cuckoldry, and the scurrilous "atheist" were all known in England. Jonson's Rabelais is, on the surface, the "dirty" writer of legend. Yet the dirt, to sane people enjoyable in itself, can serve nonfestive satirical purposes that Jonson perceived, or so one may judge from its often remarkable relevance to the new locations Jonson found for it. In Jonson's clearest recollections, at least those he recorded textually, this Rabelais is primarily the author of the later books, the tales of sea voyages, of fantastic worlds, and above all of Panurge's search to know his own will and find the bottle of bottles, the one with the answers, the one with potable words all full of truth and rapture. Jonson also recalls this bottle in lines he wrote for the Apollo Room at the Devil's Tavern:

> Welcome all, who lead or follow,
> To the Oracle of Apollo.
> Here he speaks out of his Pottle,
> Or the Tripos, his Tower Bottle:
> All his Answers are Divine,
> Truth itself doth flow in Wine.[40]

The word from Rabelais's Oracle of the Bottle is "Drink!," good advice in either a temple or a tavern, and it, too, repeats the old claim that in wine is truth. It is poignant to reflect how often Jonson mentions this bottle, as though his mind kept returning to its promise of poetic inspiration, self-knowledge, and freedom from deception. A whole tun of sack, for all the real pleasures to be found there, must have seemed a poor substitute.

Notes

1. *Rabelais in English Literature* (Cambridge, Mass.: Harvard University Press, 1933), 81–94. Brown did not know that Jonson owned Rabelais's works, and in any case the parallels he lists need a new look, especially for context. I ignore some I think improbable or for which editors find better sources and intertexts.

2. John Lemly, "Masks and Self-Portraits in Jonson's Late Poetry," *ELH* 44 (1977): 248–66. See also Frank Whigham, "Reading Social Conflict in the Alimentary Tract: More on the Body in Renaissance Drama," *ELH* 55 (1988): 333–50. Bruce Thomas Boehrer, "Renaissance Overeating: The Sad Case of Ben Jonson," *PMLA* 105 (1990): 1071–82, notes the remarkable fact of "a famous fat man and legendary drunkard constructing a cult of personality around his own excessive girth while excoriating his contemporaries for eating and drinking too much" (1072). Thanks to slander and his adopted persona, Rabelais himself gained a false reputation as a fat drunk.

3. E.g., Don K. Hedrick, "Cooking for the Anthropophagi: Jonson and his Audience," *Studies in English Literature* 17 (1977): 233–45; Joseph Loewenstein, "The Jonsonian Corpulence, or The Poet as Mouthpiece," *ELH* 53 (1986): 491–518.

4. "Satiric and Ideal Economies in the Jonsonian Imagination," *English Literary Renaissance* 19 (1989): 44.

5. Loewenstein, "Jonsonian Corpulence," 508–11, referring to Mikhail Bakhtin, *Rabelais and His World,* trans. Helene Iswolsky (Cambridge, Mass.: M.I.T. Press, 1965).

6. From *Pantagruel* (ca. 1532) to the *Tiers livre* (1546) Rabelais underwent something like the shift away from medieval attitudes toward festivity that Jonathan Haynes traces in *The Social Relations of Jonson's Theater* (Cambridge, England: Cambridge University Press, 1992), chap. 5. Bakhtin's great book can be misleading: see Richard M. Berrong, *Rabelais and Bakhtin: Popular Culture in "Gargantua and Pantagruel"* (Lincoln: University of Nebraska Press, 1986) and, complicating Bakhtin's binary terms, Samuel Kinser, *Rabelais's Carnival: Text, Context, Metatext* (Berkeley: University of California Press, 1990), chap. 10.

7. Shelf number 1081.k.2; noted by Stephen Rawles and M. A. Screech, *A New Rabelais Bibliography: Editions of Rabelais before 1626* (Geneva: Droz, 1987), no. 80. I have worked from a microfilm of the relevant section. I thank Robert C. Evans and H. R. Woudhuysen for confirming to me that most glosses are Jonson's (the latter being 90% certain); Professor Evans kindly sent me photocopies of pages in Jonson's Martial for comparison. The glosses are mentioned by Richard Proudfoot in "Richard Johnson's *Tom a' Lincoln* Dramatized: A Jacobean Play in British Library MS Add. 61745," in *New Ways of Looking at Old Texts: Papers of the Renaissance English Text Society 1985–1991,* ed. W. Speed Hill (Binghamton: MRTS 107, 1993), 97; Rabelais is not listed in published catalogues of Jonson's library.

8. Bruce Thomas Boehrer, "The Poet of Labor: Authorship and Property in

the Work of Ben Jonson," *PQ* 72 (1993), 289–312, ascribes Jonson's dropping the "h" to his sometimes self-defeating views of language, authorship, and selfhood.

9. *Calendar of State Papers: Domestic Series* (1611–18), ed. Mary A. E. Green (Nenaeln, Liechtenstein: Kraus Reprint, 1967) 8, 351–53. Thomas was nephew-in-law to Sir William Smith, who writes Lord Zouch that he was a well-traveled and accomplished youth. The Calendar also mentions a master gunner, dead by 1630, and a man whose creditors were suing his estate in the early 1630s: see the *Calendar of State Papers: Domestic Series* for Charles I, ed. John Bruce (Kraus Reprint, 1967), for 4 May 1626, 20 February 1630, and 24 June 1636. The *Guide to Reports* 1911–57 for the Historical Manuscripts Commission, ed. A. C. S. Hall (London: Her Majesty's Stationery Office, 1966) 2, lists a secretary to the Merchant Adventurers in ca. 1648. I thank my student Sae Yun Kim for her help in tracking down various Skinners.

10. *Tiers livre* 25; "'Do you want,' asked Herr Trippa, 'to know the truth more fully by fire-divination, by sky-divination (made famous by Aristophanes in his *Clouds*), by water-divination, by bowl-of-water-divination (so celebrated among the Assyrians and recently used by Ermolao Barbaro?) In a basin of water I will show you your future wife tumbling about with two knaves.' 'When,' said Panurge, 'you put your nose in my ass remember to take off your glasses.'" I quote the edition by Pierre Jourda (Paris: Garnier, 1962). Unless otherwise identified, all translations are mine.

11. On Cotgrave see Vera E. Smalley, *The Sources of "A dictionarie of the French and English tongues" by Randle Cotgrave (London, 1611)* (Baltimore: Johns Hopkins University Press, 1948), and Peter Rickard, "Le 'dictionarie' franco-anglais de Cotgrave (1611)," *Cahiers de l'Association Internationale des Etudes Françaises* 35 (1983): 7–21. I quote William S. Wood's facsimile edition (Columbia: University of South Carolina Press, 1950). About 475 entries have a "¶Rab."

12. The latter method was famous in ancient Rome. Jonson would have read (in, for example, Cicero's *De natura deorum* [2.7]) how Publius Claudius, taking the auspices during the first Punic War, was vexed when the chickens refused to eat; telling them to drink instead, the general had them thrown into the ocean—and lost the battle.

13. *Ben Jonson* (Oxford: Basil Blackwell, 1986), chap. 3.

14. I find no sign that Jonson used Nicot's French-Latin dictionary or that of Robert Estienne; perhaps he used a French-English dictionary and simply thought of Latin equivalents for the English definitions.

15. See Martin Elsky, "Words, Things, and Names: Jonson's Poetry and Philosophical Grammar," in *Classic and Cavalier: Essays on Jonson and the Sons of Ben*, ed. Claude J. Summers and Ted-Larry Pebworth (Pittsburgh: University of Pittsburgh Press, 1982), 91–104.

16. 4.9.3–4. I quote the edition of Jonson's *Works* by C. H. Herford, Percy Simpson, and Evelyn Simpson (Oxford: Clarendon Press, 1954 ed.), 11 vols.

17. The fullest treatment of Panurge's etymology is by Ludwig Schrader, *Panurge und Hermes: Zum Ursprung eines Charakters bei Rabelais* (Bonn: University of Bonn, 1958); Jerome Schwartz, "Panurge's Impact on Pantagruel (*Pantagruel*, Chapter IX)," *Romanic Review* 67 (1976): 1–8, has a summary.

18. Michael Downes, "Panurge, Ulysse et les 'gens curieux,'" *Etudes rabelaisiennes* 13 (1976): 139–45, links Panurge, "curiosity," and courtiership.

19. Venice, 1571 ed.; Terence's *Andrea* 198–200 has something similar when a slave is warned not to be "callidus" (i.e., panurgic) or "te in pistrinum . . . dedam."

Professor Greg Crane kindly checked his database for the word "panurgia" in Plautus but to no avail.

20. *The Knights (Hippeis)*, ed. and trans. Benjamin B. Rogers (London: Bell, 1910), ll. 44–45.

21. M. T. Cicero, Loeb edition, vol. 6, trans. John Henry Freese (Cambridge, Mass: Harvard University Press, 1967), sections 27–32; the verdict is lost. Schrader mentions the case in passing.

22. Trans. Edward Hoby (London: 1585), sigs. N2ᵛ–N3.

23. Jonson found his miser in Plautus's *Aulularia* but evokes the Bible's Laban by giving the child he stole the name "Rachel." Even this suits a "panurgo": tricky himself, Laban is outfoxed by his son-in-law Jacob, with whom Rachel conspires to abscond with some valuables (sitting atop them on her camel and refusing to be searched because, she says, she is menstruating; Gen. 30). Laban is broken-hearted, but to many exegetes he represented the Old Law and needed no pity; cf. John S. Coolidge, "Law and Love in *The Merchant of Venice*," *Shakespeare Quarterly* 27 (1976): 243–63 (who does not mention *Case*). For a time Jaques thinks Rachel has robbed him and cries, "my gold's gone, Rachel's gone, / Al's gone! (5.5.20–21).

24. Huntington Brown, ed. *The Tale of Gargantua and King Arthur by François Rabelais* (Cambridge, Mass.: Harvard University Press, 1932), gives the evidence for a translation; my research suggests a date ca. 1567. See also my "Reshaping Gargantua," in *L'Europe de la renaissance: cultures et civilisations*, ed. Jean-Claude Margolin and Marie-Madeleine Martinet (Paris: Touzot, 1988), 477–91, from which I adapt my comments on this scene.

25. Terrance Dunford, "Consumption of the World: Reading, Eating and Imitation in *Every Man Out of His Humor*," *ELR* 14 (1984): 131–47. Cf. Gail Kern Paster, "Leaky Vessels: The Incontinent Women of City Comedy," *Renaissance Drama* 18 (1987): 43–65, who links the "liquid expressiveness" of *Bartholomew Fair*'s urinating women to "excessive verbal fluency" (44), and, on inflation and scatology, Wayne A. Rebhorn, "Jonson's 'Jovy Boy': Lovewit and the Dupes in *The Alchemist*," *The Journal of English and German Philology* 79 (1980): 355–75.

26. For salutary if excessive skepticism, see Marcel de Grève, "Limites de l'influence linguistique de Rabelais en Angleterre au XVIᵉ siècle," *Comparative Literature Studies* 1 (1964): 15–30.

27. Jonson must have relished Rabelais's play with many "popular" languages, not just that of carnival; see Carol Clark, *The Vulgar Rabelais* (Glasgow: Pressgang, 1983).

28. *Ben Jonson: A Life* (Cambridge, Mass.: Harvard University Press, 1989), 176.

29. It may be no coincidence that the chapter in the *Quart livre* with the figs probably adopted in *Alchemist* has a young illiterate devil, as yet incapable of serious thundering, who finds himself no match for human cunning.

30. Robert C. Evans, *Jonson and the Contexts of His Time* (Lewisburg: Bucknell University Press, 1994), chap. 4, sets *Devil* in a context including political disputes over economic projection.

31. Some of these jobs are proverbial, but only Rabelais has so many of them together; the note in Peter Happé's edition of *Devil* (Manchester: Manchester University Press, 1994) finds "No close parallel" for the fleas, but they are in Rabelais.

32. The antimasque may owe a little to the *Songes drolatiques de Pantagruel* (1565), a book of grotesque figures that the title page claims for Rabelais. Inigo Jones used it when costuming Davenant's *Salmacida Spolia* and, I think, it inspired Fant'sy's dreams in *The Vision of Delight*; see my "The Stuart Masque and Pantagruel's Dreams," *ELH* 51 (1984): 407–30.

33. Evelyn Tribble, "Genius on the Rack: Authorities and the Margin in Ben Jonson's Glossed Works," *Exemplaria* 4 (1992): 317–39, sees a tension between Jonson's claims for authorship and glosses that look back to the authority of others. Be that as it may, Rabelais is here among "authorities."

34. Peter Hyland, "'The Wild Anarchie of Drinke': Ben Jonson and Alcohol," *Mosaic* 19.3 (1986): 25–33, contrasts the "gargantuan drinker" to the moralist and thinks Jonson flirted with notions of Bacchic inspiration.

35. My reading of this episode follows David Quint, *Origin and Originality: Versions of the Source* (New Haven: Yale University Press, 1983), 192–204.

36. On *Staple* and Shrovetide tradition see, for example, Anthony Parr's edition (Manchester: Manchester University Press, 1988). Parr notes such parallels in Rabelais as Carnival wars, farts from dead bodies (cf. 3.2.98; *Staple* also laughs at "projectors"), and Hearsay's college (*Cinquième livre* 30). One might add Rabelais as Diogenes, rolling his barrel up and down as the busy Corinthians prepare for war (*Tiers livre*, prologue); cf. the Induction, with Jonson in the tiring house "rolling himself up and down like a tun i'the midst of 'em": here Jonson *is* the barrel.

37. Ed. Michael Hattaway (Manchester: Manchester University Press, 1984). There is no good evidence for more than one such chapbook.

38. For example, George Hakewill complains in his *Apologie . . . of the power and providence of God* (1627, sig. Bb3ᵛ) of infectious poetical fictions like "Guy of Warwick, Bevis of Hampton, Corineus and Gog-Magog, Robin Hood and Little John, Amadis of Gaule, Pontagruel, Gargantua, and the like."

39. He was also, perhaps, the source of some of Jonson's more exotic words, including the word "exotic"; see Brown, *Rabelais,* and (on "exotic") Parr's *Staple,* 187.

40. Herford & Simpson 8.657. In a nuanced reading of Jonson's treatment of vessels and containers of all sorts, Richard Peterson, *Imitation and Praise in the Poems of Ben Jonson* (New Haven: Yale University Press, 1981), chap. 3, agrees with Herford and the Simpsons that these lines echo the *Cinquième livre.*

Jonson, Lipsius, and the Latin Classics

ROBERT C. EVANS

BEN Jonson's interest in the Greek and Latin classics is quite well known. Jonson himself often acknowledged his debt, but his interest is also clear from the lengthy list of classical works that survive from his library.[1] Valuable studies have emphasized the impact of the classics on Jonson's own creativity, and his role as one of the chief English conduits of the classical heritage has been very widely noted.[2] Yet our appreciation of Jonson's debt is magnified even further when we recall that many of the Renaissance books and authors he consulted were themselves heavily beholden to classical influences. Thus he encountered the classics not only when he deliberately sought them out, but also when he read other contemporary writers. In fact, his interest in such writers often seems to have been greatly determined by their own interest in classical texts, and he often turned to contemporary authors precisely for the access they could provide to the living thoughts of writers long dead.

There is perhaps no better example of such "mediated influence" than Jonson's heavily marked text of the *Politicorum, sive Civilis Doctrinae Libri Sex* (*Six books of politics or civil doctrine*), written by the great Flemish intellectual Justus Lipsius. This book is essentially a huge compilation of quotations, taken mainly from classical authorities, which are used to buttress Lipsius's own "neo-Stoic" political, ethical, and religious arguments. Lipsius's impact on Jonson, especially on his political thinking, has recently been discussed at length.[3] However, the value of Lipsius's book as a collection of quotations from the ancients deserves separate emphasis. While scanning the *Politica*, Jonson could become reacquainted with some of the most significant ideas and figures of the classical period—a period which, for him and most of his contemporaries, never seemed irrelevant or outdated.

Among the authors whom Lipsius cites (and whom Jonson marks) are Aeschylus, Afranius, Agellius, Ambrosius, Ammianus, Apuleius, Aristophanes, Aristotle, Augustine, Ausonius, Bernardus, Boethius, Caesar, Callimachus, Cassiodorus, Cato, Cicero, Claudian, Columella, Curtius Rufus, Cyprianus, Dio Cassius, Diodorus, Epicurus, Euripides, Festus, Florus, Herodotus, Hesiod, Homer, Horace, Iamblichus, Isidorus, Jerome, Justinian, Justinus, Juvenal, Lactantius, Lampridius, Livy, Lucan, Lucretius, Manilius, Menander, Origenes, Ovid, Pacuvius, Philo Judaeus, Plato, Plautus, both Plinies, Plutarch, Polybius, Propertius, Quintilian, Rufinus, Sallust, Seneca, Silius, Sophocles, Spartianus, Statius, Stobaeus, Suetonius, Tacitus, Thucydides, Tibullus, Valerius Flaccus, Valerius Maximus, Velleius Paterculus, Varro, and Xenophon. Even this is only a partial listing: it includes only those authors cited in the slightly more than two sections of Lipsius's treatise that Jonson obviously marked. He could have encountered quotations from other writers in other sections of the *Politica*, although we cannot be certain that he actually read the unmarked portions. In any case, his encounters with the ancients in the sections he *did* read were plentiful enough, and his enthusiastic reaction to those encounters is evident in the number and nature of his markings. For Jonson, the *Politica* seems to have served, in part, as a huge digest of classical thought, an enormous commonplace book that systematically arranged and discussed some of the wisest and most eloquent statements of the classical authors he revered.[4]

Many of the authors marked in Jonson's copy of the *Politica* are not indexed in the standard edition of his works; thus his markings in Lipsius provide us with a wealth of new information about his access to classical sources. Moreover, many of the authors he marked in Lipsius do not appear as separate listings in the standard catalogues of books surviving from his library. Professor McPherson, for instance, reports no separate volume of Cicero's works as having been owned by Jonson, and the references to Cicero in the index to the standard Herford and Simpson edition are relatively few. Yet Cicero was one of the classical authors whom Lipsius most often cited and whom Jonson most often marked. His markings in the *Politica*, then, tell us much more about his familiarity with Cicero (and many other authors) than we might assume from other available sources. Therefore, summarizing the Latin citations Jonson marked in the *Politica* seems variously worthwhile. (Limitations of space make it impossible to deal here with his borrowings from the Greeks.)

In the first place, providing such a summary can also provide a convenient overview of Jonson's second-hand familiarity with an astonishing variety of authors, texts, and ideas. Such a listing can thus supplement the list of classical works and writers already indexed in the final volume of the Herford and Simpson edition. Second, such a list and summary may also help us track previously unnoted borrowings from (or allusions to) the classics in Jonson's own writings. Third, even when specific borrowings or allusions do not exist, a listing of the specific ancient sources and ideas that Jonson noted in Lipsius can help us appreciate the larger, more general senses in which his thinking (especially his social and political thinking) was shaped by classical influences. All in all, reporting Jonson's familiarity with the classics, as filtered through his reading of Lipsius, can provide us with a handy map of the mental terrain he naturally inhabited.

Lipsius's own importance in Renaissance culture has recently been stressed by various scholars.[5] Suffice it here to say that he was one of the most significant intellectuals of his time, a man who contributed enormously to such disciplines as philology, ethics, and political philosophy. His own political views, at least as embodied in the *Politica*, were strongly influenced by Tacitus and Seneca, and so it is hardly surprising that most of the marked passages in Jonson's copy of that book also derive from those two writers. Yet Lipsius ranged far and wide for quotations to support his arguments, and Jonson, actively wielding his pencil, eagerly tracked him.

Whether Jonson's markings suggest agreement or disagreement with Lipsius is a matter that would require separate discussion of each individual case. My own assumption (expressed much more fully in *Jonson, Lipsius, and the Politics of Renaissance Stoicism*) is that Jonson generally agreed with Lipsius's basic positions. However, his markings at the very least indicate some real interest in the ideas Lipsius expresses, and my chief purpose here is simply to make those ideas more easily and widely available to other scholars. All of us will then be in a better position to argue about Jonson's use of (and attitudes toward) his sources. For instance, my own work on this project has already helped me to trace what seems to be a previously unnoted Jonsonian allusion to Seneca (apparently by way of Lipsius) in *The King's Entertainment at Welbeck*. Lines 299–300 of that work (Herford and Simpson 7:801) seem to echo almost exactly the first citation from Seneca's *De consolatione ad Polybium* (concerning a good king's watchfulness) listed below. This allusion is not reported in the standard edition of Jonson's works, but the fact that Jonson marked Seneca's phrasing when he read Lipsius provides positive proof that he was directly familiar with the Senecan passage. The fact that he also quoted that passage while praising Charles I suggests that he agreed with Seneca's sentiments; if nothing else, his allusion indicates that he found Seneca's phrasing interesting and highly useful.[6]

Things become more difficult when we try to discern, from Jonson's markings in Lipsius, his attitudes toward a more complicated issue—such as his view of women. Even the marked quotations from one source (Tacitus) express a wide variety of ideas on such topics as the traits of women and the advisability of women rulers. Jonson marks Lipsius when the latter quotes Tacitus (in the *Agricola*) as saying, for example, that the British followed women leaders (40), but he also marks Tacitus's comment (in the *Germania*) that women rulers signal cultural degeneracy (40). Nevertheless, he marks as well two ensuing passages quoted from the same Tacitean source—the claim that the Germans revered women rulers and that they valued women's advice. The poet's markings of such apparently contradictory passages can be interpreted in various ways (a matter I discuss at great length in *Jonson, Lipsius, and the Politics of Renaissance Stoicism*). It is possible that reading Lipsius encouraged Jonson to think well of women's capacities, both as citizens and as rulers.[7] However, on this matter as on others, I prefer (at least in this article) to present the hard evidence and let others use it to draw their own conclusions.

What follows, then, is a listing and summary of passages from the Latin sources cited by Lipsius and marked by Jonson. This listing summarizes only the ideas that Jonson took the trouble to underline or to emphasize in some other distinctive way (such as by drawing marginal flowers or pointing hands). The list does not, therefore, include passages marked merely by being encompassed by one of the long vertical lines that Jonson often drew in the margins of the *Politica*. However, for the sake of comprehensiveness, passages not marked in this way are reported (but not summarized) and are designated by the abbreviation "NSM" ("no special mark").

In each case where Jonson does make a distinctive mark, a brief summary of the highlighted idea is given, followed by the page number in the *Politica* on which the relevant quotation can be found. When Lipsius cites a particular ancient work or specific sections of such a work, that information is reported, although it must be emphasized that Renaissance editions of certain classical texts were often divided differently than is presently the case. Thus when Lipsius cites (say) chapter ten of a particular classical work, that citation may or may not refer to chapter ten in modern editions of the relevant text.

Although most of the ensuing summaries closely follow the phrasing of the 1594 translation of the *Politica* provided by William Jones, I do not quote Jones consistently and have departed from his exact wording on numerous occasions. Jones's renderings are almost always quite literal; his few differences from Lipsius nearly always serve simply to clarify. My own departures from Jones have usually been made to provide an even more literal or explicit rendering of the Latin (using cognates, for example), or they have been prompted by a desire to avoid words that have subtly changed meaning over the past few centuries. Furthermore, to clarify contexts, I have sometimes inserted explanatory words of my own in brackets; for instance, where Jonson sometimes marks only the adjectives describing a noun, I have sometimes reported the unmarked noun in brackets. In each of the ensuing summaries, my main goal has been to convey a given passage's chief idea. Inevitably, then, some subtleties of expression or shadings of thought may be lost. For those, the reader should consult the *Politica* directly.

When Jonson marks an author whose name is not listed in the comprehensive Herford and Simpson index (and there are many), I have indicated that fact by placing a star before the author's name. When Jonson marks an author whose works are not represented by a separate volume listed in the McPherson catalogue of Jonson's library, I have indicated that fact by inserting a raised dot (•). These symbols will allow readers to see at a glance how many of the Latin writers Jonson encountered in his copy of the *Politica* are not mentioned separately in other sources concerned with his reading. It should be remembered, however, that Jonson did have access to many Latin writers in other collections, particularly in a comprehensive anthology entitled *Chorus Poetarum* (see McPherson 36).

Primary Latin Sources of the *Politica*

•TACITUS, Publius (or Gaius) Cornelius[8]: *De vita Julii Agricolae:* 1. Be moderate in apparel and courteous in speech (30). 2. Be moderate in pursuing knowledge (36). 3. The British followed women into battle (40). 4. A prince must sometimes pretend that his people have been trained, rather than forced, to be good (52). 5. A prince should seek love rather than fear, since the latter can lead to hate (52). 6. A prince should punish capital crimes severely but deal leniently with small ones and pardon the penitent (52). 7. A prince should be neither melancholy nor arrogant (57). 8. Sometimes mildness diminishes authority and severity diminishes love (57). 9. People revere the unfamiliar (58). 10. It is more honorable for a prince to offend than to hate (59). 11. Anger should not be hidden (59). 12. Those who hide anger are malicious (59). 13. Citizens will be supportive if the prince avoids force and violence (118). 14. Citizens will not tolerate force and violence (118). *De origine et situ Germanorum:* 1. It is better to believe than to scrutinize divine works (24). 2. Female rulers signal degeneration from liberty and even from slavery (40). 3. The Germans revered women rulers (40). 4. The Germans valued the advice of women (40).

Historiae: Book 1: NSM (27). 1. All people profit when authority is vested in one (38). 2. Political change promotes instability (41). 3. Election often turns up the most worthy persons (41). 4. Inherited power is fortuitous; election implies judgment and consent (41). 5. Election bespeaks liberty (41). 6. No one exercises power well when it is shamefully gained (42). 7. A prince, once hated, will be criticized whether he does well or ill (45). 8. Nero and others were overthrown because of their own luxury and cruelty (45). 9. Any person executed without examination and trial dies innocent (49). 10. Liberality differs from prodigality; many know how to spend, but not how to give (58). 11. [A prince should not] feed the cupidity of his favorites. 12. [A good prince] is frugal with his own and the commonwealth's funds (119). 13. People measure their own losses against others' profits (119). Book 2: 1. Desire for power is ancient and inborn in mortals (41). 2. Some princes degenerate because of good fortune and bad teachers (42). 3. Refrain from spying on the rich (116). 4. Corrupt individuals are easier to dislodge than corrupt behavior (118). 5. A prince should not privately misspend public funds (118). NSM (118). 6. [A prince should not spend money on] abject and vile persons (119). Book 3: 1. Greedy princes purchase more hatred than strength (114). Book 4: 1. [Virtue is] man's proper good (21). 2. The gods aid the courageous (27). 3. Strive to be good rather than famous (30). NSM (31). 4. Seek knowledge not to disguise idleness but to serve the commonwealth by being prepared for adversity (35). 5. The Germans considered some women prophetesses and even (superstitiously) goddesses (40). 6. Nothing strengthens an empire better than numerous children (41). 7. A reputation for clemency is profitable to new rulers (42). 8. [He is evil who] uses a great fortune merely for licentiousness (43). 9. [He is evil who] ignores important matters and plays a prince in voluptuousness and lust (43). 10. Peace depends on armies; armies depend on pay; their pay depends on taxes or tributes (114). 11. [A prince should not daily] invent new ways or words to extract riches (116). Book 5: 1. There is one god who rules all things (22). 2. [The divine essence is] sovereign, eternal, immutable, and immortal (22). 3. Avoid superstition, which is the enemy of religion (24).

Ab excessu divi Augusti (*Annales*): Book 1: 1. Our body is ruled by one mind (38). 2. Monarchy as a remedy for civil discord (38). 3. [Inherited succession] strongly fortifies [a prince] (41). 4. All mortal things are uncertain, and the highest status is most slippery (56). 5.

Majesty is most revered at a distance (58). 6. [A prince who supports learning] will not lack worthy wits to record the history of his time (59). Book 2: 1. There is less hazard in receiving than in electing a prince (41). 2. [The common people] usually welcome new kings and new governments (42). 3. [Germanicus] was venerated whether he appeared or spoke, and, behaving with majesty and gravity at the height of fortune, shunned ill-will and arrogance (57–58). 4. [A prince whose] ambition empties the treasury may resort to evil to make good the shortage (58). 5. No good can exist in a mind corrupted with lust (59). 6. Studies perish when study goes unrewarded (59). 7. [People should know] that if their behavior wavers, they will not go uncorrected (121). 8. [A prince should encourage] moderation in silver plate, furnishings, and other household possessions (123). 9. [There should be special clothing for those] who excel because of order or rank (123).

Book 3: 1. Either the people, or the chief persons, or single individuals govern all nations and cities (37). 2. Women are feeble and incapable of hardship, and when they are free they are savage and ambitious (40). 3. When the succession is not uncertain, improper ambitions are restrained (41). 4. [Most princes], through their own or their servants' means, are beloved at first, but are more hated after they have taken power (42). 5. The desire to follow and imitate a prince is more forceful than legal punishments (46). 6. All do wrong through a single person's envy (47). 7. Trespasses and offenses are committed without measure (52). 8. [Bad conduct, even if not illegal,] when overlooked undermines the republic (121). 9. [Excess, unless restrained, can] break out enormously and money be widely wasted (122). 10. [The prince should ensure that] table expenses are restrained (123). 11. [The prince should ensure that] men and women are not clothed promiscuously (123). 12. [The prince will] promote restraint by conforming himself to the old ways of conduct (125). NSM (125). 13. Shame will change some people, necessity others, and satiety or loathing still others (125).

Book 4: NSM (26). 1. [Discretion or selection] discerns between the honest and the unworthy (or dishonest) and between the useful and the injurious (31). 2. Many are instructed by the experiences of others (33). 3. It is hard for power [in this case, of the many] and concord to dwell in the same place (38). 4. A woman parted from her virtue will stop at nothing (40). 5. The most corrupt republic has the most laws (49). 6. In the past, crimes proved oppressive, but now laws do (49). 7. If reproaches anger us, they seem true; if we disdain them, they pass away (59). 8. Most men are concerned with their own self-interests, but a prince needs to be concerned with his reputation (59). 9. Everything else will follow at once if you work to leave a good memory after you; by condemning renown, virtue is condemned (59). 10. [In levying taxes,] be moderate in accordance with financial constraints (115). 11. [Overtaxed people] will rebel through [the prince's] avarice rather than through any impatience to obey (116). 12. The provinces [should not be] over-burdened with new taxes (116). 13. [Levies should be made] without avarice and cruelty (116). 14. [The prince should] commit his affairs to the most respected persons (117). 15. [The prince should avoid] pressing into service [the people's] oxen, then their lands, then their bodies (118). 16. [The people, overtaxed, will resort to] anger and complaint and may even seek remedy through war (118). 17. Posterity will give every person his due (126).

Book 6: 1. [Many queens,] with a manly providence, have cast off the vices of women (40). 2. Courage as a response to the authors of fear (52). NSM (117). 3. Usury is an old evil in cities (122). Book 11: NSM (24). 1. Just as physicians profit when diseases flourish, so lawyers profit when courts proliferate (49). 2. There is nothing more vendible than the perfidy [of lawyers] (49). 3. [The prince] should seek his people's love and his enemies' fear (51). 4. The power of gold and riches is hurtful to the prince (122). Book 12: 1. [Princes often] eventually give in to pride (42). 2. [A prince] should not think in terms of despotism and servants but rather of a ruler and citizens, and he should exercise clemency and justice (51). 3. [Claudius] was submissive to his wife (59). 4. A greedy prince will always have a pretext, as if the kingdom depended on subsidies (115).

Book 13: 1. There should be no bribery in a prince's court, nor any pathway for ambition (49). 2. Show [the people] that the empire will be threatened with dissolution if the profit by which it is sustained is diminished (114). 3. Income and expenses must always agree (114). 4. [Contrived terms to justify taxes include] the hundredth part, the fortieth part, the fiftieth part (116). 5. There are other invented names for illicit exactions (116). 6. [Avoid cruelty and force,] lest what has been long endured without complaint be converted by new rigor into envy (118). Book 14: 1. [Conscience is a scourge to sin because] its enormity is known as soon as it is committed (29). 2. The persuasion of the person who has the power to command carries the force of necessity (115). Book 15: NSM (30). 1. [Some people, under a veil of learning,] are traitors and deceitful; they are dissemblers who cover their avarice and lust (35). 2. [Such persons are] false in friendship under a cover of learning or knowledge (35). 3. [Many who] profess learning with their lips never improve their minds with worthy knowledge (35). 4. Usually a woman's advice is worse. 5. [Desire for authority] is more fervent than all other affections (41). 6. The beginnings of governments are usually best, but towards the end they decline (42). 7. [A barbarous opinion:] In great fortune, what is most profitable is most just (48). 8. A reputation for modesty is not to be despised by the chiefest mortals and is pleasing to the gods (56). 9. [Subjects are more likely to respect] a person of great physical stature and imposing speech (58).

SALLUSTIUS CRISPUS, Gaius: *Unspecified source:* 1. The greatest empire is accompanied with greatest care (43). 2. [Quoting Marius:] Elegant attire is an attribute of women; labor is an attribute of men (57). *Bellum Catilinae:* 1. Virtue shines forever and is eternal (21). 2. All human endeavors take second place to virtue (21). 3. The assistance of the gods is not won by womanish prayers and supplications; by vigilance and action everything prospers (27). 4. An impure soul, troubled by men and the gods, cannot be at rest either waking or sleeping. Thus conscience consumes an unquiet mind (29). 5. Strive rather to be good than merely to seem so (30). 6. [Avoid those] who are more concerned to have a fair countenance than a good character (30). 7. This name of government [kingship] was the first on the earth (38). 8. A kingdom is most easily preserved through the same arts by which it was first brought forth (42). 9. [Be careful, lest] in changing customs one also changes one's fortune (42). 10. [Babblers] have many words but little wisdom (56). 11. [A prince] should not abuse in turpitude [money that should be honestly used] (118). 12. [A prince should reform gluttons] who search land and sea to satisfy their appetites (123). *Bellum Jugurthinum:* NSM (31). 1. [The mind is] the ruler of mankind, which does and possesses all things, and which is never in subjection (31). 2. The fairest appearance, the greatest riches, the strongest body, and other such things, quickly fade (31). 3. But worthy deeds of the mind, like the soul, are immortal (31). 4. [Quoting Marius:] that learning pleases me little that does not advance the learners in virtue (35). 5. The nature of mortal men covets to bear rule (41). 6. [Good and mild men] feel fear more than they cause it (46). 7. [Cruelty] brings more fear than power (52). 8. [Great persons often display] a disdainful mind, and pride is the common fault of the nobility (55). 9. [For a prince], it is less dishonorable to be defeated by arms than by munificence (58). *Historiae* (preserved in fragments): 1. [Be] of honest countenance and modest spirit (30). 2. (*Epist. Mithridatis*): 1. Few people desire liberty; most desire just lords (38).

Epistulae ad Caesarem senem de re publica (spurious): 1. Truly, all mortal lives are divinely observed, and our good and evil deeds are appropriately recompensed (23). 2. A person's mind or spirit holds out hope to him according to his conscience (29). 3. [Imprudence often] overthrows itself and others (32). 4. [It is a mistake to believe that] wicked kings enjoy firmer command (46). 5. The worst sort of men will with the least patience endure a commander (46). 6. [A prince] who is good himself should encourage goodness in his subjects (46). 7. Happy success comes to [rulers] who temper their authority with kindness and clemency; they are more esteemed even by their enemies than other [princes] are respected by their own citizens (51). 8. All empires governed cruelly are more troublesome than durable; no single person can cause dread in the many without feeling dread himself. Such a life is perpetual and uncertain war, for no matter where he turns he will never be assured but will always be in doubt and danger (53). 9. All the strength and virtue [of babblers] lies in their tongue (56). 10. [The censor should] restrain young people from bad practices and unlawful desires (121). 11. [The censor should discourage the elderly] from pleasures that seem dishonorable at their age (121). 12. [The censor should] encourage the people to pursue their occupations so that [through idleness] they do not harm the commonwealth (121). 13. [The censor should promote] probity and industriousness, not sumptuousness or riches (121). 14. [The censor should discourage] the use and estimation of riches, which are most pernicious (122). 15. Many kings and cities that began poor and virtuous have lost their great power through opulence (122). 16. Wherever the desire for riches invades, neither discipline nor good arts enjoy enough power (122). 17. [In such a situation,] faith, honesty, shame, chastity, and all other good things are devalued (122). 18. No mortal can raise himself up or strive for heavenly things unless he renounces money and the pleasures of the flesh (122). 19. [The censor should] suppress or discourage the desire to amass money (122). 20. [The censor should restrain] avarice, this fierce, cruel, intolerable beast (122). 21. [The censor should] set a limit to expenses (123). 22. [The censor should ensure that houses are not] adorned with pictures, tapestries, and other ornaments (123). 23. [Fools] display things rather than themselves (123). 24. [Excesses encourage] young people, after they have wasted their own resources, to do wicked acts (123). 25. [Such impoverished youth] will cause disorder and seek to acquire new things by bad means (123). 26. [Reform] will be difficult at first (124). 27. [The prince should] take the commonwealth in hand and overcome all difficulties (124). 28. [The prince should] look to the welfare of the many rather than their pleasures (124). 29. [Wise people] will account it clemency [for the prince] to restrain the foolish from their folly and deceitful pleasures (124). 30. [The prince] who tolerates vice and overlooks faults and present pleasures consents to the bad that must soon occur (124). 31. Liberty is desired by the good and the bad, by the valiant and by cowards (125).

•LIVIUS, Titus: *Unspecified source:* 1. [Assessments of wealth] indicate who is capable of bearing specific costs (120). *Ad urbe condita libri:* Book 1: 1. [History] is profitable because it provides examples beneficial to oneself and to the commonwealth and indicates what should be avoided (34). 2. A census or assessment of wealth profits and advances a kingdom (120). Book 4: NSM (24). 1. Men take risks for honor and profit (125). Book 5: 1. Those who revere the gods prosper; those who spurn worship suffer adversity (24). Book 6: NSM (27). 1. [Through government] each person is brought into awe and obedience, where before they were all fierce and singular (37). Book 7: NSM (27). Book 8: NSM (27). 1. That kingdom is most firmly established where the subjects gladly obey (50). Book 9: 1. The faithless never lack excuses for breaking pacts (54). 2. [The faithless] always cover their fraud with the appearance of doing the right thing (54). Book 25: [It is Destiny or Fate] under whose law the settled course of human affairs is ordered (26). Book 26: 1. Kingly rule is the most admirable among gods as well as men (39). Book 35: 1. Constantly viewing great persons breeds satiety and diminishes respect for them (58).

SENECA, Lucius Annaeus[9]: 1. [Quoting Augustus:] Through piety and justice princes become gods (source mentioned: "*In Ludo*"; 48). 2. No empire continued long where [the prince] was hated (no source mentioned; 51). 3. As a modest pace becomes a wise man, so should his speech be measured, not audacious (source mentioned: "*Epist.*"; 56). 4. [Some persons] became so impudent that they learned to forget shame (source mentioned: "*Ad Seren.*"; 124). 5. The best sacrifice we can offer god is a pure heart or mind (no source mentioned; 25). *Dialogorum libri XII: De ira, II:* 1. Whatever is vain and light in the mind is easily blown by the wind (55). *De providentia:* 1. The role of a good man is to obey fate (28). 2. Even if [the prince] does nothing that merits hatred, there will always be some who will hate him (126). *De clementia:* 1. Citizens are not given into [the prince's] servitude but into his protection or tutelage (no book specified; 43). 2. The republic does not belong to the prince, but rather the prince to the republic (no book specified; 43). Book 1: 1. [Government] is the chain by which the republic is linked together; it is the vital spirit which so many millions breathe; and if this soul of commanding were taken away, the commonwealth would be nothing but a burden and prey (37). 2. Rumor or report registers all the sayings and deeds of the prince (45). 3. [The prince] can no more cover himself than can the sun (45). 4. [The prince] must have care of his reputation, which, as he deserves, so will it be spread abroad (45). 5. [The prince] should apply [justice] and set it against all wrong or injury (49). 6. [Clemency] does not carry the same grace and comeliness in any other person that it does in a king or prince (50). 7. [Rulers] have more occasion to exercise [clemency], and it shows most where it has the most matter [to work on] (50). 8. Frequent severity weakens authority (52). 9. We see those [faults] most often committed which are most often punished (52). 10. Just as pruned trees shoot up, so the number of a king's enemies multiply in response to cruelty (52). 11. It is a temperate fear that restrains and bridles, but a sharp and continual [punishment] stirs up revenge (52). 12. Frequent punishments and executions are no less dishonorable to a king than frequent burials are to a physician (52). 13. A great or worthy mind befits a great fortune (59). 14. It is characteristic of [a worthy mind] to be placid and tranquil and loftily to overlook injuries and small offenses (59). 15. The prince can best abolish certain vices by enduring them (125). *De consolatione ad Polybium:* NSM (22). 1. [A good king's] vigilance defends everyone while they sleep, his labor gives all of them ease, his industry maintains their pleasure, his work provides their rest and quiet (44). 2. [A king] may sometimes pause and refresh himself but must never be dissolute (44). 3. The greatness of a prince is founded and established when everyone realizes that just as he is over them, so he is also for them (44). *De beneficiis:* Book 4: NSM (22).

Naturales quaestiones: Book 2: 1. All things depend [on god], from whom are the causes of causes (26). Book 4: 1. [Reproach as a remedy] is quotidian, and amounts to ineffective words (124). *Epistulae morales ad Lucilium:* 14: 1. A bad conscience is anxious and tormented even in solitude (29). 43: 1. You are miserable if you condemn this witness [conscience] (29). 84: 1. Nothing is hidden from god. He is present in our minds and intervenes in the midst of our thoughts (23). 89: 1. Learning is not able to give virtue but prepares our mind to accept it (35). 2. To desire to know more than suffices is a kind of intemperance (35). 3. [Faith or fidelity] is the most sacred attribute of man (53). 4. Faith is not compelled by any necessity to slip, nor is it corrupted by reward (54). 91: NSM. 95: 1. Precepts ought to be limited and certain (76). 2. If [precepts] cannot be limited or defined, they are outside the reach of wisdom (76). 98: 1. [Conscience is] an aversion, fixed within us, to whatever nature has condemned (29). 2. [Citing Epicurus:] It is possible for the guilty to hide, but not possible to be sure of staying hidden (29).

99: NSM. 107: 1. [Most people today] labor as intemperately in study as in all other things: we learn not how to live but how to debate (35). 108: 1. It is best to endure patiently what cannot be amended, and to follow god without murmur, who is the author of all events. That man is a bad soldier who grudgingly follows his commander (28). 113: 1. Calamities, reproaches, and injuries are as potent against virtue as are small clouds against the sun (22). 115: 1. Luxuries in banqueting and clothing are the symptoms of a sick city (123). *No particular epistle specified:* 1. Honesty is of little value to the man who shows excessive concern for the body (30). 2. Virtue precludes none but admits all (40). 3. [Virtue] respects neither wealth [*sensum*] nor sex (40).

Tragoediae: Particular play unspecified: 1. Whoever wants to be loved should rule with a gentle hand (50). *Hercules [Furens]*: 1. I have seen cruel and bloody dukes laid in base prisons, and tyrants murdered by the hands of the multitude (56). *Troades [Troas]*: 1. Whoever has the freest rein should exercise the most restraint (47). *Oedipus:* NSM (27). 1. Whoever fears hatred too much does not know how to rule (126).[10] *Thyestes:* 1. Where there is no shame or no care for law or justice, no sanctity, piety, or fidelity, the kingdom is unstable (45). 2. [Subversive voices argue that] sanctity, piety, and fidelity are [merely] private virtues and that kings can live as they please (45). 3. If the king desires to be honest, all persons will desire the same (47). *Octavia:* 1. [God] has given [women] reason but has denied them physical strength (39). 2. It is a worthy thing to excel among worthy men, to have regard for the interest of one's country, to pardon the afflicted, to abstain from cruelty, to temper wrath, and to administer peace and quiet to the present age; this is the highest virtue and the ready way to heaven (51).

• CICERO, Marcus Tullius: *No source mentioned:* 1. The conscience is an ample enough theater for virtue (30). "*Orat. de Arusp. respons.*" (cited source): 1. Not by cunning or strength did [the Romans] overcome all other peoples and nations but by piety and religion (78). *Pro Roscio comoedo:* 1. It is most wicked and treacherous to break faith, since that sustains life (54). *Verrines:* Book 2: 1. Taxes should be collected according to the census (120). 2. [Censors] should be permitted all power to determine estimates of worth (120). 3. The people themselves [should choose the censors], selecting with the greatest care the person in whom they have the greatest faith concerning their own [property] (120). 4. There should be two or three censors for every city (120). Book 5: 1. Everyone is influenced by religion (24). *Pro Cluentio:* 1. We receive conscience from the immortal gods, which cannot be taken from us (28). 2. [The censor is] our superintendent, and the master of the ancient discipline (121). 3. [The censor's] powers are established to give cause of fear, not loss of life (124). *De imperio Cn. Pompeii* [*Pro lege Manilia*]: 1. [Authority] avails for administering battles and military commands (57). 2. [Tributes or assessments] are the ornaments of peace and the succors of war (114). *In Catilinam:* Book 2: 1. [In bankrupt youths], the same desire persists as when they enjoyed abundance (123). 2. [Such desire] will breed a seminary of Catilines in the republic (123). *Pro Sulla:* 1. No one can suddenly be reformed or change his life or alter his nature (125). *Pro Archia:* 1. All examples would be obscured in darkness if not illuminated by learned authors (34). *In Pisonem:* 1. [The censor as] a mistress of shame and modesty (121). *Pro Rabirio Postumo:* NSM (47). *Pro Milone:* 1. [Conscience] has a double force: it renders the faultless fearless, and it keeps constantly before the eyes of the guilty their potential punishment (29). *Pro Ligario:* 1. Nothing makes humans more godlike than to give safety and well-being to other humans (51). *Pro Marcello:* 1. [All things are] thrown down, and by the force of war beaten down and prostrated (124). 2. [The prince should] call faith back, correct voluptuousness, and bind with severe laws everything that is decayed and scattered (124). *Philippics:* 8: 1. The person of the prince ought to gratify not only the minds but also the eyes of the citizens (56).

De oratore: Book 1: 1. Use [that is, practical experience] surpasses the precepts of all teachers (33). Book 2: 1. [Knowledge of governance only] comes with age [or time] (33). 2. [History is] the life of memory (34). 3. [History is] the light of truth and mistress of life (34). *Topica:* 1. Authority should be sought to build faith [or credibility] (57). 2. The concurrence of external matters helps build authority (57). *De republica:* Book 4: 1. The judgment of the censor brings nothing more than a blush of shame to the person condemned (124). Book 5: 1. The governor of a republic ought to propose and intend the happy life of the citizens (43). 2. [The prince should seek that the republic be] strengthened in wealth, abundant in riches, ample in glory, and honest through virtue (43). 3. [The office of the censor is now] decayed through forgetfulness, so that it is not only obscured but unknown (121). Book 6 (*Somnium Scipionis*): 1. [God], active, aware, mindful, rules and governs (23). *De legibus:* Book 3: 1. [Without governance] no house, no city, no nation, not the whole state of humankind, nor the nature of all things, nor even the world itself, can stand (36–37). 2. All the ancient nations were at first obedient to kings (38). 3. Princes not only commit vices but also flood the city with them and do more harm by their example than by their fault (47). 4. The censors should assess the ages, races, families, and wealth of the people (120).

Paradoxa Stoicorum: 1. Right [or law] and equity are the bonds of cities (48). *De divinatione:* Book 2: NSM (25). NSM (26). 1. A wise man protects the customs of his ancestors by preserving their sacred ceremonies (79). *De finibus:* Book 1: 1. Once we are initiated into superstition, peace of mind is never possible (25). 2. Wisdom should not only be procured but also advantageously enjoyed (35). Book 5: 1. Prudence is the art of living well as medicine is the art of healing (32). *Tusculans:* 1. [God is] a certain free and independent mind or intelligence, separate from all mortal matter, imparting sentience and movement to all, and itself in perpetual motion (22). *De natura deorum:* Book 2: 1. Worship of the gods [should] be the best, the most chaste and the most holy, and they should be venerated always with a pure, whole, uncorrupted mind and voice (25). *De officiis:* Book 1: 1. Faith is the foundation of justice (53). 2. Nothing is more appropriate to man's nature than liberality (58). Book 2: 1. Justice is so powerful that even those who support themselves through crime and wrongdoing cannot live without some particle of justice (47). 2. [The purpose of] enjoying justice was the original cause that moral men were made kings (49). 3. [Kings were selected] to maintain the higher and lower classes in an equality of right (49). NSM (114). 3. Let everyone know that if they want safety, the necessary expenses must be provided (114). NSM (118). 4. [The prince should not disrupt the privileges of certain persons but should maintain everyone under the same equity (119). 5. [A prince's] household matters should be provided for by means distant from turpitude (123). Book 3: 1. Justice is the foundation of perpetual commendation and fame: without it nothing laudable is possible (48). 2. Nothing more vigorously maintains the republic than faith or fidelity (54). 3. [Bad advisors encourage princes] to neglect everything right and honest if by doing so power may be achieved (54). 4. [Some contend] that faith or fidelity should not be kept with those who lack faith or fidelity (55). 5. [Such persons] seek a hiding place for [their own] perjury (55). *Epistles [unspecified]:* 1. In a republic, as princes are, so are the rest of the citizens wont to be (46). *Ad Atticum:* Book 4, Epistle 2: 1. [A bad prince] clips the wings so close that the feathers cannot grow again (116). Book 13: 1. [An honest man seeks] not to depart a hair's breadth from a good conscience during his whole life (29). *Ad Brutum:* Epistle 16: 1. [Solon said that] a republic is maintained by reward and punishment (125).

★•RUFUS, Quintus Curtius: *Historiae Alexandri Magni:* Book 4: 1. [The powerful are persuaded] that nothing is more efficacious in ruling the multitude than superstition (24). 2. No power can long endure that is gained by wickedness (42). Book 5: NSM (26). Book 7: 1. The tallest trees, which grow for a long time, are cut down in an hour (56). 2. Nothing is so firm that it cannot be endangered by something weak (56). 3. Sometimes the mighty lion is eaten by little birds, and rust consumes iron (56). 4. A timid dog barks more vehemently than one that bites, and the deepest rivers flow with the least noise (56). 5. [O Princes,] Hold your fortune tight with closed hands, for she is slippery and cannot be held against her will. If you bridle your felicity, you may more easily govern it (57).

•PLINIUS SECUNDUS, Gaius: *Naturae historiae* (*Naturalis historia*): Book 14: 1. Life depends on religion (24). Book 17: 1. We most credit what we have experienced (33). 2. Use or experience is the most efficacious teacher of all things (33).

Panegyricus: 1. [For women] the glory of obedience is sufficient (40). 2. [Some think that] the one who commands everyone should be elected by all (41). 3. They will most patiently endure servitude who are fit for nothing but to be slaves or servants (46). 4. [Some think that laws] are not written for a prince (47). 5. [The prince should ensure] that a city founded on laws is not overthrown by them (50). 6. [On the love of one's subjects:] this fortress is inaccessible, this fortification is unconquerable: not to need a fortress (50). 7. [The prince] should consider that he is no less a man himself, even though he presides over men (56). 8. [The prince should ensure that learning] receives, under him, spirit and the blood of life (59). 9. God hides the origins [of things], and for the most part the causes of good and evil are concealed under diverse appearance (77). 10. [The prince should sometimes publicly] make a reckoning of the cost of government (115). 11. [Greedy princes] have often been taught by us many things contrary to our own interests (115). 12. [Greedy princes] have never lacked those who, with a grave, sad, and stern countenance, have insolently promoted the profit of the ruler's purse (115). 13. [The prince should abandon those whose treasury] is a place for stripping away [the wealth] of citizens and a receptacle of blood-stained plunder (115). 14. [Alleged violations of laws against treason are sometimes] the one and only crimes of those who are free from crime (116). 15. [Greedy, deceitful officials] should lose what they have (117). NSM (117). 16. [Greedy officials] grasp at and grip onto everything, yet they want all things as if they grasped at nothing and held onto nothing (119). NSM (119). NSM (119). 17. [The prince should condemn] far-fetched culinary appetites (123). 18. [Shameless persons] should have their heads bloodied (124). 19. [When the prince corrects himself] we are thereby directed and converted (125). 20. The life of the prince is a perpetual correctress [of human conduct] (125). 21. Rewarding the good and the bad makes persons good and bad (125). 22. [The prince should ensure] that those who do well are not rewarded simply by their own consciences (125). 23. Grave verses and the perpetual honor of chronicles will make [the prince] famous, not these impermanent [contemporary comments] (126). *Epistulae:* Book 3: 1. Many people revere their contemporary reputations, but few revere their consciences (29). Book 7: 1. Veneration is badly acquired by terror. Love is a far stronger means than fear to obtain what you desire (53). 2. Repentance is the companion of sudden largesse (58).

Secondary Latin Sources

★•AFRANIUS, Lucius: 1. Use or experience begot me [i.e., Wisdom, although Lipsius argues that this would be even more appropriately said by Prudence], and memory, my mother, brought me forth (32). ★★AGELLIUS (*Source cited: Book 4, chapter 9*): 1. It is proper to be religious but impious to be superstitious (25). ★★ALPHONSUS SICILIAE: 1. The best counselors are the dead (34). •AMBROSIUS, Aurelius: *De officiis ministrorum:* 1. One ought to keep faith even with the faithless (55). ★★AMMIANUS, Marcellinus: *Res gestae:* Book 14: NSM. Book 22: 1. [It is dishonorable for a king] to exact profit on all occasions (116). APULEIUS, Lucius: *Apologia:* Book 1: 1. Fortune, like a toga, is best when it fits well rather than when it overflows (30). *Metamorphoses:* Book 9: 1. It is not possible to subvert or reform the fatal disposition of divine providence, either by prudent counsel or by clever remedy (26). ★★AUGUSTINE, St.: *De civitate dei:* Book 4: 1. If justice is removed, what are kingdoms but great robberies? (48). Book 5, Chapter 9: 1. [Destiny is] the sentence and, as it were, the voice of the divine mind (26). Book 6: 1. [Quoting Varro:] The gods are venerated by the religious person but feared by the superstitious (25). Book 21: 1. It is impossible to think of anything more pleasing than a tranquil conscience (29). *De libero arbitrio:* Book 1: 1. To esteem god best is the beginning of piety (22). *De ordine:* Book 2: 1. [God] is best known by not knowing (23). •AUSONIUS, Decimus Magnus[11]: (*Source cited*): "*in Monos*": 1. The one who does right, not the one who domineers, will be a king (44).

★•BERNARDUS, St.: *Epistulae:* 1. It is difficult [for the prince,] placed in such a high position, not to savor lofty things (55). BIBLE: See SOLOMON. ★•BOETHIUS, Anicius Manlius Severinus: *De consolatione philosophiae:* 1. Because God alone [solus] sees everything, we may truly call him the sun [Solem] (23). CAESAR, Gaius Iulius: *Commentarii de Bello Civili:* Book 3: 1. [The Romans imposed] a tax on pillars, a tax on doors (116). NSM (117). ★•CASSIODORUS Senator, Magnus Aurelius: *Variae:* Book 10: 1. [Quoting "Theodahad":] Since we have the power to do all things, let us believe that only those things are allowed to us which are laudable (48). Book 11: 1. It is fitting for a kindly prince, in the interests of clemency, sometimes to surpass the limits of equity, if only because of compassion, to which all other virtues honorably cede preeminence (52). •CATO CENSORIUS, Marcus Porcius: 1. [The Romans] desired [Faith or Fidelity] to be placed in the Capitol near great and mighty Jupiter (54). CLAUDIANUS, Claudius: *No source specified:* 1. It is admirable to forgive the wretched, and a kind of punishment to witness [an offender's] entreaties (52). *"ad Honor[inum]"*: 1. You [the prince] ought to behave as a citizen and a father; you should consider all, not just yourself; you should be moved not by your own but by public losses or injuries (43). 2. Neither sentinels nor a circle of armed men can protect [a prince] as much as love [from his subjects] (50). *Panegyricus de quarto consulati Honorii Augusti:* 1. The whole world follows the king's example (46). *Panegyricus dictus Manlio Theodoro consuli:* 1. A quiet or tranquil strength achieves what a violent power cannot, and that mandate is more forcefully urgent that comes from quiet authority (53). ★•COLUMELLA, Lucius Junius Moderatus: *De re rustica:* Book 1: 1. The ancients considered the law at its most severe the greatest injustice or torment (49). 2. [Study of the law is] snarling study, an assembly of thieves (50). 3. In the past, cities were happy enough without lawyers, and they may be so in the future (50). ★•CORNIFICIUS: See *RHETORICA AD HERRENIUM.* ★•CYPRIANUS, Thascus Caecilius: *Source cited: "in Symb."*: 1. About god it is sometimes dangerous to speak even true things (23).

•FESTUS, Pompeius: *No specific source cited:* 1. [Corrupt officers are] greedy (117). •FLORUS, Julius: *Epitoma de Tito Livio bellorum omnium annorum DCC:* Book 1, chapter 6: 1. [There are advantages of listing] differences of patrimonies, dignities, ages, skills, and offices in tabular form (120). •HIERONYMUS (JEROME): *Source unspecified:* 1. Liberality ruins liberality (58). HORATIUS Flaccus, Quintus: *Odes:* Book 3 [ode 4]: 1. [God] rules the inert earth and the windy sea, cities, and the gloomy realms [below] (23). ★•ISIDORUS: *Soliloquia* or *Synonyma de homine et ratione:* 1. Do you desire to be never unhappy? Live well [or honestly] (29). •JEROME (see HIERONYMUS). •JUSTINUS, Marcus Junianus: *Epitome of His-*

toriae Philippica (by Pompeius Trogus): Book 1: 1. In the beginning of things, the rule of peoples and nations was in the possession of kings (38). Book 8: 1. He is by right held nearest by the gods, by whom the majesty of the gods is vindicated (79). JUVENALIS, Decimus Junius: *Satires: (unspecified)*: 1. By night and day [the person with a guilty conscience] carries a witness in his breast (29). 7 [sic; 6] : 1. Effeminate riches have weakened the ages with disgraceful luxury (122).

•LACTANTIUS, Firmianus Lucius Caecilius: *De ira Dei:* chapter 8: 1. [Take away religion, and] the life of man will be filled up with stupidity, crime, and savagery (78). Chapter 12: 1. Only religion and the fear of God preserve society among human beings (78). *Divinae institutiones:* Book 1, chapter 20: 1. No other religion or worship besides that of the one God should be held or observed (79). Book 2: 1. Sometimes the multitude are wiser [than others] because they are as wise as they need to be (36). Book 5, chapter 9: 1. The whole religion of Christians consists in living without wickedness or blemish (25). Book 5, chapter 20: 1. There is nothing more excellent in human affairs than religion, which ought to be defended with the greatest force (79). ★•LAMPRIDIUS, Aelius (contributor to *Historia Augusta*): [*Life of*] *Commodus*: NSM (117). [*Life of*] *Severus Alexander*: 1. [Alexander] admitted learned men [as advisors], especially those familiar with history (34). 2. [Alexander] rarely gave gold or silver to anyone except soldiers, saying that it was a crime for him, as steward of public funds, to convert to his own pleasures and those of his favorites that which the provinces had contributed (119). ★*LIBRO DE IV. VIRT[UTIBUS]* [Probably by MANCINUS, Dominicus (A.D. fifteenth century), *De quattuor virtutibus*]: 1. [Prudence] arranges present things, provides for things to come, and remembers things past (32). 2. [Prudence] neither wishes to deceive nor is able to be deceived (32). LUCANUS, Marcus Annaeus: *De bello civili:* Book 5: 1. All follow the motion of leaders; humankind in general lives in a few (5). Book 7: NSM (27). Book 8: 1. The fortune of kingdoms is most mild or gentle under a new king (42). 2. All the power of a scepter perishes if it begins to weigh matters of justice (48). LUCRETIUS Carus, Titus: *De rerum natura:* Book 5: 1. Some hidden force crushes human affairs and tramples on the symbols of power and seems to hold them in scorn (77).

★MANCINUS, Dominicus. See *LIBRO DE IV. VIRT[UTIBUS]*. ★MANILIUS, Marcus: *Astronomica:* Book 1: 1. Through varied practice, experience makes skill or art, showing the way by example (33). Book 4: 1. Fates rule the world; all things stand upon a certain law (26). OVIDIUS Naso, Publius: *Ars amatoria*: Book 1: 1. [God] is not, like a sluggard, detained by tranquil sleep (23). *Metamorphoses:* Book 6: 1. Experience comes with old age (33). Book 8: 1. The power of heaven is immeasurable and has no limit, and whatever the gods desire is accomplished (23). Book 11: NSM. Book 13: NSM. ★•PACUVIUS, Marcus: *No source specified:* 1. I hate those men who are philosophers in words rather than works or deeds (35). •PLAUTUS, Titus Maccius: *Amphitruo:* 1. [Virtue] in herself contains all things, and whoever has virtue has everything (22). *Aulularia:* 1. [Corrupt officers] are men of the race of Gerion, having six hands, who would frustrate Argus with all his eyes (117). *Bacchides:* 1. A nightingale will always be ready with its song (115). NSM (115). *Captivi:* 1. It is truly god who hears and sees how we conduct ourselves (23). "*Milit.*" [*Miles gloriosus*]: 1. It is easy to govern the good (46). *Persa:* 1. If the inhabitants [of a state] are men of good morals, I consider it admirably fortified (45). 2. [When the inhabitants of a state are immoral], a wall reinforced a hundred times provides insufficient defense (45). *Trinummus:* 1. Truly, a wise man fashions his own fortune (32). •PROPERTIUS, Sextus: *Elegies:* Book 2: NSM (39). PROVERBS: See SOLOMON. QUINTILIANUS, Marcus Fabius: *Declamationes* [spurious?]: Book 4: 1. This is the nature and condition of princes, that whatever they do, it is perceived to instruct (46). *Institutio oratorio:* Book 3, chapter 51: 1. Even if [virtue] receives a certain impetus from nature, it must nevertheless be perfected through learning (35).

★•*RHETORICA AD HERRENIUM*: No specific book cited: 1. [Virtue] is under her own command. Everything except virtue is subject to fortune and ruled by it (22). Book 3: 1. We ought greatly to believe in preserving [faith or fidelity] (54). ★•RUFINUS, Tyrannius: *Ecclesiastical History*: Book 2, chapter 6: 1. [Citing "Moyses the Ægyptian":) Concerning a person's faith, he gives greater credit to his eyes than to his ears (25). SILIUS, Italicus, Tiberius Catius Asconius: *Punica:* Book 2: 1. Neither break covenants of peace nor consider fidelity of less account than kingdoms (55). Book 4: 1. The first cause of the crimes of miserable mortals is not to know the nature of God (23). Book 5: NSM (27). Book 13: 1. [Faith or fidelity] is better than the purple and glitterings of kingdoms (54). Book 14: 1. He is the best soldier who, first and last, remains faithful during battle (55). SOLOMON: *Proverbs:* Chapter 29 [sic; 30]: 1. Whoever blows his nose too much makes it bleed (116). STATIUS, Publius Papinius: *Thebaid:* Book 1: 1. Holy words have a grave and immutable weight, and the fates obey [God's] voice (26). Book 3: 1. From the beginning of the world this day remained fixed for battle, and this people were born to go into combat (26). SUETONIUS TRAN-

QUILLUS, Gaius: *De vita Caesarum*: *Augustus:* Chapter 2: 1. [Quoting Augustus]: It is enough if we have assurance that no one can do us harm (126). *Nero:* Chapter 20: 1. [Tyrants] think that riches and wealth have no other fruit or use than extravagant spending (119). *Vespasian:* No specific chapter cited: 1. [Flavius] imposed a tax on urine (116). Chapter 16: 1. [Corrupt officers, like sponges,] should be squeezed dry after they drink their fill (117). *Tiberius:* 1. Shear sheep rather than pull off the wool to their skin (115). ★•SPARTIANUS, Aelienus: *Source cited: "in Anton Carac."*: 1. [Bad advice: a prince] may do as he pleases (47). •TIBULLUS, Albius: 1. Although perjury may be hidden at first, nevertheless punishment eventually comes with silent feet (55).

    ★•VALERIUS Flaccus, Gaius: *Argonautica:* Book 1: 1. All created things proceed in their order, and from the beginning hold a fixed course (26). VALERIUS Maximus: *Factorem et dictorum memorabilium libri novem:* Book 1, Chapter 6: NSM (27). Book 2, chapter 9: 1. What avails it to appear attractive outdoors if we live badly at home? (121). NSM (121). Book 4, chapter 3: 1. Those households, that city, that state may long stand where lust or avarice lays claim to the fewest men (122). Book 6, chapter 9: 1. [Some people] take delight not only in enticements but in the infamy of them (124). 2. [In many people], the mind wanders in idleness but does not settle there (125). Book 6, last chapter: 1. What we call strengths and human riches are as tottering and fragile as childish playthings (56). •VARRO, Marcus Terentius: 1. [Quoted by St. Augustine:] The gods are venerated by the religious person but feared by the superstitious (25). *Fragments:* 1. [Of corrupt officers:] These dogs will entirely consume their own Acteon (117). NSM (117). ★•VELLEIUS Paterculus: *Historiae Romanae libri duo:* Book 2: 1. When [necessity] determines to change [one's] fortune, it corrupts [one's] understanding (27). NSM (27). 2. [Quoting Cato:] Never do right in order to be seen to have done so (30). 3. By doing what is right, a prince teaches his subjects to do the same (46).

Notes

1. See David McPherson, "Ben Jonson's Library and Marginalia: An Annotated Catalogue," *Studies in Philology* 71, no. 5 (1974): i–xi, 1–106. See also the listings included in the first and last volumes of the standard edition, *Ben Jonson*, ed. C. H. Herford and Percy and Evelyn Simpson, 11 vols. (Oxford: Clarendon Press, 1925–52), 1:250–71 and 11:593–603.

2. See, for example, Richard S. Peterson, *Imitation and Praise in the Poems of Ben Jonson* (New Haven: Yale University Press, 1980), and also Katharine Eisaman

Maus, *Ben Jonson and the Roman Frame of Mind* (Princeton: Princeton University Press, 1984).

3. See my book *Jonson, Lipsius, and the Politics of Renaissance Stoicism*, 2d ed. (Durango, Colo.: Longwood Academic, 1992), which also lists other relevant discussions. The title page of Jonson's copy of the *Politica* lists a publication date of 1623, thus implying that Jonson could not have read and marked this copy of the book before then. See Justus Lipsius, *Politicorum, sive Civilis Doctrinae Libri Sex* (1623), in vol. 7 of *Iusti Lipsii V. C. opera omnia* . . . (Antwerp: Ex Officina Plantiniana, apud Viduam & Filios J. Moreti, 1614). This set is presently held by the Library of Emmanuel College, Cambridge University.

4. For an intriguing discussion of the mentality associated with commonplace books, see Mary Thomas Crane, *Framing Authority: Sayings, Self, and Society in Sixteenth-Century England* (Princeton: Princeton University Press, 1992).

5. For an overview of relevant scholarship, see my book (*Jonson, Lipsius, and the Politics of Renaissance Stoicism*) and also two other studies: Anthony Grafton, "Portrait of Justus Lipsius," *American Scholar* 56 (1987): 382–90, and Mark Morford, *Stoics and Neostoics: Rubens and the Circle of Lipsius* (Princeton: Princeton University Press, 1991). For a handy selection, see the section on Lipsius in the series *Literature Criticism from 1400 to 1800*, ed. James E. Person (Detroit: Gale, 1991), 16:249–80.

6. I discuss this specific allusion to Seneca much more extensively in a note co-authored with my student Neil Probst: "Jonson, Seneca, Homer, and Lipsius: Unreported Allusions in *The King's Entertainment at Welbeck*," *Notes and Queries* 239.4 (1994): 519–20.

7. I discuss this matter much more fully in another article, co-authored with my student Lynn Bryan: "Ben Jonson, Neostoicism, and the *Monita* of Justus Lipsius," *Ben Jonson Journal* 1 (1994): 105–23.

8. The copy of Tacitus listed in McPherson's catalogue is described as a doubtful attribution (103). Having inspected it, I agree.

9. I discuss Jonson's newly discovered copy of Seneca at length in my book *Habits of Mind: The Evidence and Impact of Ben Jonson's Reading* (Lewisburg, Penn.: Bucknell University Press, 1995).

10. In my book *Jonson, Lipsius, and the Politics of Renaissance Stoicism*, this passage is not italicized but should be, to indicate Jonson's underlining.

11. I am grateful to Professor Henry Woudhuysen for informing me of a newly discovered copy of Ausonius owned and marked by Jonson. This book will be described in the expanded catalogue of Jonson's library on which Professor Woudhuysen is now at work.

Ethics and Christianity in Ben Jonson

George A. E. Parfitt

> the most luxuriantly fertile field of all is that of our moral obligations—since, if we clearly understand those, we have mastered the rules for leading a good and consistent life.
>
> —Cicero: to his son

> Teche me to no tresore, but telle me þis ilke—
> How I may saue my soule.
>
> —Langland

Ben Jonson's concern with ethics—Cicero's "rules for leading a good and consistent life"—is surely beyond dispute, and scarcely in need of demonstration. Moreover, there is plenty of evidence that his articulations of ethical principles are often derived from classical (most usually Roman) sources. For example, at *Volpone* 4.2. 232–33, where Voltore waxes sententious—

> vicious persons, when they are hot and fleshed
> In impious acts, their constancy abounds[1]

—he is drawing on Juvenal (*Satires* 13.237). In *The Staple of News* (1.3.40–41) Pennyboy Canter's

> The covetous man never has money, and
> The prodigal will have none shortly[2]

is taken from Seneca (*De remediis fortuitorum* 10.3).

But the best examples are to be found in the poems:

> what thy virtue on the times hath won,
> And not thy fortune[3]
> (*Epigrams* 63; cf. Valerius Maximus, *Factorum et dictorum* 8.15.2)

or

> Where any deed is forced, the grace is marred
> > (*Underwood* 13.24; cf. Seneca, *De beneficiis* 1.1.7)

or

> He that for love of goodness hateth ill,
> > Is more crown-worthy still,
> Than he, which for sin's penalty forbears.
> > His heart sins, though he fears.
> > > (*The Forest* 11.87–90; cf. Horace, *Epistles* 1.16.52–54)

But, as I argued many years ago,[4] Jonson's major ethical themes, however classical in formulation, remain firmly within native medieval and Renaissance traditions. The importance of self-knowledge, the need for birth and merit to coincide if there is to be social harmony, the stress upon friendship: all these, and others, are emphasized by Jonson, but all are medieval and Renaissance commonplaces. The articulation may be classical but the sentiments have become part of the native heritage.

Cicero speaks of a "good and consistent life," and the need to be constant to ethical good is one of Jonson's major themes, his career being dominated by the search to find, to maintain, and persuasively to articulate enduring moral positives. But although serene enactment of such positives is a Jonsonian ideal—"sing high and aloof, / Safe from the wolf's black jaw" (*Underwood* 23.35–36)—the reality is that these positives are being constantly tested and threatened, in his work, by Jonson's acute awareness of human frailty. The realism for which Jonson has been consistently praised is a facet of this: his observation of the messy facts of existence. The weakness, gullibility and wickedness of humankind come close to swamping *Volpone,* while in *Sejanus* virtue is obliterated. Over and again Jonson's writing takes fire as it voices vice and folly, vivid details making these features into existential facts; and at times the power of the writing nearly sweeps away the possibility of sustaining moral principles, for, in the poetry's view

> 'Tis grown almost a danger to speak true
> Of any good mind, now: there are so few.
> > (*The Forest* 13.1–2)

Bearing in mind that Jonson's satirical evocation of vice and dissipation is almost always local and contemporary, it is possible to see the tension in his work as not only between the ideal and the actual, but also as between statements of classical ethics and the observed reality of Jonson's society. This raises the question of why Jonson sought affirmations of moral certainty in the writings of classical, pagan authors. Two main reasons suggest themselves, the first being the contemporary prestige of the classics and the second the durability of their ethical propositions in Western culture. Together these constitute "authority" (Latin "auctoritas"). The fact that so many ethical views in the Christian era are rooted in classical thought may have suggested to Jonson that this, together with the respect Christian thought accorded to virtuous pagans, gave it an authority anterior to Christianity, while being compatible with that religion.

Where, then, does this leave Jonson in relation to Christianity?[5] Biographical evidence suggests that Christianity was important to him and that he was no "free thinker." He became a Catholic when such a conversion can have been of no advantage to him. His Catholicism put him in some danger at the time of the Gunpowder Plot and his reconversion to the English church seems to have come about only after protracted theological discussions. In "An Execration upon Vulcan" Jonson speaks of the burning of

> twice twelve years stored up humanity,
> With humble gleanings in divinity;
> After the Fathers, and those wisest guides
> Whom faction had not drawn to study sides.
> *(Underwood* 43.101–04).

This is clearly the remark of a man who took theology seriously.

But, when we turn back to Jonson's art after noting such biographical material, we are presented with what seems to be a paradox. For that art shows little imaginative engagement with the great mysteries of the Christian faith. In the first place, Jonson wrote few explicitly religious poems and no play or masque that could reasonably be called religious. Second, of his religious poems only "To Heaven" (*The Forest* 15) can be considered among Jonson's finest, and even there the emphasis is upon the poet figure's human sinfulness. Where in his writing is there any sign of powerful response to the nativity of Christ, his passion, crucifixion, or ascension? Where is the Virgin or any early Christian martyr?

It has been suggested to me in conversation with James Crawley that Jonson may have curtailed the Christian element in his art because of modesty; that he may indeed have seen his "gleanings in divinity" as "humble" beside the work of the Christian Fathers and the best of their successors. This, the argument would have it, might explain the lack of response just mentioned, and it could be added that Jonson—concerned as he was with promoting the poet as consistent public figure—may have felt that his religious convictions were a private matter. Perhaps, but Jonson was not usually humble (in life or literature) about his own scholarship, and—in any case—what is at stake here is not so much theological expertise as emotional response. In their different ways Donne, George Herbert, and Vaughan all produced public versions of what (says the poetry) was acute emotional turbulence over matters of faith. Jonson does not. Nor do we find anything much like, say, the religious (or antireligious) distress of Marlowe's *Dr. Faustus* or the fine expression of firm belief in Webster's *Duchess of Malfi*.

On a smaller scale, Jonson, I think, never expresses the complexity of response found at the end of Carew's "To my worthy friend Master Geo. Sands." What is communicated on such occasions is the sense of an emotional commitment that cannot be suppressed. (This is what the writing says: biographical truth does not matter here.) Jonson, however, does not seem to have this kind of commitment to express or suppress. He does, of course, make use of the Bible, but this is normally to express ethical propositions or to take a biblical character as an illustration. In any case, such usage is rare when compared with that of classical, pagan sources. Moreover, when we consider what Jonson takes from his classical sources we see that his borrowings (where they are religioethical) correspond to the dominant stresses in Roman literature. For such as Horace, Juvenal, and even Seneca the gods seem to be primarily manifestations of Fate, Fortune, and unpredictability, this being also the impression given by Vergil's *Aeneid*—and by Ben Jonson's work. In his art metaphysics means little more than the disturbance caused by the omens in *Sejanus* or the abrupt and melodramatic salvation of Celia in *Volpone*.

In using the phrase "seem to be," I do not mean to suggest that Jonson ever doubted (let alone denied) the existence of the Christian god (or, for that matter, that Horace or Vergil doubted the existence of the gods of the Graeco-Roman pantheon). But I am suggesting that Jonson's art is rarely imaginatively penetrated by religious mystery. "How I may saue my soule" is not a pressing topic in Jonson's work.

What follows? If the account above is correct, we have in Jonson a writer who, in an intensely metaphysical age, shows little interest in metaphysics—at least so far as his art is concerned; and this suggests affinity with such skeptics as Machiavelli and Montaigne. But if Jonson is a skeptic, his skepticism must be seen to include doubts about the *efficacy* of Christianity. There is no necessary contradiction here between Art and Life. In the first place, Jonson's doubts may only have surfaced under the pressure of artistic creation and, second, he may have believed in the essential truth of Christianity while doubting mankind's ability to make it efficacious in this life. This latter might suggest a Calvinist streak in Jonson (who would have hated such an idea), and it also provides a link with Marlowe (whose *Dr. Faustus* is sometimes seen as Calvinist) and the more diffuse world of "Jacobean doubt."

Yet, as soon as connections are made with Marlowe and "Jacobean doubt," we need to confront an important difference. The tragedy of the failed efficacy of Christianity in such plays as *The Jew of Malta, Hamlet, King Lear,* and *The Duchess of Malfi,* in the face of human vice and folly, involves imaginative response to the metaphysical; and this, I have already argued, is largely absent in Jonson's writing, in which there is nothing to correspond to Faustus's last speech, or Lear on the heath, or the ghost of Hamlet's father, or the death of the Duchess of Malfi. In Jonson God and the gods are largely aloof. Never an atheist, he seems to have seen ethics, rather than metaphysics, as the potential means of salvation for the individual and society. In other words, if humankind is to be saved from its own folly—if it is to succeed in achieving and sustaining "a good and consistent life"—it will do so with the help of accumulated, time-honored, ethical wisdom and not through Christ's sacrifice or by placating Jupiter.

So, on one level, Jonson's answer to Piers Plowman's "telle me þis ilke— / How I may saue my soule" is clear enough: follow Cicero's advice to his son. But Jonson's chief concern does not seem to be with his, or anyone's, soul. Instead we are encouraged to think of concepts like "honor" and "reputation"—words carrying social significance. In the comedies such words have to be downgraded, for what we are shown with Face, Overdo, and Epicure Mammon is a concern with social appearance; appearance without substance. *Sejanus* creates a world from which ethical virtue has been almost drained. Appearance ("face") is all that remains. As Sabinus says right at the play's opening, its Romans are "Like snails, on painted walls."[6] By contrast, the masques and some of the poems show us what honor and reputation should mean: the quiet, but social, life alleged to characterize the Sidneys at Penshurst. Most of what Jonsonian honor includes may be found in *Epigrams* 98 ("To Sir Thomas Roe"):

> He that is round, within himself, and straight
> Need seek no other strength, no other height.

But Jonson is neither philosopher nor theologian. He is a creative writer; and the real greatness of his art lies in his persistent effort to relate theory to practice, ideal to actuality. Often, to see the full extent and nature of this effort, it is necessary to compare work in different genres, for Jonson was genre conscious, has the satirist's tendency to work in black and white, and has the related didactic desire to encourage reform or renewed commitment to virtue by presenting extreme contrasts. If "To Penshurst" represents social harmony, *The Alchemist* may be set against it, as embodying a perverse and selfish antisocial harmony. Frequently, some reminder of one extreme will tinge the representation of the other. So "To Sir Robert Wroth" (*The Forest* 3) uses satirical passages to heighten through contrast the virtue of Wroth's life in the country; the virtue of Celia (much less pallid than she has often been thought to be) seems weak and defensive against the power of vice and folly in *Volpone;* and the good characters in *Sejanus* are well aware of their impotence in the world of Sejanus, Macro, and Tiberius. "To Penshurst" needs *The Alchemist* (and vice versa) if we are to respond fully to the struggle at the center of Jonson's art. But a frequently neglected major poem, "A Speech according to Horace" (*Underwood* 44) does, I think, epitomize the struggle at its most tense. The poem might be subtitled "A search for social virtue." Its location is firmly contemporary in time and space (the artillery yard in the early seventeenth century), and it is a poem about social responsibility, or, rather, the lack of it. In the poem's view, the aristocracy has abandoned its role of leadership and its sense of social responsibility:

> What need we know?
> More than to praise a dog or horse? Or speak
> The hawking tongue?
>
> (70–72)

The gap this leaves in the social hierarchy is symbolized by noble neglect of the traditional obligation to lead and direct civic military readiness in a state with no standing army, and this gap is being filled by plebeians—"those newer men, / As Stiles, Dike, Ditchfield, Millar, Crips, and Fen" (53–54). The poem makes it clear that this is a disastrous social development; these "newer men" cannot successfully fill the gap created by the nobles' withdrawal, and so social disharmony is imminent. The politics of the poem are clearly not democratic or egalitarian, but what is important is the sense of social danger created by the abandonment of ethical virtue. The felt tension of the situation is magnificently caught in the closing lines:

> These carcasses of honour, tailors' blocks,
> Covered with tissue, whose prosperity mocks
> The fate of things: whilst tottered virtue holds
> Her broken arms up, to their empty moulds.

Thus far "my" Jonson is obviously a serious, even sober artist, and I have been rebuked in the past for allegedly understating Jonsonian laughter. There are, of course, critics who see Jonson as becoming progressively more "genial" as his career continues. According to this view, Jonson's satire becomes less bitter as he becomes more tolerant of human folly with the passing years, more forgiving (and perhaps more Christian?). So *Bartholomew Fair* may be seen as the triumph of this more "mature" Jonson. It strikes me that an effort is being made here to fit Jonson into a predetermined view of artistic development, the analogy being with the inescapable broad pattern of human life. This effort parallels that sentimental view of Shakespeare as ripening through a period of disillusionment into a serene last-phase acceptance of the human condition as ultimately harmonious under a benevolent god. But it also strikes me that to see Jonson's career in this way depends to a disturbing extent on selection and misreading. How, from this position, do we explain *Catiline*, or poems like the *New Inn* ode and the attacks on Inigo Jones, or the pressure put on virtue in the most developed of the masques? My main point here, however, is that the nature of Jonsonian laughter has often been misunderstood.

To start with the most obvious point, Jonsonian laughter is often cruel. In *Epigrams* we are invited to laugh at folly:

> For all night sins, with others' wives, unknown,
> Colt, now, doth daily penance in his own.

$$(39)$$

or

> Groin, come of age, his state sold out of hand
> For his whore: Groin doth still occupy his land.

$$(117)$$

True to their generic nature, Jonson's satirical epigrams invite grim humor and no sympathy at all for the victims. Dramatic episodes like the humiliation of Crispinus in *The Poetaster* seem designed to elicit a similar response. The ethic of the play has it that such as Crispinus are a threat to social harmony and, therefore, that destructive laughter is both necessary and appropriate. The famous senate scene in *Sejanus* includes the grim comedy of the vacillating senators ebbing and flowing around the doomed figure of Sejanus himself.[7] Moreover, dark humor also plays upon the bewildered Sejanus.

It is only a step from this to Jonson's use of laughter to wrong-foot the watcher or reader, especially in his plays. We have, for instance, every reason to know how corrupt Volpone and Mosca are, but their energy and creativity draw us to laugh with them. It is an extraordinary comment upon these qualities and upon our moral weakness that such laughter recurs even after Volpone's attempt to rape Celia, surviving then up to the epilogue, where Volpone himself—and it is important that the actor remains in character—seeks (and gets?) the approval of the audience: "fare jovially, and clap your hands." Volpone tries to make us approve of "his" comedy, that is, his version of the play; to make us laugh at what amuses him. But if/when we remember what Volpone and Mosca are, can laughter be an adequate final response? There is a similar pattern in *The Alchemist*, where, however, both the "joviality" and the trickery are even more subtle (sic!). We are drawn to laugh with Subtle, Face, and Doll because of their creative ingenuity and their own enjoyment of it; and how can we not laugh gratefully at what they create? Yet here again we know perfectly well that what is created is designed to humiliate human frailty (some of it pretty trivial) and when Lovewit, the gentleman owner of the house, returns, we are encouraged to expect the renaissance of harmony, with appropriate punishment of the tricksters and reparation made to the victims. Instead we laugh at Lovewit's enactment of his own name—at the wit which outfaces Face and seizes ill-gotten gains, instead of restoring them. There *is* a new harmony, but this is a new coalition of knaves—Face and Lovewit—and the former has the epilogue, wherein he invites the audience to be feasted as his guests, with the money he has swindled from other guests! Such neatness and audacious suavity represent comedy at its best, but—if we think what it would be to be Face's guests—we might realize that all that has finally changed is that a gentleman has abandoned the responsibility of his role. We are in danger of laughing ourselves into Mammons and Dappers.

Another way of seeing this use of laughter is to relate it to the idea of comic conversion, whereby a foolish or malign character is brought to some degree of real or seeming penitence (Webster's Bosola, Shakespeare's Malvolio, Gratiana in the *Revenger's Tragedy*). In his early comedies Jonson imposes conversion on figures like Crispinus, but precisely that maturity which marks the great middle period of his drama involves laughter being used to cover the absence of conversion. Volpone is sardonic to the end. His exit line—"This is called mortifying of a Fox"—calls for laughter which endorses his defiant refusal to be converted (although the dim Avocatori cannot see this). The adroit comic maneuvers of Face and Lovewit produce delighted laughter, but the Face of the epilogue, rather than promising reform, displays his natural tricks (not reform, but "re-form" of a knavish pact). *Bartholomew Fair* is still more complicated, but not very different. The Puritan Busy, out-argued by Puppet Dionysius, is converted: "I am changed, and will become a beholder with you" (5.3.613–14).[8] But this means joining Cokes as an uncritical beholder of third-rate art. Justice Overdo is converted from his verbose complacency and is asked by Quarlous to remember that he is "but Adam, flesh and blood" (5.3.721). Yet two questions have to be asked. In the play's terms, what is it to be "Adam, flesh and blood"? The best answer would seem to be to become Ursula Pig-woman. Second, isn't Overdo already showing signs of reinflation by the end? What, moreover, are we to make of Grace's conversion to wife-to-be? Or of Win's joyful conversion to whore? *Bartholomew Fair* is packed with conversions, but they can scarcely be said to mate laughter with moral propriety. The Jonson who can evoke laughter with such mastery might, paradoxically, be seen as somewhat suspicious of it.[9]

Such observations raise questions about the nature of harmony in Jonson's work. His concern with ethics importantly includes the idea of a fullness and completeness of the individual (like Sir Thomas Roe) operating harmoniously with others in social accord. Such harmony is the ideal, but, far from being taken for granted, this ideal is tested upon Jonson's alertness to human vice and folly. One of the most attractive versions of this ideal is the poem "Inviting a Friend to Supper" (*Epigrams* 101) with its emphasis on moderation and innocent friendship. Typically, however, Jonson puts pressure on the ideal by suggesting a surrounding world of excess, spies, betrayal, and guilt: the devil is always threatening to enter paradise.

A supper or feast is among the most common symbols of social harmony (the conclusion of Dekker's *The Shoemakers' Holiday* is a good example of this), but Jonson uses the symbol wryly in both *The Alchemist* and *Bartholomew Fair*. We have seen the irony in Face's offer to the audience "To feast you often." At the end of *Bartholomew Fair* Justice Overdo says, "I invite you home with me to my house for supper" (5.3.734), and Cokes ends the play by supporting the justice: "Yes, and bring the actors along, we'll ha' the rest of the play at home." Obviously, there are intimations of harmony here, but they seem to me to be indications of harmony at the lowest common denominator: the debased art of the puppet show, the humiliation of Busy and Wasp, the stupidity of Cokes.

Another of comedy's great images of harmony is that of the dance, mention of which brings Jonson's masques to the fore. The nature of that courtly genre means that (partly, at least, for the purpose of getting repeat commissions) Jonson, pragmatically, needed to produce convincing representations of courtly harmony intended to suggest national unity. Dance is the soul of masque, and the verbal text is meant only to set off and reinforce the climactic dancing by courtiers. But Jonson worked hard at writing masques, producing some of his most carefully wrought and fully annotated texts. Yet it is interesting that his most important contribution to the form was the development of the antemasque. This represents a challenge to the masque proper (as *anti*masque), and, although the challenge is always repelled by the masque itself, it amounts to a threat against the harmony of the proceedings. And, although Jonson's attacks on the form itself, which he once called "the short bravery of the night" (*The Forest* 3.10), are mainly the direct product of the famous quarrel with Inigo Jones, it is possible that they resonate beyond the immediate occasion. After all, one of Jonson's favorite targets throughout his career was the relationship between appearance and reality. His antemasques challenge courtly values, and Jonson was quite capable of emphasizing the vice and folly behind the practices and claims of the masque. It is at least possible that, in his masques, and while preserving decorum, Jonson saw the shallowness of its conventions: in which case, the laughter induced by the antemasque would be pretty hollow.

A final issue may draw things together. A cliché has it that Jonson cannot create convincingly virtuous characters. It is largely true that he does not, but this, of itself, is no proof of inability to do so. In *Cynthia's Revels* and *The Poetaster* he is struggling to make virtue interesting, but the difficulty is more to stop the virtuous characters from seeming priggish and dull than to make them convincing. There is such a thing as dull virtue. Those who think Jonson cannot create convincing virtue seem to rule out the possibility that he finds it hard to believe in such virtue thriving, or even surviving, in society as he sees it. The poems, in fact, suggest that a convincing representation of idealized virtue is well within Jonson's grasp—for example, in "To Penshurst," "Inviting a Friend to Supper," the Roe epigrams, and the epistles to the Countess of Rutland and Lady Aubigny (*The Forest* 12, 13). But it is interesting that virtue, in the poems, sometimes exists in retirement from the corrosion of urban social life (Wroth, the Sidneys at Penshurst) or is seen under siege (Rutland,

Aubigny). It is plays like *Volpone, Sejanus*, and *Bartholomew Fair* that have attracted most of the adverse criticism relevant here; and in such plays it is true that virtue emerges as under pressure and largely ineffectual in the face of the vitality of vice and folly. Celia, in *Volpone*, is by no means as passive as some critics have suggested. There is an obdurate sanctity about her which shades at times into baroque Catholic masochism; and this, while unattractive (except, presumably, to baroque Catholic masochists) is neither weak nor unconvincing.[10] Her virtue emerges as weak because it is given a negative definition by the force of the vicious comedy. Celia is saved by a melodramatic entry which seems to mock the idea of divine intervention, but only (like Castiza in *The Revenger's Tragedy*) to go into a life of exile or retreat. She converts no one. In *Sejanus* the virtuous have almost given up. In the very first moments of the play Arruntius says:

> the men,
> The men are not the same; 'tis we are base,
> Poor and degenerate from the exalted strain
> Of our great fathers

and then asks

> Where is now the soul
> Of god-like Cato?

These self-defeated virtuous figures are terribly vulnerable, and they make little impact because (says the play) this Roman society is too powerfully antipathetic to virtue. Vice in *Sejanus* may be self-destructive in the case of Sejanus himself, but he is not replaced by virtue (weak or otherwise). Instead Macro takes Sejanus's place and Tiberius weaves in the background. Vice endures. In *Bartholomew Fair*, the significantly named Grace Welborn is a caricature of virtue. Snobbish and lightweight, she—like Lovewit in *The Alchemist*—survives through compromise. Trust the tale rather than the teller. The tale suggests, not that Jonson could not create convincing virtue, but that, at times at least, he could not believe in its efficacy. If, therefore, there were occasions when he could hardly heed Cicero's advice, he certainly could not answer Langland's question.

Notes

Cicero, *Selected Works*, trans. Michael Grant (Harmondsworth: Penguin, 1971), 160.William Langland, *Piers Plowman: The Prologue and Passus I–VII*, ed. J. A. W. Bennett (Oxford: Clarendon, 1972), passus I, 83–84.

1. *Volpone,* ed. David Cook (London: Methuen, 1962).

2. *The Staple of News,* ed. Anthony Parr (Manchester: Manchester University Press, 1988).

3. *Complete Poems,* rev. ed., ed. George Parfitt (Harmondsworth: Penguin, 1988). This is also the edition used for all subsequent quotations of Jonson's poetry.

4. George Parfitt, "Ethical Thought in Ben Jonson's Poetry," *SEL* 9 (1969): 123–34.

5. My remarks on this topic have been influenced by conversation with Dr. James Crawley of the University of Delaware.

6. *Sejanus,* ed. Philip Ayres (Manchester: Manchester University Press, 1990).

7. Since *Sejanus* is so seldom produced, its comic effects are often ignored, but the play contains a body of black comedy which is reminiscent of *Volpone* and helps give the play its peculiar flavor.

8. *Bartholomew Fair,* ed. Maurice Hussey (London: Benn, 1964).

9. "Nor is the moving of laughter always the end of comedy" (Jonson, *Discoveries, Ben Jonson,* ed C. H. Herford, Percy Simpson, and Evelyn Simpson [Oxford: Clarendon Press, 1925–52], ll.3253–54).

10. At 4.2.155–6 Corvino associates Celia with Catholicism (which we should expect, since Venice was a Catholic state). The Quarto, issued when Jonson was Roman Catholic, has "Christian." Interestingly, critics of *Measure for Measure* do not seem to find Isabella's extreme virtue unconvincing, although some do find it repellent.

Volpone: The Double Plot Revisited

Alexander Leggatt

SINCE its appearance in 1953, Jonas A. Barish's classic article "The Double Plot in *Volpone*" has been the standard reading of the Politic Would-be subplot. Barish sets out to defend the subplot against the charge that it is "irrelevant and discordant, because of its lack of overt connection with the main plot." He finds the connections, characteristically for the criticism of that period, "on the thematic level."[1] In doing so, he implicitly confirms the claim made in the play's prologue that this is not an eclectic entertainment but a carefully structured one: "Nor made he'his play, for iests, stolne from each table, / But makes iests, to fit his fable" (27–28). (The claim is, in fact, twofold: the jests fit the play; and the jests are made for the sake of the play, not the other way around.) This produces a reading in which Volpone and Sir Politic, for all their obvious differences, are part of the same system, and ultimately subject to the same judgment: "The relative harmlessness of Sir Pol's downfall serves to differentiate his folly from the viciousness of the Venetians, but the many parallels between his catastrophe and theirs warn us that his kind of folly is sufficiently virulent after all, is closely related to graver sins, and if it persists in imitating them, must ultimately fall under the same condemnation."[2] Their names identify Sir Pol and his lady as parrots and, as Barish points out, parrots mimic.[3] Sir Pol is an imitation Volpone. His fate is to do badly what Volpone does well: "he is the would-be politician, the speculator *manqué*, the unsuccessful enterpriser. Volpone, by contrast, is the real politician, the successful enterpriser, whose every stratagem succeeds almost beyond expectation."[4] In this reading, incompetence does not excuse Sir Pol from the final judgment; the mere fact of his imitating Volpone is enough to make them "two aspects of evil" brought together "into the same moral universe and under a common moral judgment."[5] Even his Englishness has serious implications; his comic panic at reports of prodigies is a joke that recoils on the audience: "Sir Pol's prodigies are distant echoes of the moral earthquake rocking Venice, a looking glass for England whereby that country is warned to heed the lesson of the Italian state lest its own follies turn to vices and destroy it."[6]

As the last passage shows, Barish's determination to find thematic parallels leads to some forcing; yet his essential argument has proved compelling, and most discussions of the subplot fall in line behind his. The quest for unity always exerts a magnetic fascination (later in this essay I will be unable to resist it myself), and the popularity of Barish's idea of a hierarchy of competence testifies that the concept of the Great Chain of Being, however it may have functioned in the Renaissance, held powerful sway in the mid-twentieth century. Thus Judd Arnold, for whom "Barish's study showing Sir Pol's place in the thematic structure of the play makes further comment along these lines unnecessary," notes "a range of competence. . . . At the top of the scale is Volpone. . . . at the bottom is Sir Politic, the hopelessly inept intriguer."[7] Alvin B. Kernan sees both characters, and everyone in between, committing the same offense: "Each of the gold seekers, from Volpone to Sir Politic, thinks of himself as rising in both the social and the hierarchical scale by his efforts."[8] Both discussions belong to the 1960s; but more recent critics have displayed Barish's continuing influence. R. B. Parker, in the introduction to his 1983 Revels edition, calls the main function of the Would-bes "to bridge the gap between the Italian setting and the English audience and to provide farcical parallels to the main action." He sees "the 'parrot' subplot" as "another example of the theme of degrading imitation."[9] Robert N. Watson, in a book published in 1987, praises Barish's essay, then goes on to apply Barish's approach to his own metatheatrical concerns: "The Would-Be subplot is a would-be main plot."[10] John W. Creaser, in an article published in 1976 and reproduced with variations in the introduction to his 1978 edition of the play, takes Barish to task for excessive parallel-hunting and for an overly solemn reading of the Would-be scenes. He declares, "Sir Politic has no contact with vice, and virtually none with Italy. . . . he seems in no danger of corruption." Nonetheless, even for Creaser "Sir Politic . . . is a kind of parody of Volpone. . . . Both are dominated by self-love" and while Volpone is "a great actor" Sir Pol is "little more than a mimic, an unwitting and confused imitator."[11]

In the reading provided by Barish and his followers, Sir Pol is an imitation Volpone, and in the end both characters are brought into the same courtroom where a single judgment awaits them. But subplots work through a play of similarity and difference: without some contacts, there would be no point in putting the stories together; without some differences, the duplication of effects would be simply redundant.[12] The Barish reading, for all its virtues, may go too far in the direction of smoothing over internal differences for the sake of unifying the play. I want to reawaken a sense of those differences, arguing that Sir Pol is distinguished from Volpone by more than just a different level of competence. My purpose is not to render the play incoherent but to suggest that its coherence is a more complex matter than the traditional reading supposes, and that its internal relations work not so much by imitation and combination as by opposition and otherness.

The value of a sense of otherness in a two-plot play can be seen by glancing at one of the earliest English examples, the Wakefield *Secunda Pastorum*. Like *Volpone,* it can be seen, up to a point, as unified by internal parallels, linking the Yorkshire action of Mak, Gill, and the shepherds with the story of the shepherds' visit to Bethlehem. When the sheep Mak has stolen is disguised as a baby and placed in a cradle, when Gill offers to eat it, when the shepherds return to give it presents, we can see the two stories linked by parodic imitation. Yet the theatrical effect is that the play actually breaks in two: the Yorkshire action is a story in its own right, and only after it is completed does the angel appear to announce the birth of Christ. When the shepherds go to Bethlehem, Mak and Gill are not only left behind but totally forgotten; it is as though a different play has begun. The play can be staged with Mak's cottage doubling as the Bethlehem stable, and with Mak and Gill doubling as Joseph and Mary; this keeps the parallels theatrically alive. But I have seen it staged with Bethlehem and Yorksire as different spaces, and Mak and Gill sitting apart, silent and forgotten, as the shepherds adore the Christ child. This separation reflects the sharp break in the writing of the play, and the effect is both more poignant and more disturbing than straightforward parody: what happens at Bethlehem is supposed to be for all humanity, but somehow it does not touch Mak and Gill. There is salvation, no end of salvation, but not for them. The parallels that draw the stories together only make this sense of isolation sharper by highlighting how far apart Mak and Gill are from what they parody.

Parallelism and difference are both built into the text of *Secunda Pastorum,* and the play draws its full life from a paradoxical, ironic interplay between the two. The stories make contact in order to drive each other apart; their relationship lies in their separateness. So it is in *Volpone.* The initial impression the subplot makes on readers and audiences is its curious otherness, and this impression is important.[13] While Volpone presides over an intrigue whose technical workings and satiric intent are crystal clear, Sir Pol appears in a loose collection of scenes that don't seem to add up to a plot, and whose overall intent is left murky by their lack of any obvious narrative link with the main story. To some critics, Sir Pol seems to belong to a different sort of play, the comical satires of Jonson's pre-*Sejanus* phase,[14] showing the relaxed observation of folly rather than (as in the main plot) a tight action propelled by crime. When Sir Pol's wife Lady Pol enters the main action as one of Volpone's dupes she does not operate in parallel with the others: the emphasis is not on her greed and low cunning but on her foolish, incessant chatter. A morning in the life of Volpone, as we see it acted out before us in act 1, consists of a hightly structured series of encounters with his dupes, each with the single purpose (on both sides) of gain. A morning in the life of Sir Pol, as we hear when Peregrine reads extracts from his diary (a much looser form than drama), is a random collection of events: buying toothpicks, arguing with a Dutch merchant, getting his stockings mended, urinating at St. Mark's (4.1.135–44). Volpone's morning, like his story, adds up; Sir Pol's does not.

Given the intensity of the main plot, the looseness of the subplot has a certain technical value: it provides breathing space, relaxation for the audience. The harmless folly of Sir Pol also sets off the criminal behavior of Volpone and Mosca by contrast.[15] Yet the Sir Pol scenes are not just interludes, comic relief in a comedy that needs it. On closer inspection, the sheer otherness of Sir Pol, like the otherness of Mak and Gill in *Secunda Pastorum*, has a paradoxical effect. Jonson's boast that he makes jests to fit his fable holds true. Volpone and Sir Pol are linked not by the latter's inadequate imitation of the former, but by his head-on opposition to him. In his nature, in his agenda, in the kind of action he inhabits, he is so sharply opposed to Volpone that we can after all find it profitable to think of them together. The result, however, is not a play unified by bringing the characters together under a common judgment that consolidates our responses; it is a play blown apart by a centrifugal force that may be even more powerful and systematic in its operation than the centripetal force other critics have argued for, a force that makes response difficult and judgment impossible.

Each character's opening position—Volpone begins act 1, Sir Pol act 2—is set firmly before us. Volpone is in his bedroom, his center of power, which his language turns into a private universe with its own sun and its own religion. Volpone's concentration on the shrine that contains his treasure is a clue to other kinds of concentration, notably the centering of all values on gold: "Thou art vertue, fame, / Honour, and all things else!" (1.1.25–26). Human relations fall away; gold is

> the best of things: and far transcending
> All stile of ioy, in children, parents, friends,
> Or any other waking dreame on earth.

(1.1.16–18)

Volpone's is a life of pleasure and self-indulgence—including, we soon see, indulgence in power—centered on himself. There is, for him, virtually no one else:

> What should I doe,
> But cocker vp my *genius*, and liue free
> To all delights, my fortune calls me to?
> I haue no wife, no parent, child, allie. . . .

(1.1.70–73)

Sir Pol opens act 2 in an undefined public space, as voluble and full of self-display as Volpone but talking to Peregrine where Volpone talks to his gold, revealing a way of life as diffuse as Volpone's is concentrated:

> Sir, to a wise man, all the world's his soile.
> It is not *Italie*, nor *France*, nor *Europe*,
> That must bound me, if my fates call me forth.
> Yet, I protest, it is no salt desire
> Of seeing countries, shifting a religion,
> Nor any dis-affection to the state
> Where I was bred (and, vnto which I owe
> My dearest plots) hath brought me out; much lesse
> That idle, antique, stale, grey-headed proiect
> Of knowing mens minds, and manners, with VLYSSES:
> But, a peculiar humour of my wiues,
> Laid for this height of *Venice*, to obserue,
> To quote, to learne the language, and so forth—
> I hope you trauell, sir, with licence?
> *Per.* Yes.
> *Pol.* I dare the safelier conuerse—

(2.1.1–15)

When Volpone travels it is in his bedroom, in his fantasies of dressing up Celia as a French, then a Tuscan, then a Spanish lady, "Or some quick *Negro*, or cold Russian" (3.7.226–32). Volpone is a loner operating in private; Sir Pol is respectful of the state (which Volpone ignores) and anxious to ensure that Peregrine is traveling "with licence" before he converses with him. Volpone virtually creates his own moral language, in which words like virtue, fame, and honor are redefined; Sir Pol intends to learn the language of the country he is visiting. While Volpone has one grand scheme, which he appears to have devised himself, Sir Pol boasts of a versatility triggered by the climate: "I should be loath to draw the subtill ayre / Of such a place, without my thousand aymes" (4.1.66–67). (Here we could totally confuse the play's beast-fable by pointing out that Volpone is the hedgehog and Sir Pol is the fox.)

While calling himself an observer, Sir Pol disclaims any interest in "knowing mens minds, and manners" (2.1.10). Volpone and Mosca, on the other hand, study their dupes closely and comment on them with critical precision. That is because Volpone is out to control the behavior of others and impose his vision on the world. Sir Pol would rather have the world impose on him: he has a "chameleon's willing-ness to do as the Romans and take on the moral coloring of his surroundings."[16] He is respectful of authority, and patriotic; he is anxious to know if Peregrine has been with the English ambassador, and keen to hear news from England (2.1.17–18). He is shocked to hear that Peregrine has come abroad "Emptie of rules, for trauaile" (2.1.112). Lady Pol is equally patriotic and equally concerned with rules. Dissatisfied with her appearance, she berates her maids:

> Besides, you seeing what a curious nation
> Th'*Italians* are, what will they say of me?
> The *English* lady cannot dresse her selfe;
> Here's a fine imputation, to our countrie!
>
> (3.4.32–35)

In the event, neither of the Would-bes does much for England's reputation abroad. Lady Pol is Volpone's least favorite visitor, and (assuming the merchants who assist in Sir Pol's final humiliation are also English) there may be a touch of hurt national pride when the second merchant remarks of Sir Pol, "If you could ship him away, 'twere excellent" (5.4.3).

On the matter of religion, Volpone invents his own: "Open the shrine, that I may see my *saint*" (1.1.2). Sir Pol advises Peregrine,

> And then, for your religion, professe none;
> But wonder, at the diuersitie of all;
> And, for your part, protest, were there no other
> But simply the lawes o'th'land, you could content you:
> NIC: MACHIAVEL, and monsieur BODINE, both,
> Were of this minde.
>
> (4.1.22–27)

Volpone is committed to his religion; Sir Pol will commit to nothing. The variety of religion is something to be observed, not (as in Donne's Satire 3) a challenge that demands a response. If a decision must be made, it is not a personal choice of faith but a politic respect for the religion of a particular state. (Sir Pol goes on to lecture Peregrine on table manners, putting the two issues on the same level of importance.) Sir Pol is a patriot in religion; when he hears of a whale in the Thames, he is fearful for England in its cold war with the Papist powers of Europe: "'Twas either sent from *Spaine*, or the *Arch-dukes!*" / SPINOLA'S whale, vpon my life, my credit!" (2.1.50–1).

Sir Pol's religion is not something he has argued himself into, but something he has picked up from his reading of continental authors, Machiavelli and Bodin. Lady Pol reads even more superficially, not for content but simply to add to her collection of names:

> *Volp*. The Poet,
> As old in time, as PLATO, and as knowing,
> Say's that your highest female grace is silence.
>   *Lad*. Which o' your Poets? PETRARCH? or TASSO?' or
>   DANTE?
> GVERRINI? ARIOSTO? ARETINE?
> CIECO *di Hadria?* I haue read them all.
>
> (3.4.76–81)

For her, even authors are collectors, not creators; their business is to steal from the most fashionable models (3.4.87–92). In the Scoto scene Volpone is the inventor and performer, Sir Pol the delighted audience. He and his lady are not inventive or critical spirits, but collectors, devices for the indiscriminate recording of whatever sounds they happen to pick up.

Sir Pol does have aspirations as an inventor, but his motives and Volpone's are radically opposed. Volpone is a grasper and a consumer; he has, to put it mildly, no notion of being useful to society. He takes pride in the things he does not do:

> I vse no trade, no venter;
> I wound no earth with plow-shares; fat no beasts
> To feede the shambles; haue no mills for yron,
> Oyle, corne, or men, to grind 'hem into poulder.
>
> (1.1.33–36)

All of these trades are potentially useful; but Volpone chooses to ignore their usefulness and see only the destruction they entail, so that he can present himself, ironically, as a great public benefactor because he abstains from them. Sir Pol, on the other hand, genuinely sees himself as public-spirited. He sees even a project to sell herrings as serving the state (4.1.50), and he boasts to Peregrine,

> I haue, at my free houres, thought vpon
> Some certaine goods, vnto the state of *Venice*,
> Which I doe call my cautions: and, sir, which
> I meane (in hope of pension) to propound
> To the great councell, then vnto the forty,
> So to the ten.
>
> (4.1.70–75)

The hope for a pension hardly sounds like his central motive; it is admitted in a brief subordinate clause, and it is only a hope. What really drives his speeches, besides the fascination of the schemes themselves, is a delight in being useful. His scheme to use onions to detect plague in incoming ships is designed to save time, trouble, and money:

> And, where they vse,
> To lie out fortie, fifty daies, sometimes,
> About the *Lazaretto*, for their triall;
> Ile saue that charge, and losse vnto the merchant,
> And, in an houre, cleare the doubt.
>
> (4.1.104–08)

His scheme for the licensing of tinderboxes—anyone, he points out, could take so small an object into the Arsenal—is equally public-spirited. It also shows the satisfaction he takes in the notion of state regulation. Just as he looks forward to taking his schemes through the decision-making structures of Venice—"To the great councell, then vnto the forty, / So to the ten" (4.1.74–75)—so he envisions a system of control from which even the patriotic will not be exempt:

> I, therefore,
> Aduertise to the state, how fit it were
> That none, but such as were knowne patriots,
> Sound louers of their countrey, would be sufferd
> T'enioy them in their houses: and, euen those,
> Seal'd, at some office, and, at such a bignesse,
> As might not lurke in pockets.
>
> (4.1.93–99)

In him breathes the spirit of every public servant who has schemed to regulate the most trivial actions of the most innocent people for the sake of the general good.

There is no malice in these schemes; like so many nuisances, Sir Pol thinks he is being helpful. It is in this spirit that he offers Peregrine a torrent of trivial, useless advice. It is not just that he is "less venal than the crow or vulture."[17] Though Creaser may be going too far in calling him "generous and warm-hearted,"[18] he is right to note that Sir Pol "lacks the nastier qualities" of the Machiavel: "Rather than disparaging others, he is often ready with undiscriminating praise, and cruelty and malice are in him replaced by comically ineffective innocence."[19] Or, as Douglas Duncan puts it, the play confirms the view that "the English were too nice or too stupid to make good Machiavels."[20] Sir Pol's good nature shows up particularly when we compare his marriage with that of Corvino and Celia. Volpone is amused by the freedom Sir Pol allows his lady:

> 'For heauen, I wonder at the desperate valure
> Of the bold *English*, that they dare let loose
> Their wiues, to all encounters!
>
> (1.5.100–02)

Shortly thereafter, Mosca describes Corvino's treatment of Celia:

> Shee's kept as warily, as is your gold:
> Neuer do's come abroad, neuer takes ayre,
> But at a windore.
>
> (1.5.118–20)

Sir Pol is eager to introduce his lady to Peregrine, intending both a treat for his new acquaintance and a compliment to her:

> 'Tis shee indeed sir, you shall know her. She is,
> Were she not mine, a lady of that merit,
> For fashion, and behaviour; and for beauty
> I durst compare—*Per.* It seemes, you are not iealous,
> That dare commend her.
>
> (4.2.11–15)

Peregrine takes a guarded, cynical attitude not unlike Volpone's; but Sir Pol sees nothing wrong with praising his wife and introducing her to another gentleman.

While Volpone is the great deceiver, Sir Pol is totally frank; he could not keep a secret if his life depended on it (as in Venice it might). Having warned Peregrine, "beware, / You neuer speake a truth" (4.1.16–17), he proceeds to tell him all his schemes. He boasts that if he had a trusted friend he would make him rich,

> With certaine proiects, that I haue:
> Which, I may not discouer. *Per.* If I had
> But one to wager with, I would lay odds, now,
> He tels me, instantly. *Pol.* One is, (and that
> I care not greatly, who knowes) to serue the state
> Of *Venice,* with red herrings, for three yeeres. . . .
>
> (4.1.46–51)

His very name declares his nature:

> *Per.* This fellow
> Do's he gull me, trow? or is gull'd? your name, sir?
> *Pol.* My name is POLITIQVE WOVLD-BEE.
> *Per.* O, that speaks him.
>
> (2.1.23–25)

Volpone is the creative center of a grand deception that, with its make-up and disguise, has the characteristics of a play within the play. His theatricality is quite self-conscious, as when he recalls to Celia his stunning performance as the young Antinous (3.7.157–64). Peregrine sees Sir Pol as a figure in a play (which he is), the difference being that the knight is quite unconscious of playing a role:

> O, this Knight
> (Were he well knowne) would be a precious thing
> To fit our *English* stage. . . .
>
> (2.1.56–58)

His one deliberate connection with the theater lies not in creation but in the more characteristic activities of copying and collecting. His politic notes turn out to be "Drawne out of play-bookes" (5.4.42).

Perhaps the most striking contrast between the two characters is that while Volpone is for the most part supremely confident, master of his world (the reservation is important, and we will return to it) Sir Pol, however he may trust his wife, is fearful of everything else:

> Now, heauen!
> What prodigies be these? The fires at *Berwike!*
> And the new starre! these things concurring, strange!
> And full of omen! Saw you these meteors?
>
> (2.1.35–38)

Frightened though he is, he keeps asking for more: "Worthie sir, / Some other newes" (2.1.52–53). Volpone demands to be fed with things—gold, plate, jewels—all of which confirm his sense of power; Sir Pol demands to be fed with news, all of which frightens and upsets him. Encouraged by Peregrine, he fears that Corvino's attack on Celia is in some way directed against him, and adds that it is all part of a grand design: "This three weekes, all my aduises, all my letters, / They haue beene intercepted" (2.3.13–14). This private outburst of jealousy is "Some trick of state, beleeue it" (2.3.10). By assuming that there are no innocent events in the world in which he moves and that everything is part of a grand network of menace and surveillance, Sir Pol anticipates a powerful strain in New Historicist criticism. One critic who belongs to that school has paid tribute to him: he may have his facts wrong, but he is "perfectly correct in principle."[21]

Throughout this discussion I have been indulging in the old critical game of parallel hunting. My argument, however, is that the play rewards such activity not by revealing hidden similarities, showing all the characters as participating in the same evil, distinguished only by degrees of competence, but by revealing a series of sharp oppositions, as though the subplot were made of a kind of antimatter resistant to the matter of the main plot. There are a few passages that suggest underlying similarities, but they tend to be odd, incidental touches, easy to miss: the sort of thing a reader might happen to notice on the first reading, or the fifth, or never; the sort of thing an audience might pick up subliminally if at all. The fool Androgyno is allegedly one of Volpone's offspring; Sir Pol is so upset by the death of Stone the fool that Peregrine asks, "He was no kinsman to you?" to which Sir Pol replies guardedly, "That I know of" (2.1.62). Sir Pol's contact with the powers of Venice is "A *commandadore* . . . a common sergeant" (4.1.78), the type of officer Volpone impersonates in act 5. Sir Pol's account of the fate of the Baboons, who failed as spies because they "Were so extremely giuen to women, as / They made discouery of all" (2.1.92–93), anticipates the risk Volpone takes over Celia. Other links are matters of suggestion—Androgyno's soul has wandered through bodies as Sir Pol wanders through countries (1.2.1–62)—or slight verbal echoes, as when the Avocatori call Celia and Bonario "prodigies" (4.6.55).

These are connections to be worked out (or not) in the study. There are others that are more likely to have an impact in performance, and these are more important. What they show is not, as in the usual critical model, Sir Pol trying to rise to Volpone's level, but Volpone unexpectedly sinking to his. Moments after Sir Pol's panic

over the Celia episode, with his fear that his letters have been intercepted, we see Volpone, also shaken by Corvino's intervention, un-
characteristically flustered: "Is not the colour o'my beard, and eye-
browes, / To make me knowne?" (2.4.30–31). Mosca quickly reas-
sures him, but it is the first time Volpone's confidence has cracked.
(The parallel may be set up by Volpone's impersonation of Scoto—
who, with his grand schemes, his claim to have the public interest
at heart, and his oil that is *the fruits of my trauels* [2.2.185], for
the first time brings Volpone close to Sir Pol.) Though in his principal
scenes he is alone with Peregrine, Sir Pol fantasizes about himself as
a public man who understands the state. Yet he also lives in perpetual
anxiety, imagining the public world as one of constant surveillance,
in which exposure and humiliation, or worse, await those who do
not follow the rules. Volpone's power is exercised behind closed
doors, and when Bonario rescues Celia, he panics at the thought of
public power invading his private space, even his body:

> I heare some footing, officers, the *Saffi*,
> Come to apprehend vs! I doe feele the brand
> Hissing already, at my fore-head: now,
> Mine eares are boring.
>
> (3.8.16–19)

Dragged into the courtroom and forced to play his role there, he
declares, "here, 'twas good, in priuate, / But, in your publike, *Caue*,
whil'st I breathe" (5.1.3–4). Later he will voluntarily risk public
exposure, disguising himself as an officer of state, seeking out his
dupes to torment them in the street, participating in the trial—all
steps that lead to his undoing. When he enters Sir Pol's world—the
public arena, the machinery of state—he becomes in his own way
as fearful, as vulnerable, as out of his depth as Sir Pol himself.

To work properly his scheme depends on purely oral invention;
nothing is written down, and nothing should be. Sir Pol, on the
other hand, claims he has everything written down; he just can't find
his notes (4.1.84,127). When Volpone's scheme starts to unravel in
act 5, paper starts to figure in the action for the first time: as the
dupes read through the will, Mosca reads out a long inventory of
his goods. The tricksters have gone from the safety of purely oral
scheming to the risk of using documents, forgetting that schemes
like theirs require there should be nothing in writing. Oral inventions
can be denied, forgotten, kept private. What is written is public.
When Voltore changes tack in the last court sequence, he has to

repudiate a document in his own hand. Sir Pol, realizing he is in the same danger, burns his notes.

As Volpone enters Sir Pol's world, showing some of his vulnerability and capacity for panic, so Sir Pol makes one Volpone-like error, and it undoes him. His innocent delight in serving the state is bound up with a pride—potentially less innocent—in his own devices. As Volpone goes one step too far by pretending to be dead and leaving Mosca his heir, Sir Pol goes one step too far when he boasts to Peregrine,

> Were I false,
> Or would be made so, I could shew you reasons,
> How I could sell this state, now, to the *Turke;*
> Spight of their galleis, or their—
>
> (4.1.128–31)

When Jonathan Goldberg claims that "Like Volpone, Sir Pol is full of plots and stratagems, and his are quite explicitly aimed at overthrowing the state"[22] he gets it, as we have seen, exactly wrong. But this moment is the exception. When the disguised Peregrine turns Sir Pol's own words back on him—"That you profest to him, to haue a plot, / To sell the state of *Venice,* to the *Turke*" (5.4.37–38)— Sir Pol's plaintive self-defense, "Sir, I but talk'd so, / For discourse sake, merely" (5.4.46–47) has a ring of truth to it. It was just talk, meaning nothing. But for once Sir Pol's talk was aimed in a particular direction, making him sound like what Volpone truly is—a powerful, dangerous man. Each character, in short, enters the other's territory, to his undoing.

In the end, however, the separation between them is restored. We expect that in a play with double or multiple plots the stories will come together at the end; Jonson pointedly refuses to satisfy this expectation, just as he refuses to bring Celia and Bonario together for a romantic ending. As Mak and Gill never get to Bethlehem, Volpone and Sir Pol are disposed of in separate operations, Volpone in public and Sir Pol in private. For Barish this is an appropriate way of distinguishing between vice and folly[23]; but it is also an ironic reversal of each character's career. Each, having got into the other's territory, is caught and punished there. Sir Pol, who seems to spend his days wandering the streets chatting with people, is humiliated not in some public arena but in the privacy of his own lodgings; the tortoise shell is an enclosure within an enclosure. Volpone is judged and condemned in public. He is forced into Sir Pol's fantasy role of public benefactor when all his goods are confiscated and given "To the hospitall, of the *Incurabili*" (5.12.120). The great shape-shifter is fixed in one shape, that of his principal disguise: "Thou art to lie in prison, crampt with irons, / Till thou bee'st sicke, and lame indeed" (5.12.123–24). The role he played from time to time in his bedroom he will play forever in a theater provided by the state. Volpone clapped in irons may seem an echo of Sir Pol trapped in his tortoise shell; but the actual effect is rather different:

> *Wom.* My lady's come most melancholique, home,
> And say's, sir, she will straight to sea, for physick.
> *Pol.* And I, to shunne, this place, and clime, for
>   euer;
> Creeping, with house, on backe: and thinke it well,
> To shrinke my poore head, in my politique shell.
>
> (5.4.85–89)

While Volpone and Mosca are doomed to perpetual imprisonment, the Would-bes are on the move again. We do not know where they are going, and it would spoil the effect if we did; aimless wandering has always been the essence of their lives. Sir Pol's "And I" implies that he will join his lady, but the rest of his speech suggests that they are taking different routes out of the country, she by water and he by land, still creeping under his tortoise shell. They are both too preoccupied with their own misfortunes to seek or give comfort; they slink away from Venice and from each other. If Sir Pol seems determined to stay in his disguise, it is at least a mobile disguise, and it offers protection. Having eagerly collected gossip, Sir Pol knows that he will now be gossip himself:

> O, I shall be the fable of all feasts;
> The freight of the *gazetti;* ship-boyes tale;
> And, which is worst, euen talke for ordinaries.
>
> (5.4.82–84)

He has sought public recognition, but not this sort; and while Volpone is forced out of his enclosure, Sir Pol, who has always been so artlessly open and public, retreats to his for shelter.

Though each character is appropriately disposed of, the judgments themselves are subject to irony. Volpone and his cohorts are condemned by the Avocatori, who are as venal as any of them and as stupid as the dupes. They have not exposed Volpone; he has betrayed himself, knowing his danger is real but confronting it boldly in order to end the action on his own terms, spreading destruction as he does so: "Nay, now, / My ruines shall not come alone" (5.12.85–86).

Conversely, when Sir Pol fears that officers of state have come to arrest him, his danger is unreal. The state knows nothing of him, and his punishment is not torture but humiliation, which he brings on himself by hiding out of fear in his tortoise shell—unlike Volpone, who precipitates his fate by uncasing himself out of bravado. Sir Pol could have escaped the punishment designed for him if he had not been so easily frightened by a larger punishment that was pure illusion. Yet the ultimate irony in the subplot is the one that affects Peregrine. He strikes at Sir Pol out of sheer misapprehension, assuming that the innocent knight is actually a machiavel conducting a sexual intrigue, assuming that his name—which in fact is a full revelation of his nature—has to be decoded to get at the hidden truth:

> Sir POLITIQVE WOULD-BEE? no, sir POLITIQVE bawd!
> To bring me, thus, acquainted with his wife!
> Well, wise sir POL: since you haue practis'd, thus,
> Vpon my freshman-ship, I'le trie your salt-head,
> What proof it is against a counter-plot.
>
> (4.3.20–24)

Like Volpone and Sir Pol, Peregrine has got himself into the wrong plot. His assumption that the world is a great con game would be safe enough if he were in Volpone's story; here it is misplaced, and he himself becomes a mirror image of his dupe, responding to an imaginary threat, another politic would-be. Unlike his victim, he never learns the truth.

Peregrine has seemed to be the *raisonneur,* if not of the play, at least of the subplot. His failure in that role is not theatrically conspicuous; but it is a clue to the play's fundamental questioning of the whole business of judgment, including the final judgment to be passed by the audience. In the epilogue Volpone asks for our decision: applaud the Fox or not. If we applaud, as audiences tend to do automatically, he has played his last and most successful trick on us. Yet even as we applaud we may feel that the decision is not so easy, that the play presents us with a more disconcerting challenge than that of weighing Volpone's evil against his entertainment value. When we put Volpone together with Sir Politic (even the first syllables of their names rhyme) we see two radically opposed ways of living: the one selfish, enclosed, unnatural, socially and morally destructive; the other amiable, innocent, public-spirited, anxious for good relations, eager to serve the community. Volpone is antisocial man; Sir Pol, social man. Yet Sir Pol with all his virtues is a total idiot while Volpone with all his vices is creative and intelligent. Volpone understands the world he exploits; Sir Pol wants to serve the world, but knows not the first thing about it. If Sir Pol were not in the play, we could, after making due allowance for Volpone's skill and intelligence, condemn him as inhuman, judging him by implied standards of decency, good nature, and social usefulness. The trouble is, those standards are not just implied, they are embodied in Sir Pol.[24] By the same token, if Sir Pol had the play to himself, we could easily dismiss him as an idiot by the implied standards set by clever people who know the world; but those standards are embodied in Volpone.

The choice Jonson confronts us with is in one respect like the choice between the Houyhnhynms and the Yahoos: each presents an extreme but recognizable possibility, neither is tolerable, and (in Gulliver's perspective at least) no other choice is offered. In Barish's essay Volpone and Sir Politic converge and are judged together. But there is also a centrifugal force in the play, propelling its vision to radical extremes, making judgment impossible, leaving us stymied. We cannot, even, detach ourselves from the narrator and escape that way, as we can at the end of *Gulliver*. There is no narrator. There is only what we have seen and heard, unmediated, and we are responsible for what we do with it. We may want to infer a reasonable middle ground, a mean between Volpone and Sir Pol, but the play has offered no image of this; only judges as venal as the criminals they condemn, and a *raisonneur* who acts through self-deception. In the end we make our decision, or pretend to, by applauding Volpone, and so escape from the theater; but the play will continue to haunt us, as it would not do if it were as closed within a single system of judgment as the traditional reading imagines.[25]

Notes

All quotations from Jonson's works in this essay are taken from *Ben Jonson*, ed. C. H. Herford, Percy Simpson, and Evelyn Simpson, 11 vols. (Oxford: Clarendon, 1925–52).

1. Jonas A. Barish, "The Double Plot in Volpone," quoted from *Ben Jonson: A Collection of Critical Essays*, ed. Jonas A. Barish (Englewood Cliffs, N.J.: Prentice-Hall, 1963), 93. First published in *Modern Philology* 51 (1953): 83–92.

2. Ibid., 104.

3. Ibid., 93–94.

4. Ibid., 94.

5. Ibid., 105.

6. Ibid., 95.

7. Judd Arnold, "The Double Plot in *Volpone*: A Note on Jonsonian Dramatic Structure," *Seventeenth-Century News* 23.4 (Winter 1965): 51, 48.

8. Alvin B. Kernan, Introduction to *Volpone* (The Yale Ben Jonson: New Haven and London: Yale University Press, 1962), 19.

9. R. B. Parker, Introduction to *Volpone, or the Fox* (The Revels Plays: Manchester: Manchester University Press, 1983), 39–40.

10. Robert N. Watson, *Ben Jonson's Parodic Strategy: Literary Imperialism in the Comedies* (Cambridge, Mass.: Harvard University Press, 1987), 94.

11. John W. Creaser, "A Vindication of Sir Politic Would-be," *English Studies* 57 (1976): 512–13.

12. On double and multiple plots in general, see William Empson, *Some Versions of Pastoral* (London: Hogarth Press, 1986), 27–86; and Richard Levin, *The Multiple Plot in English Renaissance Drama* (Chicago: University of Chicago Press, 1971), passim.

13. See, for example, Douglas Duncan, *Ben Jonson and the Lucianic Tradition* (Cambridge: Cambridge University Press, 1979), 162.

14. John Gordon Sweeney, III, *Jonson and the Psychology of Public Theater* (Princeton: Princeton University Press, 1985), 97; Parker, introduction, 41.

15. Creaser, "Vindication," 514.

16. Thomas M. Greene, "Ben Jonson and the Centered Self," *Studies in English Literature* 10 (1970): 341.

17. Barish, *Ben Jonson*, 103.

18. Creaser, "Vindication," 509.

19. Creaser, Introduction to *Volpone, or the Fox* (The London Medieval and Renaissance Series: London: Hodder and Stoughton, 1978), 48.

20. Duncan, *Lucianic*, 161.

21. Jonathan Goldberg, *James I and the Politics of Literature* (Baltimore and London: Johns Hopkins University Press, 1983), 73.

22. Ibid., 72.

23. Barish, "Double Plot," 103.

24. Celia and Bonario, who are beyond the scope of this essay, present a similar problem: their virtue is real, but so helpless in the state of Venice as to be futile.

25. I am grateful to the members of the Work in Progress in English group at the University of Toronto for their comments on an earlier version of this essay.

Cynicism and the Futility of Art in *Volpone*

JAMES HIRSH

THE knavish characters in *Volpone* cynically believe that everyone is either a knave or a fool and that language itself is an instrument by which knaves manipulate fools. The play actually confirms and even deepens their cynical view. Language is shown to operate as described by the knaves. Although the knaves do eventually expose their own folly, this eventuality, rather than undermining their cynical viewpoint, merely refines that viewpoint. Instead of being divided into knaves and fools, the world of *Volpone* is divided into naive fools and knavish fools. Foolishness, of one sort or another, is inescapable and incurable. Consequently, it is futile to seek either a preventive or a cure. To do so would itself be an act of folly. The play establishes a series of interlocking analogies among a variety of means for supposedly curing what ails characters. These include Scoto's elixir, Sir Politic's projects, the schemes of the gulls to inherit Volpone's gold, Volpone's gold itself, Volpone's ruses, and Mosca's stratagems. All prove futile. But the corrosive cynicism of the play and the series of interlocking analogies extend to other areas. Poetry, drama, and philosophy are also shown to be futile. A writer who seeks to cure incurable foolishness by means of writing is a naive fool, whereas a writer who believes that foolishness is incurable but claims to be able to cure foolishness is a con artist, a mountebank selling a phony elixir.

At numerous moments in *Volpone*, knaves comment on the way of the world. Hoping to inherit Volpone's estate, Corvino tries to convince his wife to join Volpone in bed. When she argues that this would damage Corvino's honor, he responds,

> Honor? tut, a breath;
> There's no such thing in nature: a mere term
> Invented to awe fools.[1]

(3.7.38–40)

According to Corvino, moral concepts are devices used by knaves to manipulate fools. Later in the same scene, Volpone makes a similar point in ironically seeking the same goal as Celia's husband. When Celia resists his seduction and appeals to his "conscience," Volpone responds, "'Tis the beggar's virtue" (211). When Volpone himself reveals some respect for learning, Mosca responds,

> Hood an ass with reverend purple,
> So you can hide his two ambitious ears,
> And he shall pass for a cathedral Doctor.
>
> (1.2.111–13)

Elsewhere Mosca declares that "almost / All the wise world is little else in nature, / But Parasites and Sub-parasites" (3.1.11–13)—the rest are "clods and Clot-poles" (9). While impersonating Scoto, Volpone declares that "to be a fool born is a disease incurable" (2.2.159).

Although the cynical comments of Corvino, Volpone, and Mosca are convenient rationalizations for their own behavior, the action of the play disturbingly supports their suggestions that moral concepts are instruments of knavish manipulation and that the entire cultural and political system is pervaded by knavishness and foolishness. The play confirms, for example, that "conscience" is "the beggar's virtue." Near the end of the play, Voltore appeals to the Avocatori:

> now struck in conscience, here I prostrate
> Myself at your offended feet, for pardon.
> . . . .
> It is not passion in me, reverend fathers,
> But only conscience, conscience, my good sires,
> That makes me, now, tell truth.
>
> (5.10.11–12, 16–18)

Not only is Voltore a beggar, but he is also a knave cynically using the concept of "conscience" in an effort to manipulate the Avocatori. Similarly, Mosca uses the concepts of "conscience" and "gratitude" to manipulate Corbaccio; according to Mosca, Volpone will leave Corbaccio his estate "out of conscience, and mere gratitude" (1.4.108). Corbaccio himself does not have a conscience or feel gratitude, but he believes that the dying Volpone does. Corbaccio's mistake is that he is not cynical enough; he places too much faith in the existence of conscience in others.

Like Volpone, Corvino also equates conscience with weakness. Early in the play he hesitates when Mosca offers to murder Volpone, but he later chides himself, "Ay, a plague on't, / My conscience fools my wit" (2.6.89–90). Mosca associates conscience with losers, with those who have been duped, when he facetiously tells Voltore: "You, that have so much law, I know ha' the conscience / Not to be covetous of what is mine" (5.3.97–98). Mosca knows that Voltore does not have a conscience, but Mosca believes that Voltore is as helpless in this battle of knaves as if he had one, as if he were a naive fool. Among would-be knaves, this is the supreme insult.

Moral terms have been so emptied of their conventional meaning that they can be expropriated by knaves for the expression of a knavish system of values. According to Mosca, his "conscience" tells him that Voltore deserves "to be cozened" (5.2.43, 47). A knave has a moral obligation to cozen fools, and one is presented with unlimited opportunities. So many fools, so little time.

In some instances the word "conscience" is used in two different cynical ways simultaneously. Mosca uses the word to convince Voltore that he will aid him unscrupulously to gain the fortunes of Volpone and Corbaccio:

> Truth be my comfort, and my conscience,
> My only aim was, to dig you a fortune
> Out of these two old rotten sepulchers.
>
> (3.9.37–39)

The "conscience" to which Mosca here alludes is that which requires a knave to cozen fools. But Mosca is lying to Voltore. Like the real tinsel that lies beneath the phony tinsel of Hollywood, a deeper cynicism lies beneath Mosca's surface cynicism. Mosca is making a fool of Voltore by appealing to Voltore's sentimentalism, to his faith in honor among thieves. In an earlier episode Mosca used the word "conscience" to explain his desire to help Volpone seduce Corvino's wife:

> I'm bound in conscience,
> No less than duty, to effect my best
> To your release of torment, and I will, sir.
>
> (2.4.15–17)

At the time this passage occurs, a naive playgoer may believe that Mosca is what he seems to Volpone to be at the time, a conscientious knave working unselfishly for his knavish master's benefit. Such a naive playgoer will be disillusioned when Mosca eventually tries to make a fool out of his master. As soon as his own interests and those of Volpone's diverge, Mosca acts for himself. In retrospect, then, the passage just quoted does not differ in kind from the passage involving Mosca and Voltore. In each case, the cynical surface use of the term "conscience" obscures a deeper cynical function of the word. In both cases, by frankly revealing his cynicism, Mosca builds a rapport with a character whom he will later betray. Iago uses a similar technique in *Othello* (another Venetian play in the repertoire of the King's Men): Iago's reputation for cynicism, for brutal honesty, allows him cynically to deceive the other characters.

The play also confirms Corvino's cynical assertion about "honor." Whether or not the concept was invented to awe fools, it is used by knaves for that purpose in the play. As Scoto, Volpone repeatedly uses the word "honorable" in addressing his audience (2.2.69, 87, 173, 182, 187), whom he regards as a congregation of dupes. Corvino himself used the term in an attempt to awe Celia. He rebuked her for her behavior in regard to the mountebank Scoto: "Death of mine honor" (2.5.1). Corvino's ability to see moral concepts as mere inventions to awe fools and his own willingness to use such terms for such purposes distinguish him in his own eyes from such fools. When he dismisses the concept of honor, he is again trying to awe Celia, to manipulate her into obeying his will, this time by emphatically denying the very category he earlier emphatically affirmed. Corvino is not troubled by his apparent dishonesty; honesty, like the related concept of honor, is merely another concept used to awe fools. Playgoers are encouraged to view Corvino as a contemptible character. But the main ground for this contempt is his foolishness, not his knavery. He earnestly says, "I trust thee, Mosca" (4.6.76), but he is a fool to believe that Mosca is trustworthy, that there is honor among thieves. As in the cases of Voltore and Corbaccio, Corvino's mistake is to be insufficiently cynical.

Like Scoto's audience, the Avocatori are insistently called "honorable," as well as "your honors," or "honored fathers," most often by Voltore (at 4.5.29, 4.5.63, 4.6.35, 4.6.43, 5.10.3, 5.12.46), but also by Lady Wouldbe (4.6.9), Corvino (5.12.103), and others. Voltore uses the word as a rhetorical device, as flattery. He no more values "honor" than Corvino does, and he is here trying to manipulate the judges. As it happens, the Avocatori are not particularly honorable. They resemble the gulls; they are easily manipulated and mercenary. When they learn that Mosca is heir to Volpone's fortune, their attitude toward him immediately and radically changes:

Avocatore 4: We have done ill, by a public officer,
   To send for him, if he be heir.
Avocatore 2:   For whom?
Avocatore 4: Him, that they call the parasite.
Avocatore 3:   'Tis true,
   He is a man of great estate, now left.

> *Avocatore 4:* Go you, and learn his name; and say, the court
>   Entreats his presence, here; but to the clearing
>   Of some few doubts.
>
> (5.10.37–42)

When Mosca enters in the next court episode, the Avocatori show deference to wealth and hope to become allied with it:

> *Avocatore 3:* A stool.
> *Avocatore 4:* A proper man! and were Volpone dead,
>   A fit match for my daughter.
> *Avocatore 3:*   Give him way.
>
> (5.12.49–51)

When Mosca later asserts that he has inherited Volpone's fortune, the Fourth Avocatore's reaction is not that of a disinterested judge: "It is a match, my daughter is bestowed" (5.12.62). Perhaps fearing that another Avocatore may beat him to the punch, he raises the issue in the midst of the court proceedings: "Sir, are you married?" (5.12.84). The Fourth Avocatore's eagerness to sell his daughter resembles Corvino's eagerness to prostitute his wife and Corbaccio's eagerness to disinherit his son. The severity of the punishments meted out by the Avocatori suggests that they are less concerned with justice than with exacting revenge for having been made fools of. They give prominence to Mosca's offense against themselves: "[You] Have, with your impudence, abused the court" (110). The Avocatori are also driven by snobbism; Mosca's crime is exacerbated because he is "a fellow of no birth or blood" (112).[2] Corvino's comment about honor haunts the scenes in which the "honorable" Avocatori show themselves to be governed by the same knavish and foolish impulses as the rest of the characters. When in the course of his testimony Corvino compares Celia to various supposedly lecherous animals, Notario warns him, "Preserve the honor of the court" (4.5.120). The honor of the court depends on the maintenance of decorous language. Although Corvino tries to awe Celia with his use of patriarchal terminology, he is in turn silenced by the greater patriarchal power of the city fathers.

The concept of honor is used by Corvino to browbeat Celia, by several characters to flatter the Avocatori, and by the Avocatori themselves to maintain control. All these conspicuous uses of the word confirm Corvino's explicit assertion that the term is an instrument of interpersonal or social control. Even if the term was not specifically "invented" for this purpose, it has by now been compromised by this insistent usage and so expropriated by scoundrels that

Volpone can use it without irony in praising Mosca: "Thou art mine honor, Mosca, and my pride" (3.7.68).[3] *Volpone* is even more cynical than Volpone, however. Mosca does not honor his relationship with his master. Like the other gulls, Volpone places too much faith in Mosca's honor. Volpone makes the same mistake as Corbaccio: he is not cynical enough.

In the context of the play the word "honor" sounds hollow even when used by characters who are not obvious scoundrels. Bonario also calls the Avocatori "honored" (4.5.93). He does so not in his first speech addressed to them but only after Voltore has repeatedly applied the epithet to them. This creates the disturbing impression that Bonario is learning to flatter, is learning how to use such terms. The very last use of the term occurs only thirteen lines from the end of the play (5.12.146) when "All" the other characters in unison use it to express their awe of the Avocatori. This would seem to be a final confirmation of Corvino's cynical observation.

In the conspicuous use of the term "honorable" in the Scrutineo scenes of *Volpone*, regular patrons of the King's Men (the theatrical company that gave the first performance of *Volpone*) were invited to recall the conspicuous use of the same word in another play in the repertoire of the same company. In a famous episode in *Julius Caesar*, Marc Antony repeatedly calls Brutus and the other assassins of Caesar "honorable men" (for example, at 3.2.83) in the context of eliciting sympathy for Caesar and revulsion against the conspirators.[4] By the end of his speech the word "honorable" has come to mean its opposite for the onstage listeners. Voltore and other characters in *Volpone* use the word "honorable" as flattery rather than as sarcasm, but both episodes foreground the cynical use of the word to manipulate others. Both plays encourage playgoers to be skeptical or cynical when they hear such terminology used outside the theater. But the concept of honor is undermined even more in *Volpone* than in *Julius Caesar*. Whatever his flaws, Brutus is a far more attractive character than any of the "honorable" Avocatori. Shakespeare's play problematizes the concept of honor but does not necessarily empty it of all meaning.

Another word emptied of meaning in *Volpone* is "father." In his initial appearance, Corbaccio tells Mosca, "I do not doubt to be a father to thee" (1.4.127). Corbaccio has just shown a willingness to disinherit his own son, so "to be a father" rings hollow. The hollowness of the concept of fatherhood resounds through the later part of the play. In the first Scrutineo episode, Voltore addresses the Avocatori as "Fathers" or "father-hoods" or "sires" a total of nine times. A motive for Voltore's particular and particularly insistent use of the term is noted by Alvin Kernan:

> By his frequent references to the judges as fathers he establishes a prejudice on their part for the outraged father, Corbaccio; makes them feel the wrongs done Corbaccio the father are done to them, the fathers of the city. Volpone, a splendid rhetorician himself, is properly appreciative of the fine points of Voltore's art and comments particularly on this device, 5.2.33–7.[5]

Kernan does not point out, however, that the association between the father Corbaccio and the Avocatori is designed to have a quite different rhetorical effect on playgoers than on the Avocatori themselves. Playgoers are aware that, by his actions, Corbaccio has abandoned whatever moral authority he may have had as Bonario's father. The very same association that might incline the Avocatori to sympathize with Corbaccio would undermine playgoers' respect for the Avocatori. As R. B. Parker points out, "the *Avocatori* fail to live up to the responsibilities implied by their title of 'fatherhood'" (30). At least one aspect of their failure is, ironically, their apparent susceptibility to flattery based on their status as city fathers. Because the Avocatori have been so insistently associated with fatherhood, the term is another, like "honor," that has been compromised.

Voltore is not the only character to address the Avocatori as father. Before Voltore ever speaks in court, Mosca addresses them as "your father-hoods" (4.5.13), and when Mosca appears as Volpone's heir, he addresses them as "Most reverend fathers" (5.12.55) and "father-hoods" (81). Corvino addresses them three times as "your father-hoods" (4.5.117, 5.10.28, and 5.12.94) and five times as "grave fathers" (4.5.145, 5.10.20, 5.10.24, 5.10.50, 5.12.8). In disguise as an officer, Volpone addresses them twice as "grave fathers" (5.12.11, 71). After revealing his identity, Volpone addresses them as "reverend fathers" (5.12.92). Many of these expressions occur in quick succession, as if the characters were in competition with one another to paternalize the Avocatori. The climax of this process seems to occur when Corvino and Mosca, each desperate to plead with the court, simultaneously shout "Most honored fathers" (5.12.103). But this choral outburst is topped a short while later when "All" characters exclaim "Honored fathers" (145) in response to the sentences meted out by the Avocatori.

As if other ironies had not already undermined playgoers' respect for the Avocatori enough, the sentence these judges mete out to

Corvino just before they themselves are universally acclaimed as fathers shows deference for another father:

> And to expiate
> Thy wrongs done to [thy] wife, thou art to send her
> Home, to her father, with her dowry trebled.
>
> (5.12.142–44)

The wrongs done to Celia are expiated not by restitution made to Celia herself but by restitution paid to Celia's father, who showed little concern about Celia's welfare in marrying her off to the odious Corvino. That offstage thoughtless father has an onstage analogue in the Fourth Avocatore who was thoughtlessly and conspicuously eager to marry his daughter to Mosca simply because of Mosca's presumed wealth. Both Corvino and the Fourth Avocatore are also compared implicitly with an imaginary father whom Mosca described to Corvino. When the doctors supposedly prescribed that a young woman lie next to Volpone, "One o' the Doctors offered, there, his daughter" (2.6.60). The doctor's supposed action called for a corresponding action by Corvino, who equated his own action with that of the doctor-father and did so by means of the concept of honor: "In the point of honor, / The cases are all one, of wife, and daughter" (72–73). It is significant that at his most passionate moment in his attempt to coerce Celia to enter Volpone's bed, Corvino utters the oath "Heart of my father!" (3.7.90). In this play Jonson goes out of his way to associate fatherhood with unseemly coercion.

The knaves are not the only characters who "father" the Avocatori. After a speech in which Voltore calls them "fathers" three times and "father-hoods" once, Bonario addresses them as "Most honored fathers" (4.5.93). Two can play that game. If Voltore's use of the term can be regarded as a cynical rhetorical device, then so can Bonario's use of the term. By referring to the judges as fathers, Bonario attempts to establish himself as a respectful son and to elicit paternal sympathy from the Avocatori toward himself. When Corbaccio denounces him, Bonario declares,

> Sir, I will sit down,
> And rather wish my innocence should suffer,
> Than I resist the authority of a father.
>
> (4.5.112–14)

If his assertion were spoken in an aside, it would be simply an expression of extraordinary if misplaced filial respect. But it is spoken aloud before the Avocatori, whom Bonario has just addressed as "Most honored fathers," and is presumably intended to make a favorable impression on those fathers. When the case begins to go against him, he desperately attempts to get a hearing by calling them "Fathers" (4.5.139), but to no avail. Bonario may not be as experienced or adept at such rhetorical strategies as Voltore, who is after all a lawyer, but he is not above attempting to employ them. Playgoers are encouraged to hear the word "father" as another term used in the effort to awe fools.

The Avocatori appear in only three episodes but are addressed with a paternal epithet a total of thirty-five times. It is hard to imagine how a word could be more conspicuously foregrounded in a play. In this context, it is something of a joke that the father Corbaccio himself never addresses the Avocatori as "fathers"—presumably he is too stupid to use this obvious rhetorical ploy. It is noteworthy, furthermore, that Voltore addresses the Avocatori as fathers at least as insistently, in the second court episode, when he is no longer allied with Corbaccio the father, as he did in the first court episode. The term is used so insistently, and the Avocatori are so foolish, that it is hard not to see the play as a devastating attack on patriarchy. "Fatherhood," like "honor," has become tainted.

The play hollows out other conventional terms of approbation. The Avocatori are also frequently called "grave" (e.g., at 5.10.26). The foregrounding of the term, like that of "honorable," also emphasizes its irony. The gravity of the Avocatori is superficially conferred on them by the dignified decorum of the courtroom. In fact, they are intellectual lightweights easily swayed by their prejudices and by the manipulations of unscrupulous characters. They are ready to take Mosca's assertions about Celia at face value because of preconceptions about women: "This woman has too many moods" (4.5.142). The play confirms Mosca's cynical assertion: "Hood an ass with reverend purple, / So you can hide his two ambitious ears, / And he shall pass for a cathedral Doctor" (1.2.111–13). After having made a fool of Voltore, Mosca contemptuously and sarcastically calls him "Reverend sir" (5.3.82). The Avocatori, who are often called "reverend" (e.g., by Corvino at 4.5.121 and by Voltore at 5.10.16), are as asinine as the gulls.[6]

The concept of wisdom has been expropriated by the scoundrels and reduced to worldly wisdom or cynicism. Mosca refers to the "wise world" (3.1.12) that is dominated by scoundrels and would-be scoundrels. In attempting to seduce Celia, Volpone urges her, "If thou hast wisdom, hear me" (3.7.212). This expropriation of the concept of wisdom encourages playgoers to adopt a cynical attitude toward the Avocatori, who are addressed by Voltore as "your wisdoms" (4.5.146, 5.10.32). Furthermore, once the terms "honorable" and "father" used in regard to the Avocatori have become tainted, all other terms of approbation similarly applied to the Avocatori, even though used less often, become similarly tainted in a cascading effect.

Knavish characters have also appropriated the word "virtue." Mosca responds to Bonario's allegations as "eas'ly stuck on virtue, when she's poor" (3.2.13). Mosca claims to act out of "an interest in the general state / Of goodness, and true virtue" (3.2.47–48). In response to the Second Avocatore's reference to Bonario's reputation for honesty, Voltore declares,

> So much more full of danger is his vice,
> That can beguile so under shade of virtue.
>
> (4.5.61–62)

Voltore is here engaged in the very practice of which he is accusing Bonario. Shortly before Voltore warns against the danger of vice that "can beguile so under shade of virtue," Voltore referred to the Avocatori themselves as "your virtues" (19). Because the word has been so contaminated, his use of it immediately raises cynical doubts about the Avocatori, doubts that are shortly confirmed, as indicated above. When Celia offers to apply the word "virtuous" to Volpone, he is offended and supplies the cynical connotations of the word "virtuous" in this wise world: "Think me cold, / Frozen, and impotent, and so report me?" (3.7.260–61). Because almost all the characters in Celia's world are cynical knaves, it is foolishly naive of Celia to believe that "virtuous" could carry the same uncynical meaning for her interlocutor as it does for her.

The language of religion has been expropriated by the scoundrels. Volpone praises Mosca as both his "better Angel" (2.4.21) and a "fine devil" (5.3.46); in this world the two terms are interchangeable. The following passage indicates an effect of the disruption of religious terminology:

> *Mosca:* Patron, go in, and pray for our success.
> *Volpone:* Need makes devotion; heaven your labor bless.
>
> (3.9.62–63)

Volpone cynically observes that people feel religious when they need something. Although he suggests that he himself is not immune to such a feeling, he and Mosca have expropriated the conventional formulas of religion merely for the expression of their knavish hopes. Their religion inverts conventional piety. When Volpone attempts to rape Celia, she shouts "O! just God!" (3.7.266). Volpone declares that her invocation of the name of God is "In vain," but at that precise moment Bonario enters to rescue Celia. Rather than salvaging conventional pieties, however, the episode encourages cynicism by presenting the triumph of virtue as pat melodrama. As George A. E. Parfitt has commented, "The experience is so unconvincing as a manifestation of how God looks after his own as to seem almost parodic."[7] Furthermore, the rescue is cynically dramatized as actually the result entirely of an earthly cause, the fallibility of the knaves. Mosca has placed Bonario where he can overhear Celia's shout. The knaves have overextended themselves in attempting to juggle too many plots simultaneously. The final resolution of the play is attributed to God by certain characters:

> *1st Avocatore:* The knot is now undone, by miracle!
> . . . .
> *Bonario:* Heaven could not long let such gross crimes be hid.
> (5.12.95, 98)

Celia earlier declared that "heaven . . . never fails the innocent" (4.6.17). But, again, playgoers are presented with a cynical, earthly cause for the turn of events: conflict among the knaves, each of whom is motivated by selfishness or revenge. No supernatural causes are dramatized or necessary to explain the turn of events, and in the context of a play that so relentlessly holds credulity up for ridicule, the belief in divine intervention is made to appear hopelessly naive.

Corvino expropriates the language of compassion in his attempt to coerce his wife to get into bed with Volpone: "A pious work, mere charity, for physic, / And honest policy" (3.7.65–66). The play also dramatizes a cynical attitude towards compassion and trust. When Mosca weeps in 3.2, Bonario reacts with sympathy in an aside: "What? does he weep? the sign is soft, and good! / I do repent me, that I was so harsh" (18–19). Playgoers are encouraged to feel contempt for Bonario's compassion, which allows Mosca to make a fool out of him.[8] In a world in which most people are knaves, compassion for others is foolishly naive. Mosca himself pretends to be compassionate later in the same episode:

> You have too much wrong,
> And I do suffer for you, sir. My heart
> Weeps blood, in anguish.
> (68–70)

The play suggests not only that people should resist compassionate impulses in themselves, but that they should mistrust the expression of apparent compassion in others. Such an expression is likely to be a tactic in a con game. This consideration in turn provides a further reason for resisting compassion in oneself. In a cynical world where expressions of compassion are suspicious, people make themselves suspicious by expressing compassion. After Celia pleads in her last words in the play for "mercy" (5.12.105) for the husband who has abused her, the First Avocatore warns her: "You hurt your innocence, suing for the guilty" (106). After his own compassion is abused by Mosca, Bonario apparently learns his lesson. In court he gloats over the discomfiture of his enemies, and he lusts for revenge ("O, sure vengeance!" [5.10.24]). This behavior markedly contrasts with his earlier expression of compassion for Mosca. Bonario is the only character in the play who undergoes a decisive transformation in attitude. He gains knowledge of the ways of the world and gives up his compassion. He learns to be suspicious and vengeful; he learns that if one is surrounded by would-be knaves it is foolish to be trusting and forgiving.

Corvino's cynical observation about honor, that it is a "mere term / Invented to awe fools," is echoed in the following passage:

> *Volpone:* The parasite will straight be here, grave fathers.
> *Fourth Avocatore:* You might invent some other name, sir varlet.
>
> (5.12.11–12)

The patriarchy here explicitly demands the cynical invention of euphemisms to honor those with money. (A further irony in the exchange is that the last "name" used by Volpone is "grave fathers" which is another term invented to awe fools; the Avocatore's response is a kind of Freudian slip.) A short time earlier, the Fourth Avocatore, asked to identify Volpone's heir, responded, "Him, that they call the parasite" (5.10.38)—he does not yet have another name for this person but he does not want to be guilty himself of directly applying a derogatory term to a wealthy man. The Avocatori use the threat of physical coercion to enforce their demand that Mosca be described only in dignified terms. When Volpone calls Mosca "this creature" (5.12.73) and Mosca objects to this "insolence," the Avocatori vigorously and promptly order the offender to be taken away, whipped, "And taught to bear himself / Toward a person of his rank" (79–80).

Jonson remarks in *Discoveries,* "Wheresoever manners and fashions are corrupted, Language is" (954–55). In *Volpone* the conventional language of morality has been expropriated and corrupted, if not invented, by scoundrels. Once moral concepts have been used insistently and conspicuously by knaves for cynical purposes, once knavish characters explain the usefulness of such terms for knavery, those terms themselves become compromised, and it becomes difficult to use them with a straight face, as if they were uncontaminated. To do so would seem hopelessly naive. Corruption has permeated the linguistic as well as the social system.[9]

Volpone is not the only play of the period to raise such issues. Many of the plays discussed by Jonathan Dollimore in *Radical Tragedy* do so. For example, the title character in *Selimus* (1594) asserts that "The names of Gods, religion, heaven, and hell" were invented to keep the populace in "quiet awe."[10] The passage anticipates Corvino's comment that "honor" is "a mere term / Invented to awe fools." According to Dollimore,

> *Selimus* is a good instance of how even a relatively unsophisticated play could problematize religion by probing its status as ideology. . . . nothing in the play effectively contradicts Selimus' argument that religion is mystification of the social order, and "meere fictions" cannot continue to work effectively in that respect when successfully exposed. (86)

Volpone is a much more sophisticated play that problematizes the whole system of moral discourse. Certain comedies could be as "radical" or as cynical as the tragedies of the period.[11]

The play supports and extends Volpone's assertion that "to be a fool born is a disease incurable." As Parfitt has pointed out, "one of the great functions of comedy, to bring wisdom and understanding to the immature and foolish, is denied here: the miscreants refuse to learn."[12] *Volpone* implies that foolishness is not only incurable but inescapable. Would-be virtuous characters are presented as foolishly naive and the shrewdest would-be knaves turn out to be just as foolish as the foolishly naive characters.[13] Neither Volpone's gold nor his shrewdness prevents his "substance" from being confiscated and turned over "To the hospital of the *Incurabili*" (5.12.120). Foolishness seems to be as pervasive and as incurable in *Volpone* as melancholy is in Robert Burton's *Anatomy of Melancholy*, published a few years after the first performance of Jonson's play. On the basis of the play, the "hospital of the *Incurabili*" would seem to be all of human society.

Verbal and thematic patterns were one kind of evidence used by New Critics to argue that individual works of literature both exhibit and promote unity and harmony. But verbal and thematic patterning may be used to tear down as well as to build up. *Volpone* undermines the whole system of conventional morality by a series of analogies among the cynical uses of terms like "honor," "conscience," "father-hood," and so forth. A comparable set of analogies cynically under-mines the value of human endeavor and of natural agency. As Harriett Hawkins has argued, "By establishing thematic relationships between folly, disease, and various panaceas offered as cures for the incurable (gold, Scoto's oil, beds shared with young ladies, Lady Wouldbe's prescriptions), Jonson binds together the first scene and the last, the variety of characters, the main plot and the subplot."[14] Some of these analogies are explicit. For example, Mosca compares gold to an elixir:

> Why, your gold
> Is such another med'cine, it dries up
> All those offensive savors! It transforms
> The most deformed and restores 'hem lovely,
> As 't were the strange poetical girdle.
>
> (5.2.98–102)

Neither Volpone's gold nor his plots ultimately cure what ails him. Nor does Mosca's cleverness cure what ails him. Reliance on gold or knavery turns out to be a fool's game, and so each is ultimately analogous both to the phony elixir and to Sir Politic's more obviously foolish projects.[15]

But the network of implicit and explicit analogies extends to other areas. *Volpone* dramatizes cynicism about philosophy, poetry, and drama. The same linguistic corruption that applies to other terms of approbation applies to terms used in these fields. The word "art" has been expropriated by scoundrels. Scoto describes the preparation of his phony elixir as an "art" (2.2.114), and Mosca applies the same term to the activities of a parasite (3.1.30). In an evaluation of their knavish machinations in the courtroom Mosca expropriates a term appropriate to works of art: "This is our masterpiece" (5.2.13).[16]

Furthermore, Jonson sets up a series of disturbing analogies be-tween the arts of the knaves and the art of the dramatist. In the view of Stephen Greenblatt,

Scoto's pitch for his worthless snake oil seems to me a brilliant and bitter parody of the central Renaissance defense of the stage. The mountebank tells us that his product is a sovereign cure for all ailments. . . . Is this not derisive laughter at those who never tire of telling us that . . . plays cure all our moral hernias? Is this not the disturbing self-mockery of the man who in the Dedicatory Epistle to *Volpone* . . . wrote with a straight face of the "impossibility of any man's being the good Poet, without first being a good man"?[17]

As Greenblatt points out, the epistle also contains "extravagant claims for the poet" (104). Indeed, the analogy is much closer than Greenblatt suggests. According to the epistle, for example, poetry can "keep old-men in their best and supreme state or, as they decline toward child-hood, recover them to their first strength" (25–27).[18] Scoto's elixir supposedly has the same property: "Would you be ever faire? and young? / Stout of teeth? and strong of tongue? . . . / Here's a med'cine for the nones" (2.2.194–95, 203). Scoto describes the supposed effects of the powder he offers: "where ever it but touches, in youth it perpetually preserves, in age restores the complexion" (244–45). The epistle's account of the supposed beneficial effects of poetry seem even more blatantly tongue-in-cheek if one considers other parts of the play to which this epistle is attached.

> *Corbaccio:* I may ha' my youth restored to me, why not?
> *Mosca:* [aside] Your worship is a precious ass—
>
> (1.4.129–30)

Only an ass would believe that poetry or anything else has the ability to "recover" old men "to their first strength." A short while later Volpone gives an extended disquisition on the foolishness of old men who believe that youth can be recovered:

> their limbs faint,
> Their senses dull, their seeing, hearing, going
> All dead before them; yea, their very teeth,
> Their instruments of eating, failing them.
> Yet this is reckoned life! Nay, here was one,
> Is now gone home, that wishes to live longer!
> Feels not his gout, nor palsy; feigns himself
> Younger, by scores of years, flatters his age,
> With confident belying it, hopes he may
> With charms, like Aeson, have his youth restored.
>
> (1.4.147–56)

According to the epistle, all Corbaccio needed to do was to read some good poetry. In fact, old age is incurable (except by death). The play implies that foolishness, too, is incurable. And foolishness is inescapable. Volpone's expressed contempt for Corbaccio's delusion of recovering youthfulness carries dramatic irony since Volpone himself is an old man who fools himself into believing in his youthfulness. Volpone elsewhere prominently and repeatedly uses a key word from the epistle in the passage about old men. He repeatedly expresses hopes of "recovery": "O, my recovery shall recover all" (5.3.109); "the Advocate / Had betrayed all; but now, it is recovered" (5.12.52–53). Recognizing the foolishness of others does not prevent one from being foolish oneself and may even contribute to one's foolishness by encouraging one's complacency. The epistle itself slyly distances the writer from the improbably large claims for poetry. Those claims are presented as hearsay: the poet "is said to be able" (23–24) to perform such feats.

Scoto's attack on rival mountebanks specifically resembles the attack in the epistle on rival poets:

> [They] spread their cloaks on the pavement, as if they meant to do feats of activity, and then come in, lamely, with their mouldy tales out of Boccaccio. . . . these meager, starved spirits, who have half stopped the organs of their minds with earthy oppilations, want not their favorers among your shriveled salad-eating artisans. (2.2.49–65)

> As for those, that will (by faults which charity hath raked up, or common honesty concealed) make themselves a name with the multitude, or (to draw their rude, and beastly claps) care not whose living faces they intrench, with their petulant styles; may they do it, without a rival, for me. (70–75)

The epistle ridicules some rivals for stale imitation of past poetic materials: "fools, and devils, and those antique relics of barbarism retrieved, with all other ridiculous, and exploded follies" (79–81). Scoto ridicules other mountebanks on the otherwise odd grounds that their performances are stale imitations of past literary materials. Scoto attacks "the calumnious reports of that impudent detractor, and shame to our profession (Allessandro Buttone, I mean)" (2.2.43–44). Similarly, Jonson complains in the epistle that his reputation is "subject to the petulancy of every vernaculous Orator" (98–99).

In the epistle Jonson acknowledges that current writers lack the powers he has described:

> But it will here be hastily answered that the writers of these days are other things; that, not only their manners, but their natures, are inverted; and nothing remaining with them of the dignity of Poet, but the abused name. (31–35)

The epistle goes on to defend Jonson's own poetry at first not on the positive ground that it has the powers listed earlier but primarily on the negative ground that it contains no personal invective. Even this negative ground is removed by the threat that closes the epistle. In response to the "vile and slothful" who denigrate poetry, poetry "shall out of just rage incite her servants (who are *genus irritabile*) to spout ink in their faces, that shall eat, farther than their marrow, into their fames" (134–41). Surrounded and baited by knaves and fools, a poet is brought down to the level of his society, and nothing remains "of the dignity of Poet, but the abused name." Other words have been expropriated or contaminated by scoundrels, and so has the name of poet.

As indicated earlier, Mosca compares gold to an elixir (5.2.98–102). But the same passage simultaneously establishes an analogy between those two items and poetry because the passage again recalls the passage in the epistle about the supposed restorative powers of poetry. The poet can "keep old men in their best and supreme state or . . . recover them to their first strength." Similarly gold, like an elixir, "transforms / The most deformed, and restores 'hem lovely, / As 't were the strange poetical girdle." The phrase "the strange poetical girdle" carries a double meaning. It refers to Cestus, the girdle of Venus that had magical properties described in Homeric poetry. But the "poetical girdle" may also be poetry itself, which, according to the epistle, has magical properties like those of Venus's girdle.

There are also specific analogies between the prologue to the play and Volpone's harangue as Scoto.[19] Both speeches offer a product to the public, specify its properties, explain its supposed beneficial effects, describe its manner of production on the basis of time-honored practices, denigrate competitors, and respond to detractors. The analogy suggests that a playwright is a kind of mountebank and alerts playgoers to be skeptical even of Jonson's own art. Scoto responds to "calumnious reports" (2.2.43) against him and provides a hypothetical example: "may some other gallant fellow say, 'O, there be diverse that make profession to have as good, and as experimented receipts, as yours'" (144–47). In the prologue, Jonson responds to "some (whose throats their envy failing) / Cry hoarsely, 'All he writes is railing'" (9–10). Scoto describes the supposed effect of his elixir: "this rare extraction . . . hath only power to disperse all malignant humors" (94–95). According to the prologue, the cheeks of playgoers will be "red with laughter" and "They shall look fresh, a week after" (35–36). According to Scoto, his elixir is "an abstract of the theoric, and practice in the Aesculapian art" (113–14). According to the prologue, the playwright has followed the theoric and practice of the dramatic art: "As best Critics have designed, / The laws of time, place, persons he observeth, / From no needful rule he swerveth" (30–32). Scoto offers a liquid to the public: "this my oil, surnamed *oglio del Scoto*" (135–36). The prologue uses a liquid metaphor for what Jonson offers to the public: "All gall and copperas, from his ink he draineth" (33). The passage already quoted in which Scoto attacks rival mountebanks resembles not only the epistle's attack on rival poets but the prologue's attack on rival dramatists. Like the other mountebanks denigrated by Scoto, the other dramatists denigrated in the prologue are contemptible for their crude and old-fashioned methods, which appeal to the rabble:

> no eggs are broken;
> Nor quaking custards with fierce teeth affrighted,
>   Wherewith your rout are so delighted;
> Nor hales he in a gull, old ends reciting,
>   To stop gaps in his loose writing;
> With such a deal of monstrous and forced action.
>
> (20–25)

The play dramatizes a cynical attitude toward the effects of poetry. Lady Wouldbe shows a familiarity with literature:

> Which o' your Poets? Petrarch? or Tasso? or Dante?
> Guarini? Ariosto? Aretine?
> Cieco di Hadria? I have read them all.
>
> (3.4.79–81)

But she is none the wiser for having read these writers. The satire cuts two ways. On the one hand, Lady Wouldbe's foolishness is dramatized as incurable. On the other hand, literature is dramatized as incapable of curing foolishness. In the very same passage, Volpone alludes to Sophocles ("The Poet, / As old in time as Plato" [76–77]). Volpone tries to seduce Celia by suggesting that they re-enact episodes from "Ovid's tales" (3.7.221). Volpone himself seems to be well-read, but his reading has deterred him neither from knavery nor, as it turns out, from foolishness. Playgoers who resemble the characters on stage in *Volpone* are not likely to be improved by the play. Indeed, throughout his career Jonson often expressed a deeply cynical attitude toward the actual audiences of his plays.[20]

When Volpone declares to Lady Wouldbe that his mind is "perturbed" (3.4.98), she responds, "Why, in such cases, we must cure our selves, / Make use of our philosophy—" (99–100). The satire here again cuts two ways. On the one hand, Lady Wouldbe's pretension to learning is ridiculed. On the other hand, by putting in Lady Wouldbe's mouth the assertion that philosophy can cure a perturbed mind, Jonson makes the assertion suspect. Lady Wouldbe goes on to spout conventional wisdom: "And, as we find our passions do rebel, / Encounter 'hem with reason" (101–02). Playgoers are encouraged to associate such advice with the foolish Lady Wouldbe and to recognize that neither the speaker nor the hearer of this advice is capable of applying it. To offer advice that no one can apply is foolish. If they have no curative effect, philosophy and literature thus resemble the phony elixirs offered by Scoto. Kernan comments on Lady Wouldbe's advocacy of "golden mediocrity" (3.4.47):

> the phrase operates . . . to remind us of ideals being violated and to define the moral status of the characters and action. Here the ideal referred to is the "golden mean," that classic guide to conduct which dictates "nothing in excess," and which has been lost completely in Volpone's world where men pursue gold and power and lust to the exclusion of all else, becoming in the process "golden mediocrities."[21]

But if the ideal "has been lost completely" then it would seem to be beyond recovery by Jonson's art, like the youth that old characters in the play foolishly wish to recover.

Volpone's suggestion, noted above, that foolishness is "incurable" is odd in the context of a speech about an elixir that is supposedly a cure-all. The elixir cannot cure the foolishness that makes people buy it. But if foolishness is inescapable and incurable, art cannot be anything but a phony elixir or a con game. If the world is incurable, then "true medicine" cannot exist, and a contrast between true and false medicine is invalid.[22] *Volpone* expresses Jonson's bitter frustration as a would-be healer faced with an incurable patient. Jonson's desire to believe in art as moral therapy was undermined by his cynical perception of society as incurably ill.[23] A writer who naively believes that a play can cure foolishness is—like Politic Wouldbe with his ridiculous projects—a fool himself. A writer who cynically abandons the notion that art should involve moral instruction is—like Nano or Castrone or Androgyne, who present frivolous antics for the idle amusement their master—a professional fool. A writer who believes that foolishness is incurable but who nevertheless offers his art as therapy is—like the Scoto that Volpone impersonates—a mountebank.[24] In a world composed entirely of knavish fools and naive fools, a world that Jonson dramatized with exuberantly thorough cynicism in *Volpone*, an artist cannot avoid being one or the other.

Notes

1. Ben Jonson, *Ben Jonson*, ed. C. H. Herford, Percy Simpson, and Evelyn Simpson, 11 vols. (Oxford: Clarendon Press, 1925–52). All quotations from Jon-

son's works are based on this edition, but spelling and punctuation have been modernized.

2. "The *Avocatori*'s savagery relates them to the strain of sadistic superiority that runs throughout the play," according to R. B. Parker, ed. *Volpone* (Manchester: Manchester University Press, 1983), 43.

3. Conversely, Volpone turns a conventional term of disapprobation into a term of approbation: "Rare, Mosca! How his villainy becomes him!" (5.3.61).

4. William Shakespeare, *The Riverside Shakespeare*, ed. G. Blakemore Evans (Boston: Houghton Mifflin, 1974).

5. Alvin B. Kernan, ed. *Volpone* (New Haven: Yale University Press, 1962), 222–23.

6. Anne Barton has remarked that in *Volpone* "Institutionalized justice, . . . the court presided over in Venice by the Avocatori, is a farce. And there are no strong, good characters . . . who can amend as well as recognize human viciousness and crime" (*Ben Jonson, Dramatist* [Cambridge: Cambridge University Press, 1984], 106).

7. "Virtue and Pessimism in Three Plays by Ben Jonson," *Ben Jonson: Quadricentennial Essays*, ed. Mary Olive Thomas, *Studies in the Literary Imagination* 6 (1973): 25.

8. Robert N. Watson has argued that "If we try to perceive Celia and Bonario entirely as heroes, the play calls us fools; if we try to perceive them entirely as fools, the play calls us rogues" (*Ben Jonson's Parodic Strategy: Literary Imperialism in the Comedies* [Cambridge: Harvard University Press, 1987], 91). But at least in this particular case the choices do not seem balanced. Not only are playgoers encouraged to see Bonario as a fool, but his foolishness consists precisely in his failure to be cynical.

9. George A. E. Parfitt notes how pervasively Jonson's "characters misuse words" and how Volpone and Mosca specifically "delight in using words to deceive others" (*Ben Jonson: Public Poet and Private Man* [Totowa: Barnes & Noble, 1976], 100, 101). Parfitt elsewhere maintains, nevertheless, that Jonson uses "a fairly small stock of terms which define his basic moral position," terms which include some of those discussed in the present essay, such as "virtue" and "honor," and that these terms "are given definition by context" (92). If the "context" is the pervasive and exuberant "misuse" of those terms, however, the misuse overwhelms and supplants the uncynical use. According to Martin Elsky, "the particular social context of Jonson's day . . . portended ethical subversion of language's referential function, and . . . this threat of corruption . . . gives moral urgency to Jonson's muscular attempt to hold words and things together" ("Words, Things, and Names: Jonson's Poetry and Philosophical Grammar," *Classic and Cavalier: Essays on Jonson and the Sons of Ben*, ed. Claude J. Summers and Ted-Larry Pebworth [Pittsburgh: University of Pittsburgh Press, 1982], 102). In *Volpone*, however, Jonson dramatized a world in which the threat of linguistic subversion has been realized. Commenting on the "cant orations" of Volpone as Scoto and of Voltore in court, Peter Womack has argued that

> What immediately underlies these more or less cynical formalisms is a contradiction in the rhetorical heritage itself. . . . So far from regularizing and underwriting the referentiality of language, rhetoric in this sense tends . . . to redirect verbal energy away from reference; to thicken words, as it were, rendering them free-standing and opaque. (*Ben Jonson* [Oxford: Blackwell, 1986], 101)

Womack goes on to suggest that throughout his career Jonson dramatized what he saw as a larger problem with language in general:

Living speech, speech as polymorphous social interaction, appears by the dry light of the absolutist Latin ideal to be a monster, endlessly doubling, compartmentalizing, contradicting and parodying itself, travelling ever further outwards, in its illicit dynamism, from some pristine centre of truth and sense. (103)

10. Quoted by Dollimore, *Radical Tragedy: Religion, Ideology and Power in the Drama of Shakespeare and His Contemporaries* (Chicago: University of Chicago Press, 1984), 85.

11. Dollimore's inclusion of Jonson in the "radical" camp may be misleading. As Katharine Eisaman Maus has argued,

Jonson seems to resemble more recent critics of capitalism, but his 'anti-acquisitive attitude' has different motives and consequences. . . . For Jonson, virtue requires the minimizing or the repudiation of material motives and a material basis. ("Satiric and Ideal Economies in the Jonsonian Imagination," *English Literary Renaissance* 19 [1989]: 56).

Furthermore, because folly in *Volpone* is dramatized as inescapable and incurable, the cynicism of Jonson's play applies not just to the present social order but to any possible social order and is not "radical" in the sense of intentionally seeking or encouraging a reformation of the social system. According to Alvin Kernan, Jonson exhibits a "deep-rooted pessimism about the possibility of change" ("Alchemy and Acting: The Major Plays of Ben Jonson," *Ben Jonson: Quadricentennial Essays*, ed. Mary Olive Thomas, *Studies in the Literary Imagination* 6 [1973]: 7).

12. Parfitt, "Virtue," 33.

13. In commenting on Jonson's *Discoveries*, Parfitt has noted "Jonson's awareness of the resistance of human nature to even obvious moral truths," his "sad resignation," and his "awareness of the . . . intractability of human nature" (*Ben Jonson*, 31–32).

14. Harriett Hawkins, "Folly, Incurable Disease, and *Volpone*," *Studies in English Literature* 8 (1968): 337.

15. The parallels between the main plot and the subplot, explored by Jonas A. Barish (in "The Double Plot in *Volpone*," *Modern Philology* 51 [1953]: 83–92) and by Alexander Leggatt in the present collection, constitute only a small part of this dense, interconnected web of analogies.

16. Noting that "Volpone, Morose, and Sir Epicure all think of the garbing of their paramours as 'art,'" Jonas A. Barish has suggested that "By placing the sacred term 'art' in the unhallowed mouths of these characters, Jonson acknowledges the bond between himself and them even as he repudiates it" ("Jonson and the Loathèd Stage," *A Celebration of Ben Jonson*, ed. William Blissett, et al. [Toronto: University of Toronto Press, 1973], 51).

17. "The False Ending in *Volpone*," *Journal of English and Germanic Philology* 75 (1976): 103.

18. Elsewhere in the epistle Jonson declares that he will in effect restore the youth of poetry itself:

I shall raise the despised head of poetry again, and stripping her out of those rotten base rags, wherewith the Times have adulterated her form, restore her to her primitive habit, feature, and majesty, and render her worthy to be kissed, of all the great and master-spirits of our world. (129–34)

19. Greenblatt exempts the prologue from the cynicism he finds in the epistle: "If there is a convincing defense of the stage in *Volpone*, it is not the pretensions of the humanists but the comically medical promise of the prologue" (104), the promise

that is, of simple escapist amusement. But the prologue seems no more "a convincing defense" than the epistle. It contains ironic echoes of Scoto's harangue similar to those in the epistle, and within the play the antics of Nano, Castrone, and Androgyno, put on for the amusement of Volpone, are not presented in a favorable light.

20. See, for example, the bitter "Ode to Himself": "'Twere simple fury still thyself to waste / On such as have no taste" (13–14). Although Jonson could at times be more conciliatory in regard to readers or playgoers, such passages generally seem condescending or facetious. As Alexander Leggatt comments, the problem with those frequent passages that involve "attack—direct or implied—on the stupid reader is that they make no attempt to create a bond with the intelligent reader" (*Ben Jonson: His Vision and His Art* [London: Methuen, 1981], 234). This may be so because Jonson had difficulty maintaining a belief in the genuine existence of the latter kind of audience. According to John Gordon Sweeney III, by the time Jonson came to write *Volpone*, "his experience in the playhouse had revealed the audience to be an intractable, unregenerate mass, entirely unconcerned with his program for profit and pleasure" (*Jonson and the Psychology of Public Theater: To Coin the Spirit, Spend the Soul* [Princeton: Princeton University Press, 1985], 72). Barish has argued that Jonson was one of those "playwrights who at a given moment in their careers have seen their whole enterprise as hollow" ("Loathèd Stage," 28). Barish contrasts readers and playgoers: "Readers, simply by virtue of literacy, possess a certain minimum of knowledge and discipline" and "bring cool heads and sound judgments to the act of evaluation" (35). But *Volpone* dramatizes cynicism in regard to readers as well as in regard to playgoers.

21. Kernan, *Volpone*, 219.

22. After arguing in detail the notion that "the world of *Volpone* is, from beginning to end, a comic 'Hospitall of Incurable Fools,'" Hawkins concludes that the fools in the play "are presented as fit objects for the diversion and (by way of it) the instruction of rational men" ("Folly," 336, 348). But in a world wholly populated by incurable fools, it would be foolish to believe in the existence of rational men amenable to instruction.

23. Compare Parfitt's comment that the "belief in the possibility that art may help man to be better . . . collides with Jonson's honesty in the face of experience" (*Ben Jonson*, 55).

24. Sweeney has suggested that Jonson suspected that theater "is fundamentally a form of fraud" (*Psychology*, 75).

Unmasquing *Epicoene:* Jonson's Dramaturgy for the Commercial Theater and Court

Kate D. Levin

By 1609, Ben Jonson's dual career as court entertainer and commercial theater dramatist was burgeoning. The *Masque of Queens* featured the queen and her ladies in an opulent performance at Whitehall on 2 February 1609. Jonson also completed *Epicoene, or The Silent Woman* by the end of that year, and the Children of the Queen's Revels mounted its production in the winter of 1609–10. While these two facets of Jonson's dramatic writing—his masques and his plays—have received ample critical attention over the years, that attention has almost always been bestowed on them separately. Few scholars have gotten beyond the assumption that profound and essential differences far outweigh any likenesses between Jonson's work for these two venues: the public and private stages to which I am collectively referring as London's "commercial" theater, and the royal or noble households in which entertainments, which I am calling court masques, were performed in honor of the ruling elite.[1] My aim in this essay is to counter that assumption by identifying some elements of Jonson's dramatic practice common to both kinds of work.

I want to make *Epicoene* the touchstone of my effort for three reasons—one contextual, one critical, and one personal. First, the play's chronological place in the thick of Jonson's commercial and court endeavors gives some sanction to an argument about cross-pollination between the dramatist's work in different forms. Second, *Epicoene* has inspired some exceptions to the critical habit of cordoning off consideration of the plays from the masques. Ian Donaldson has pointed out the qualities of antimasque that characterize the incursion of the uninvited wedding guests into the home of the hapless newlywed Morose in act 3, and David Riggs has made a persuasive case for viewing *Epicoene* as an outlet for Jonson's frustrations during a period of his life "when he was preoccupied with masques that either celebrate weddings or praise women"; the play "is a satire on women and marriage."[2] By focusing on *Epicoene*, I

128

thus hope to build on a few of the distinguished contributions that have been made toward an understanding of Jonson's stagecraft that embraces both plays and masques. Third, the experience of having directed the play has magnified my awareness of a range of structural peculiarities—peculiarities, I will argue, that it shares in greater and lesser degrees with all of Jonson's dramatic work.[3]

This is a motley collection of justifications for my focus on *Epicoene;* the kinds of evidence I will marshal are similarly varied. My discussion will be organized around three elements of Jonson's dramatic practice in the play: the construction of two characters (one principal, one minor), the management of entrances and exits, and the comprehensibility (or lack of it) of several major plot developments. An essential caveat: although for most of this essay I will be pointing out fissures and elisions in *Epicoene*'s dramaturgy, my criticisms do not mean that I think the play is "bad." I am picking on *Epicoene* because, along with the myriad elements that make it a dramatic achievement of the first rank, the play makes available for scrutiny certain essential aspects of Jonson's technique as a theater artist. Accordingly, after exploring an aspect of *Epicoene*'s stagecraft, I will place it in relation to Jonson's other commercial theater plays and to his court entertainments. In the course of ranging among the plays and masques, I hope to define certain predilections of Jonson's dramatic imagination; his engagement with some aspects of stagecraft, and lack of interest in—even neglect of—others.

1

Epicoene is strikingly generous even within Jonson's comic oeuvre in giving all its characters at least one opportunity, however fleeting, to captivate an audience's attention—whether on the page or on the stage. This generosity extends from the operatic endurance contests written for Truewit and Morose to the wordless responses of Morose's mute servant, responses painstakingly indicated in Jonson's marginalia for the 1616 folio play text.[4] It is therefore notable, given Jonson's imaginative largess in peopling the play, that on closer examination two characters are half-conceived: Clerimont does not consistently display a distinct personality, and Trusty seems to have been abandoned mid-play. These characters illuminate Jonson's tendency throughout his dramatic writing to compose in a series of spectacular vignettes. His deployment of a given character is not allied to any principle of characterological consistency or development, but rather is dependent on how useful that character can be in moving an exchange to its climax.[5] In the plays, this utilitarian approach can lead to odd disjunctions: characters are suddenly stranded, left with nothing to do. As Jonson develops the masque form, however, its aesthetic and ideological impact becomes dependent on these same disjunctions: the masque's basic structure becomes a succession of brilliant, pithy episodes whose personnel and settings are no sooner established than they are abandoned.

Clerimont, a major player in *Epicoene*'s intrigues as one of the triumvirate of Wits, provides a subtle illustration of this tendency. The play starts out auspiciously for the character. Following the prologue,[6] the play's action begins with Clerimont's entrance; indeed, for its opening twenty lines, Clerimont *is* the play, is apparently its lead and major object of interest as he spars with his cheeky young male servant. Not until Dauphine's entrance almost two hundred lines later, well after Truewit has entered, is it clear that Clerimont is only one of a group of men-about-town who will be bidding—against each other and against other groups and individual characters—for the role of the play's "hero." By positioning Clerimont center stage at the outset, Jonson lures his audience into assuming that the character is the star of *Epicoene*—the first of many mistaken assumptions in the course of a play that explodes expectations with each twist of the plot, duping would-be masterminds (in the play and in its audience) over and over. Having fulfilled his role as an authorial gambit to destabilize readers and viewers, Clerimont then devolves into a prop for the more consistently drawn characters of Truewit and Dauphine.

Jonson's practice of deploying Clerimont as the straight man to his wittier colleagues is previewed in his opening exchange with the Boy. The scene begins promisingly enough for Clerimont with lines that suggest some sharp, specific character traits: he is restless, sexually sophisticated, given to domineering behavior. Yet for all these attention-getting attributes, Jonson gives Clerimont none of the more admirable (or at least entertaining) characteristics of wit or inventiveness. Throughout this scene the Boy, not his master, gives the greater impression of cleverness, in his saucy suggestion that Clerimont's verse will earn its author "the dangerous name of *Poet* in towne" (6–7), his breezy description of his handling by the lady and her followers (13–18), and his sadistic stratagems for tormenting Morose with noise (169–79). Although Clerimont has authored the lyric eventually sung by the Boy, its wit and polish are consistent with what we have heard the youth, not his master, say. Clerimont has been established as the inspiration of and sponsor for this model of precocious depravity; but, perhaps banking on the audience appeal of a scene-stealing turn by the very youngest member of a boy's company, Jonson has created a character (the Boy) who consistently outshines his master.

Clerimont comes in a distant second again in his first exchange with Truewit. Truewit can elaborate on the idleness of the age—the urge to "Harken after the next horse-race . . . spend aloud, that my lords may heare you; visite my ladies at night, and bee able to give 'hem the character of every bowler, or better o' the greene" (34–39)—in one breath and, in the next, touch on the terrible fear that lurks beneath his studied ennui: "this time, because it is an incorporeall thing, and not subject to sense, we mocke our selves the fineliest out of it, with vanitie, and miserie indeede: not seeking an end of wretchednesse, but onely changing the matter still" (52–55). By comparison, Clerimont is at best a cardboard sensualist. The most vivid lines he can muster express the insipid demand that Truewit talk "of pinnes, and feathers, and ladies, and rushes, and such things: and leave this *Stoicitie* alone, till thou mak'st sermons" (64–66). This first exchange establishes Truewit's kindled imagination, and even a Hamlet-like touch of melancholy alienation in his claim to participate in the exercises of fashionable men only "for companie" (40–41). Clerimont, by comparison, is merely one of those fashionable men, the easily upstaged sketch of a vicious, self-proclaimed esthete.

Indeed, Clerimont spends most of the play being upstaged, most often—although not exclusively—by Truewit. Of the three Wits, Clerimont is easily the least distinguishable. Truewit's verbal flash is simply unbeatable, and Dauphine is perennially deferred to as the Wits' leader and principal beneficiary of their plotting. Part of Clerimont's problem is that the few individualizing attributes given him by Jonson do not remain exclusively associated with his character: anything he can do, someone else can do better. The streak of bullying cruelty is first appropriated by the Boy as outlined above and then, more spectacularly, by Truewit and Dauphine. Clerimont is quick to intimidate LaFoole after intentionally misunderstanding his hyperaffected attempt to issue dinner invitations, assuring him that the "doubtfulnesse o' your phrase, beleeve it, sir, would breed you a quarrell, once an houre, with the terrible boyes, if you should but keepe 'hem fellowship a day" (1.4.15–18). Truewit, however, is far more menacing—for example, in 3.6 when his taunts drive Morose to ask the Collegiates if Truewit is their "*Bravo*" (109) or hired bully. The tone of Truewit's response is positively chilling: "As god helpe me, if you utter such another word, I'll take mistris bride in, and beginne to you, in a very sad cup, doe you see? Goe too, know your friends, and such, as love you" (110–13). And while Clerimont

has all the affects of a gentleman sadist, it is Truewit who devises
and engineers the beating of Daw and LaFoole. Dauphine, of course,
outdoes them both, most notably in his suggestion, never recanted,
that Truewit amputate Daw's left arm (4.5.133), and in his final dismissal of the emotionally and financially eviscerated Morose, promising not to "trouble" the old man "till you trouble me with your
funerall, which I care not how soone it come" (5.4.215–17).

Even Clerimont's few displays of initiative are overshadowed.
Granted, in 3.3 it is Clerimont who accomplishes the first step in
transforming LaFoole's dinner party into Morose's bridal feast by
double-talking Daw into believing himself slighted. Dauphine, however, completes the second phase of the operation, convincing La-
Foole to bring the food; moreover, credit for the whole scheme
belongs to Truewit, who proposes it in 2.6. Clerimont is certainly
formidable in his only independently initiated plot, in 5.1 when he
lures Daw and LaFoole into bragging that they have had carnal
knowledge of Epicoene. The character of Clerimont comes into
sharp focus for this brief scene as he crudely bullies the two terrified
gulls, insisting that, as Epicoene "is married, now . . . you cannot
hurt her with any report, and therefore speake plainely: how many
times, yfaith? which of you lead first? Ha?" (86–88). Yet even here
Clerimont does not seem to sustain Jonson's interest long enough to
supply the scene with dramaturgically coherent closure. The instant
that Daw and LaFoole have made their scurrilous—and pathetic—
assertions, Jonson brings the scene to an abrupt end. Clerimont
began with flattery, telling the gulls, "you two governe the ladies,
where e're you come" (30–31). And yet, at the end of the scene, Daw
and LaFoole are meant to find the following lines of Clerimont's an
invitation to exit: "Speake softly: here comes [Dauphine], with the
lady Haughty. Hee'll get the ladies from you, sirs, if you looke not
to him in time" (97–99).

The peculiarity of this transition is the more pronounced because
Clerimont does not escort Daw and LaFoole offstage, but is made
to wait around in full view of the audience for the first forty-five
lines of the next scene until he becomes useful again by helping
Dauphine to gloat over his successive flirtations with the Collegiates.
Clerimont's continued presence is not by definition a problem: it is
consistent with the often-used convention in Renaissance drama that
allowed characters to overhear others but escape notice themselves.[7]
Nevertheless, Jonson's handling of the convention here makes it very
difficult to achieve a coherent stage picture. When I directed this
scene, I had the actor playing Clerimont alternate between yearning
and envy in observing the goings-on, but the character could not be

positioned too near Dauphine and the Collegiates or—conventions notwithstanding—his invisibility to the other onstage characters was implausible. If, however, I placed Clerimont too far from the action, any physical movements or even facial expressions large enough for an audience to register proved an annoying distraction from the deliciously farcical and intricately timed comedy of Dauphine and the Collegiates. This experience reinforced my sense that the scene had been structured with little consideration for the character (or for the actor playing the character); I cite it here as evidence that Jonson's investment in Clerimont is limited to the ways in which he can bolster others or assist in matters of exposition.

Perhaps the most transparent example of Jonson's ruthless use of Clerimont is the character's involvement, or lack of it, with Lady Haughty. In 1.1, Truewit describes the "new foundation . . . here i' the towne, of ladies, that call themselves the Collegiates" (74–75)—a "foundation" of whose existence, oddly enough, Clerimont seems unaware. When Truewit names Lady Haughty as the group's "president," Clerimont, with characteristic violence, identifies her as the object of his rejected suit: "A poxe of her autumnall face, her peec'd beautie: there's no man can bee admitted till shee . . . has painted, and perfum'd, and wash'd and scour'd but the boy here; and him shee wipes her oil'd lips upon, like a sponge" (85–89). Having established Clerimont's interest in (and hostility toward) his wished-for lover, Jonson does not follow through on it. Clerimont acknowledges no special interest in Haughty when he joins her on stage for the first time in act 3.7. To be sure, the relationship is resurrected briefly in act 4.1 when Clerimont, in a thinly disguised non sequitur, announces to his fellow Wits, "Me thinks, the lady Haughty lookes well to day, for all my dispraise of her i' the morning" (32–34). It is impossible, however, to take this line as a serious declaration of the heart; Clerimont as a closet romantic is patently absurd. A more plausible reason for giving him these lines is to set up Truewit's series of lengthy monologues anatomizing cosmetic beauty, and advocating date rape (among other methods of impressing the female sex). Truewit's misogynistic arias are, in fact, the focus of this scene; in 4.1 Jonson has again used Clerimont primarily as a means of introducing important information and showcasing other characters.

Why then has Jonson created the character of Clerimont at all? Largely, it seems to me, because the presence of a third Wit adds an essential element of competition to Truewit's bid for Dauphine's admiration and affection, competition that Jonson uses to fuel many of the play's intrigues. The Wits' "love triangle" is evident from Dauphine's first entrance. The response of Truewit and Clerimont is telling: Dauphine quite literally takes their breath away, as his initial line makes clear ("How now! what aile you sirs? dumbe?" [1.2.1]). In the jockeying for pride of place with Dauphine that follows his first entrance, Clerimont leaks the secret of Epicoene's procurement and lodging, setting in motion Truewit's attempt to dissuade Morose from marrying. Other plot developments are similarly propelled by this competition between Truewit and Clerimont for Dauphine's attention. In 4.5, for example, Truewit and Clerimont have a vitriolic exchange over the latter's desire to "be in at" the gulling of LaFoole. Truewit rejects this bid for shared billing in the performance being mounted for Dauphine's delectation. Later in the same scene, however, he endorses Clerimont's follow-up proposal to have the "ladies" be present for "the *catastrophe*" (241) of Daw and LaFoole's corporal punishment—as long as Dauphine is given credit for the whole operation.

On the one hand, by creating Clerimont to compete with Truewit for Dauphine's affections, Jonson has devised a sophisticated means for enriching and advancing the play's labyrinthine plot. On the other hand, Jonson doesn't seem to have bothered with making Clerimont much more than a serviceable placeholder in the competition. By comparison, Truewit's crush on Dauphine seems to have inspired Jonson to supply touches of emotion that are unusual in his dramatic writing. The starkest example of this comes at the end of 4.5, when Dauphine has completed the beating of Daw and LaFoole. After returning both victims to their hiding places, Truewit blurts out, "Dauphine, I worship thee" (350), before acknowledging that the Collegiates are swarming onto the stage from their hiding place. Even if this remark is understood as one strategically uttered to further enhance Dauphine's appeal for the listening Collegiates, the raw, slavish emotion conveyed by the words is undeniable. The whole episode has been orchestrated by Truewit to revenge the gulls' disparaging talk about Dauphine; in the brutal world of *Epicoene*, this is what passes for an act of love. Taken in tandem with Truewit's earlier profession of horror at Dauphine's implacable cruelty ("What, maime a man for ever, for a jest? what a conscience hast thou?" [4.5.135–36]), the moment suggests a characterization of psychological complexity in addition to surface brilliance. Jonson has thus opened the door to experiencing Truewit as a character tinged with pathos, if not tragedy. Clerimont, however, is never more than the doorstop.

At least Clerimont gets a full night's work out of the various dramaturgically thankless tasks relegated to him. The actor playing Trusty, however, must scrounge for employment during the character's several wordless appearances and endeavor to salvage the one (botched) joke that the character was specifically created to perform. Like Clerimont, the play initially promises far better things for Trusty than it in fact supplies. As a lady's maid, Trusty is by definition an expendable marker of her mistress' social status, but Jonson goes to considerable lengths in establishing this minor character for *Epicoene*'s audience—which suggests that she will play a role of some consequence. In 1.4, after listing the Collegiates invited to his dinner party, LaFoole is quick to add that "mistris Trusty, my ladies woman, will be there too" (54–55). When the ladies sweep into Morose's house in 3.6, Daw introduces Trusty to Epicoene along with the others. Trusty is not, however, part of the Collegiates' next appearance, in 4.3, and Haughty must send for her at line 102 of 4.4 to take part in the group consultation about Morose's putative madness. Here is the entire exchange concerning Trusty:

> *Hau.* Where's Trusty, my woman? . . . I pr'ythee, Otter, call her. Her father and mother were both mad, when they put her to me.
> *Mor.* I thinke so. Nay gentlemen, I am tame. This is but an exercise, I know, a marriage ceremonie, which I must endure.
> *Hau.* And one of 'hem (I know not which) was cur'd with the *Sick-mans salve;* and the other with *Greenes Groates-worth of wit.*
> *Tru.* A very cheape cure, madame.
> *Hau.* I, it's very feasible.
> *Mrs. Ot.* My lady call'd for you, mistris Trusty: you must decide a controversie.
> *Hau.* O Trusty, which was it you said, your father, or your mother, that was cur'd with the *Sicke-mans salve?*
> *Trus.* My mother, madame, with the *salve.*
> *Tru.* Then it was the *Sicke-womans salve.*
> *Trus.* And my father with the *Groates-worth of wit.* But there was other meanes us'd: we had a Preacher that would preach folke asleepe still; and so they were prescrib'd to goe to church, by an old woman that was their physitian, thrise a weeke—
> *Epi.* To sleepe?
> *Trus.* Yes forsooth: and every night they read themselves asleepe on those bookes.
> *Epi.* Good faith, it stands with great reason. I would I knew where to procure those bookes.
> *Mor.* Oh.
> *LaF.* I can helpe you with one of 'hem, mistris Morose, the *groats-worth of wit.*
> *Epi.* But I shall disfurnish you, sir Amorous: can you spare it?
> *LaF.* O, yes, for a weeke, or so; I'll reade it my selfe to him.
> *Epi.* No, I must doe that, sir: that must be my office.
> *Mor.* Oh, oh!

(101–36)

The exchange achieves several things. The Collegiates' intellectual pretensions are exploded by the seriousness they accord Greene's sensationalist death-bed confession and Thomas Becon's tract (in which, according to its title page, "all faithful Christians may learn both how to behave themselves patiently and thankfully in the time of sickness, and also vertuously to dispose their temporal goods, and finally to prepare themselves gladly and godly to die").[8] LaFoole, too, in his willingness to spare the *Groat's-worth of Wit* "for a week or so" is mocked. Reference to the preacher "that would preach folks asleep still" is presumably a brief variation on the antipuritan satire that runs through so many of Jonson's plays. Morose's yelps of dismay at the contemplated "cure" register the escalating horror of his situation—and his powerlessness to stop it.

The vignette is thus consistent with a number of Jonson's comic and satiric aims in the play. It is also, however, just this side of superfluous: these lines add bulk to the precariously long act 4 without establishing anything new—or enhancing what we already know—about any of the characters. The Collegiates' claims to learning are already suspect (see lines 83–100 of the same scene), and the infinite varieties of LaFoole's foolishness have been minutely documented by this point in the play. Truewit's witticism about the "Sick woman's salve" is, for him, noticeably feeble, and Morose's agony here is not particularly intensified or augmented.

The structure of the exchange suggests that its raison d'etre is some kind of joke, for which Trusty is meant to supply the punchline. Jonson provides all kinds of signposts pointing toward that punchline, but it never materializes. Comic energy is generated before Trusty's entrance by the malevolent gusto with which all the characters endeavor to have a good time at Morose's expense. Trusty herself is billed as an avatar of the absurd: she is an authority on madness because her "father and mother were both mad" (101–02). Jonson also cues us to expect some kind of comic epiphany by constructing an elaborate entrance for the character—an entrance that also features the laugh-inducing Mistress Otter—although Trusty could easily have been on stage already, having entered with the Collegiates at the beginning of 4.3. Jonson has thus gone to some lengths to build our expectations—Trusty, the supernumerary, slips on a verbal banana peel and becomes a star—but the character's actual lines are anticlimactic at best. Trusty's lines center on two pamphlet titles, but naming these tracts cannot be the comic surprise we have been waiting for because both the *Sicke-mans salve* and the *Groat's-worth of Wit* have already been named by Haughty.[9] Trusty's own embellishments on the subject of Becon and Greene, while endearingly earnest, are far from riotous, and the conversation moves past her almost immediately. It is possible that Trusty is meant to crown the scene's satire against quack cures—one of Jonson's favorite targets over the years. In that case, the comic payoff of this part of 4.3 is Morose's torment at the prospect of having tracts read aloud to him. Again, though, this particular torment is not an especially radical advance over the other kinds being showered on Morose, and it hardly justifies Trusty's creation and inconsistent deployment.

Following this scene—which contains Trusty's only lines in the play—the character is listed only once more, as part of the group entry that takes place in 4.6 when the Collegiates are brought in to observe the beatings of Daw and LaFoole. In 5.2 Lady Haughty names Trusty to Dauphine as an accessory to their proposed trysting, but the character is not included in the Collegiates' final entrance for the play's denouement in 5.4. Unlike the Mute, no stage business is ever indicated for Trusty, and Jonson's interest in the character deteriorated to the point where he apparently forgot to include her in the final scene. It is as if the *idea* of the maidservant had far more potential for Jonson than the actual character: he takes a great deal of trouble to establish her existence, but her part, as written, consists only of three lines in a joke that falls flat.

Let me summarize my argument about these two characters before I discuss them in relation to Jonson's other works. Clerimont is essentially a more nuanced and extended version of Trusty: both characters are the product of fitful attention on Jonson's part; neither character is deployed with much consistency—or much consideration for the actors playing either role. Clerimont is a fuzzily defined third wheel to Truewit and Dauphine, devised primarily to flesh out their conversations and conflicts. Trusty is the vestigial punchline of a half-hearted comic effect; she is discarded in the course of completing the play. As constructed, Clerimont and Trusty don't "ruin" *Epicoene;* the kinds of inconsistencies I've pointed out are likely to nag at a reader or viewer only momentarily, if at all. These characterizations do, however, suggest to me a dramaturgical habit of mind evident in Jonson's other theatrical writing, a habit of mind that values the climax—verbal fireworks, spectacular plot developments, extreme comic effects—over the patient stagecraft leading up to those moments.

This dramaturgical tendency has different repercussions in different plays. Jonson's best works for the commercial stage, *Epicoene* included, place superabundantly energetic characters in propulsively unfolding plots. Other plays, however, seem to consist of occasionally brilliant sequences erupting from lumbering, episodic writing.

Two brief examples of his enormous gift for composing concentrated vignettes (as distinct from sustained characterizations) should help to place my assessment of Jonson's dramatic practice in *Epicoene* in the context of his career as a whole.

I want to look first at the Children in the Induction to *Cynthia's Revels* (1601). Their pungent, brawling wit is a far cry from the sodden and tendentious play that follows. The contention over which child will get to speak the prologue, the Third Child's scene-stealing summary of the play's plot, and the Second Child's parody of defective audience members—including those "whom it hath pleas'd nature to furnish with more beard, then braine" (206–07)—are infinitely more lively than is Crites' hectoring morality. The role of the First Child shares some similarities of conception and construction with the characters I've been discussing in *Epicoene*. The First Child commandeers the audience's attention at the start of the Induction, as he defends his claim to recite the prologue. Once he has succeeded, however, the other two children completely efface him with their antics. As a sign of his abandonment by Jonson, the First Child is given nothing to say for the last eighty-five lines of the scene.

Jonson creates and abandons a similarly juicy group of characters at the end of his career as well. *The Magnetick Lady* (1632) also features an energetic "Induction or Chorus" consisting of the audience delegates Mr. Probee and Mr. Damplay, and the Boy left in charge of the "Poetique Shop" (6). These characters appear at the close of each act, debating the merits of *The Magnetick Lady* in particular, and of plays and playgoers in general, in a stream of acerbic commentary far more consistently engaging than the rather flaccid plot and characters of the play proper. The "Chorus" concludes act 4 with a raging debate about the need for the play to continue into a fifth act. Damplay complains that "every one here knowes the issue . . . already, or may in part conjecture" (23–24), while the Boy argues (with Probee's support) that the Poet will surely justify his decision to have a fifth act by springing "some fresh cheat, to entertaine the *Spectators,* with a convenient delight, till some unexpected, and new encounter breake out to rectifie all, and make good the *Conclusion*" (28–31). The value of Jonson's elemental dramaturgical impulse is up for debate here: is the playwright's penchant for the dazzling surprise, for pulling a rabbit out of the hat, able to sustain an audience's attention? For Jonson, apparently act 5 is its own answer: the chorus never reappears to make good *its* conclusion. Instead, an eight-line rhyme dubbed "Chorus changed into an Epilogue: to the King" is tacked on. This spiritless verse "waives" the opinion of the viewers and appeals instead to the King whose judgment of the play is preferred "'fore all the Peoples hands" (8). Jonson's decision to jettison his lively and engaging chorus in favor of this muted plea for King Charles's favor—a plea apparently not heard by the play's live audience—is unfortunate inasmuch as it gives *The Magnetick Lady* an oddly truncated feeling. With hindsight, the epilogue by which Jonson shortchanges the play seems a particularly sorry choice given the relative failure of his efforts, here and elsewhere, to garner Charles's approval.

Jonson's tendency to work up and then discard brilliant little vignettes and the characters in them may have had uneven consequences for his commercial stage work, but this dramaturgical habit is the basis for his success in the masque form. His court theatricals are built of short, dazzling episodes, with no need to worry about sustaining or extending the characterizations.[10] It is worth noting that in the one masque for which Jonson was asked to write a sequel (the *Masque of Beauty*, performed in 1608, "completed" the 1605 *Masque of Blackness*), he did not avail himself of the expository continuity that characters from the first masque might have given the second. The narrator figures of Oceanus and Niger from the 1605 court entertainment are replaced three years later by the completely new team of Boreas, Januarius, and Vulturnus.

Jonson's didactic impulses occasionally lead to excessively long speechifying (the dialogue between the Lady of the Lake and Merlin in *Prince Henry's Barriers* is a particularly stupefying example), but almost all his court entertainments feature sparkling, well-paced exchanges. Truth and Opinion in *Hymenaei*, the Satyrs in *Oberon, the Faery Prince*, Christmas, Cupid, and Venus in *Christmas His Masque*, and the Poet and Cook of *Neptune's Triumph* are only a few examples of Jonson's formidable dramatic handiwork for the masque that share the wit, timing, and linguistic richness of his best writing for the commercial stage.[11]

2

I have extrapolated from my argument about two characterizations in *Epicoene* to consider like aspects of Jonson's dramatic practice in his other plays and his masques. I now return to *Epicoene* to launch a related investigation, this time of Jonson's attention to the technical matter of entrances and exits. A number of these transitions are strikingly awkward. While they can be rationalized (and staged), the degree of ingenuity required suggests strongly that Jonson was not always successful at this aspect of stagecraft in his work for the commercial theater. By comparison, Jonson's development of the masque form relied on elaborate and precisely timed entrances and exits, often by large groups of performers. In his court masques, Jonson's weaknesses were compensated for by the technical innovations of his frequent collaborator, Inigo Jones.

Let me begin with *Epicoene* by considering Truewit's entrance at 2.4, an entrance that precipitates a lengthy and perplexing set of onstage maneuvers. Truewit's arrival, fresh from his initial visit to Morose, occasions a conversation (that includes Dauphine, Clerimont, and eventually Cutbeard) about the various schemes for Epicoene's marriage. This discussion is, however, manifestly inappropriate for Daw and even for Epicoene—both of whom are still present from the previous scene—to overhear. Epicoene has just asked Daw to return his verses to her; consistent with Renaissance stage conventions, the two could be understood by the audience to be so absorbed in a separate conversation that they would not overhear the consciously guarded talk among the Wits and Cutbeard. Even so, the awkwardness of construction remains, for two reasons. First, the interpolated conversation is dauntingly long—more than eighty-five lines—and frequently contentious. Second, Daw and Epicoene are reintegrated into the scene at different times. Truewit insists on being introduced to Epicoene before she is led off by Dauphine for further instructions (88–94); Daw is thus bereft of his conversational partner for a number of lines until Truewit turns to entertain him. While Daw's unique brand of asinine obtuseness is a helpful cover for these transactions, the fact that he doesn't realize that Epicoene has exited for another twenty lines (115) is extreme even for him. The choreography of this scene—on the stage or in a reader's imagination—is clumsy at best.

A briefer version of the same problem occurs in 3.2. There, the Wits have arrived at the house of Mistress Otter, the hostess of LaFoole's dinner party, and are in the midst of their smooth, cruel flattery when the ubiquitous Cutbeard (with his bloodhound's ability to track down Dauphine) pops in to report that the marriage of Morose and Epicoene has been successfully performed. This conversation, somehow out of Mistress Otter's earshot, takes just under twenty lines and concludes with Truewit abruptly declaring that he must leave to watch for and divert the Collegiates' coaches to Morose's house. Mistress Otter's query, "Is master Truewit gone?" (54) two lines after his departure confirms her ignorance of the exchange between the Wits and Cutbeard that has led up to that exit, but Jonson has given no definitive clues about how to orchestrate Truewit's participation in the exchange itself. The muddle is com-

pounded by the social illogic of Truewit's exit since he, as an established acquaintance of Mistress Otter's, has sponsored the
introduction of Dauphine and Clerimont to her. I was tempted to
stage the scene with Truewit holding Mistress Otter in conversation
while Cutbeard and Dauphine talk in an "aside" as Clerimont listens.
However, Truewit's departure only makes sense if he, too, has heard
Cutbeard's news. I ended up having Mistress Otter sink into her
own fretful—and therefore characteristic—reverie over the atten-
tions being paid her by the Wits while they all conspired with Cutbeard, but it was a makeshift solution at best. Jonson is working
here in a kind of dramaturgical shorthand that is too compressed to
make much sense.

Another indication of Jonson's dramaturgical illogic is the fact that
when Truewit next appears, at Morose's house in 3.5, he arrives
alone—*without* the Collegiates or their coaches—to reprise and re-
double the tormenting of Morose begun back in 2.2. The ladies don't
arrive for a full one hundred twenty lines, when they enter escorted
by Jack Daw to start the next scene (3.6). The ladies' absence could
be seen as a compliment to Truewit's powers of persuasion—he
doesn't need to accompany them to ensure their arrival—but, in that
case, surely the carriages with their passengers would have arrived
before Truewit, who is presumably traveling on foot. Although an
extra-textual explanation can be scraped together for this apparent
dramaturgical elision, the logic of such an explanation is inevitably
as dubious as the initiating difficulty; Jonson makes an assiduous
audience (or director) work awfully hard for minimal results in the
way of dramaturgical coherence.

The last scene of act 3 contains a particularly puzzling entrance.
LaFoole and Mistress Otter arrive carrying the feast in the act's final
movement toward pandemonium, and, while Dauphine is included
in the list of characters meant to enter during the scene (3.7), it is
difficult to determine just when that entrance takes place. The only
possibility is afforded by Truewit's lines telling Morose to observe
"what honour is done you unexpected, by your nephew; a wedding
dinner come, and a Knight sewer before it . . . and fine Mrs. Otter,
your neighbour, in the rump, or tayle of it" (16–20). The sequence
in which characters are named could authorize Dauphine to enter
first, but the actual lines make clear that that place is reserved for
LaFoole, ridiculous in his maître d's towel. Dauphine has no lines
here, and two modern editors have tried to solve the problem—thus
confirming it *as* a problem—by expunging him from the scene
altogether.[12]

The last two acts of *Epicoene* give evidence of Jonson's difficulties

in motivating the group entrances of the Collegiates. For example,
in 4.3, Mistress Otter enters describing her terrifying encounter with
the sword-waving Morose to the Collegiates, Epicoene, Daw, and
LaFoole. The timing here is staccato: almost all of the seven characters who enter have lines which must follow one another rapidly
in order to establish the appropriately chaotic atmosphere for the
discussion of Morose's "madness" that follows. No matter how fleet
of foot—and tongue—the child performers were for whom Jonson
wrote the play, a traffic jam is all but unavoidable in the effort to
get all of these characters onstage while making their dialogue audible. My experience working with extremely nimble adults made it
excruciatingly clear to all of us that while such a pile-up of bodies
and voices was a comic effect fully appropriate to the moment, and
therefore quite possibly exactly what Jonson had envisioned, the
challenges of this transition placed the playwright in a position of
unusual dependence on the skill of those staging his work. Jonson
may have intended any incongruities (including garbled lines) to be
attributed to the fractious, flighty personalities of the characters,
but such a dramaturgical strategy leaves the play vulnerable to an
unacceptable level of chaos in performance.[13]

Jonson again depends on the speed of the actors and acumen of
the staging at the start of 5.4, when Epicoene must come on with
Daw, LaFoole, and the herd of Collegiates. The difficulties here are
somewhat mitigated by the fact that Epicoene is the sole speaker for
the first eight lines, but William Gifford's 1816 edition of the play
acknowledges the problem and tries to order the confusion by adding
a stage direction: "Epicoene rushes in, *followed by* Haughty, Cen-
taure, Mavis, Mistress Otter, Daw, and LaFoole" (my emphasis).[14]

Again, by pointing out assorted awkwardnesses in getting characters in and out of scenes, I don't mean to suggest that *Epicoene* is in
any sense a failure. I am arguing, though, that Jonson's uneven success at orchestrating smooth or motivated entrances and exits, evident
in *Epicoene,* had significant ramifications for all his dramatic writing.
Jonson's organization of his printed play texts certainly suggests his
ambivalence about—if not outright hostility toward—the playhouse
pragmatism necessary for managing the flow of actors on and off the
stage. Almost alone among his peers, Jonson adopted a style of act
and scene notation derived from fifteenth-century Italian editions of
classical Greek and Latin plays. In particular, he followed their practice of heading up each scene with a "massed entry" or list of all the
characters in that scene, whether or not they are present at its beginning. No further entrances or exits are indicated, although marginal
notations describe bits of stage business. In quartos of some early

plays, Jonson's practice was more relaxed; *Every Man in his Humour* (1600) contains no massed entries and indicates entrances in the margins. By the 1616 Folio, however, the massed entry system was firmly in place. Wilfred T. Jewkes has suggested that it "is quite conceivable that Jonson wrote one type of direction in a manuscript he was turning over to the playhouse in the usual way, and another type when he was later preparing his copy for the formal Folio, when he would be freer to use the classical convention." Jewkes goes on to admit, however, that the difference between quartos and folio may just as likely be the result of a distinct change in practice on Jonson's part, since the quartos following *Poetaster* are as bare as the later folio versions. Peter Wright has made an extended argument for seeing Jonson's folio stage directions for his comedies as part of a vexed attempt to both affirm the plays as literary works and still convey some sense of the theatrical experience they afforded (259–61).[15] This hypothesis is appealing; however, as my discussion of *Epicoene* indicates, playhouse solutions to a number of entrances and exits cannot be deduced from its folio text. Consciously or not, Jonson's textual practices work to suppress theatrical literacy; to discourage readers from engaging with the onstage dimensions of the play.

In his best dramas—aside from *Epicoene*—(*Volpone, The Alchemist, Bartholomew Fair*) Jonson has chosen settings that regulate or rationalize the mechanics of entrances and exits. Most of the time in *Volpone*, characters come and go through the one door into Volpone's room. It is no coincidence that the sections of the play worried over most by its critics, notably the Sir Politic Would-be/Peregrine scenes, come when the play leaves Volpone's house and moves among various locales. *The Alchemist* features only one portal from "London" into the tricksters' lair; inside the house, a series of hiding places giving onto the common stage obviates the need for subtlety in getting characters in and out of the increasingly frenzied plot. In *Bartholomew Fair*, the fairground setting eliminates the need for disciplined or motivated comings and goings, and allows the flexibility (well within Renaissance conventions of staging) of activating different parts of the stage for different scenes.

Jonson's work in the masque form accommodates his dramaturgical weaknesses—and strengths. As I have argued in the first section of this essay, Jonson developed the masques so that he could focus on the "best bits," creating and discarding groups of quickly and vividly limned characters. His refinement of the antimasque/main masque formula, in which anarchic forces are supplanted by representatives of order, supplied, in the transition from chaos to concord, a rationale for performers to clear the stage quickly. Scenarist Inigo Jones relieved Jonson of responsibility for the logistics of these comings and goings: mechanical innovations enabled settings to be changed (or revolved), screening any awkwardness of motivation or movement with visual spectacle. The *Masque of Queens* is a particularly apt example, containing as it does Jonson's first extended "foyle, or false *Masque*" (13). The antimasque of twelve witches takes up the first three hundred forty lines of the entertainment, erupting toward the end into a complex dance. The transformation, when it comes, from antimasque of witches to masque of queens is sudden and absolute: "In the heat of their *Daunce,* on the sodayne was heard a sound of loud Musique, as if many Instruments had made one blast. With which not only the *Hagges* themselves, but their *Hell* into which they ranne, quite vanishd; and the whole face of the *Scene* alterd; scarse suffring the memory of any such thing" (354–59). The witches are replaced by an elaborate House of Fame in which twelve court ladies are enthroned. Jones's technical wizardry is essential in bridging the gap between hags and queens.

Jones's increasing facility at such scenic slight-of-hand and Jonson's sense that these "Showes! Showes! Mighty Showes!"[16] were luring audience attention away from his words and ideas, has long been understood as the basis of the feud between the two men. I propose that part of what fueled Jonson's rage and contempt was his awareness, conscious or not, that Jones's machinery did more than mesmerize viewers: Jones's resources compensated for one of Jonson's major dramaturgical weaknesses. It is consistent with Jonson's difficult personality that he would find it galling indeed to be indebted to Jones over such a basic aspect of stagecraft.

3

I want to return to *Epicoene* to take up one last aspect of Jonsonian dramaturgy, the difficulty of comprehending his plot machinations. I do not mean to suggest that Jonson's intricate and ingenious plotting is unique to *Epicoene;* it has long been considered a hallmark of all his writing for the commercial stage. I do maintain, though, that the difficulty of absorbing (much less remembering) the reasons behind two of the major plot twists in *Epicoene* is organic not only to that play's central concerns, but also to Jonson's work in the masque form. In the case of *Epicoene,* much literary criticism has been expended on identifying what the play is really "about," with useful and intelligent readings pointing out issues ranging from inheritance to the persecution of misanthropy. At its most seminal level, however, the play seems to me a powerful exercise in hostility, implicating characters and audiences alike. This hostility is of a piece with Jonson's tormented relationship to his commercial theater audience, a relationship that has been documented in a number of superb analyses which draw on the life-long harangues in his plays, poetry, and prose of what he perceived to be an underappreciative public. Interestingly, though, critics hold harmless the audience of Jonson's masques: *they* are assumed to be objects of the poet's respect.[17] I contend that, to the contrary, the difficulty of comprehending *Epicoene*'s plot twists helps expose possible patterns of hostility in Jonson's court entertainments as well.

The sequence of events in *Epicoene* by which LaFoole's banquet is transferred from Mistress Otter's house to Morose's is extremely difficult to follow. This is partly because an audience's attention will necessarily be beguiled by the introduction of Mistress Otter and her husband Tom into forgetting the Wits' purpose in visiting the couple. Once reminded of that purpose, an audience is likely to find Clerimont's tortuous explanation to Daw mind-numbing:

> . . . this was the injury to you. LaFoole intended this feast to honour [Epicoene's] bridale day, and made you the propertie to invite the college ladies, and promise to bring her: and then at the time, shee should have appear'd (as his friend) to have given you the *dor*. Whereas now, sir Dauphine has brought her to a feeling of it, with this kinde of satisfaction, that you shall bring all the ladies to the place where shee is . . . and there she will have a dinner, which shall be in your name: and so dis-appoint LaFoole to make you good again. (3.3.24–34)

Dauphine appeals to an even more scrambled mixture of paranoia and revenge in convincing LaFoole that Daw has "diverted" all of the would-be guests to celebrate Epicoene's marriage, and that LaFoole should strike back by bringing the provisions to Morose's house and bid the guests "welcome to't, which shall show 'tis yours, and disgrace his preparation utterly" (71–72). To further sweeten this inane reasoning, Dauphine insists that such a move will save Mistress Otter the "care of making and giving welcome" (74) in her own home and will (somehow) improve her status: rather than be the evening's hostess, she will be "a principall guest her selfe" (75). It is nearly impossible to hold the logic, such as it is, of the Wits' arguments in one's head for any length of time. Several audience members of the production I directed commented on their frustration at being unable to keep track of these plot twists. They also remarked, though, that feeling confused and even browbeaten was so much of a piece with

what characters onstage were enduring that, rather than being alienated from the play, they had a heightened sense of participation in
act 3's increasing hysteria as wave after wave of guests swarm noisily
into Morose's house.

The motives for beating La Foole and Daw are also all but incom-
prehensible to a theater audience, and only slightly less so to a reading audience, who can at least re-read the steps leading up to the
event (as they can with the redirection of LaFoole's feast) when bewildered.[18] Truewit first hatches this particular scheme after hearing
Daw and LaFoole, in four short lines between them, suggest that
Morose's marriage has reduced Dauphine to poverty and that
(worse) he is a card sharp (4.4.162–66). Truewit then convinces Daw
that LaFoole is in a murderous rage at him for removing the dinner
guests to Morose's from Mistress Otter's. LaFoole is terrified for
reasons that are even less plausible: perhaps Daw is angry because
of LaFoole's failure to "pledge all the horse full" (175–76) in the
drinking contest sponsored by Captain Otter in 4.2; perhaps Daw
is angry at LaFoole for supplying the bridal dinner (183–85). Once
Daw and LaFoole are properly terrified, Truewit's ability to convincingly mime conversation with the adversary, along with his mind-
boggling diplomatic skills (negotiating five kicks in place of six of
Daw's teeth; turning LaFoole's refusal to bang his head against his
own sword into an agreement to have his nose tweaked) are bravura
theatrical moves that are likely to distract an audience's attention
from questions about the motives behind the brutality.

The disorientation produced by the near-impossibility of following key plot developments contributes to *Epicoene*'s relentless thematic and dramaturgical preoccupation with humiliation—of
characters in the play by other characters, and of the play's audience
(of readers as well as, although perhaps more acutely, of theater-
goers). The Collegiates are mocked for their judgment in consorting
with Daw and LaFoole; the two gulls are repeatedly ridiculed; they
get physically assaulted, as does Captain Otter; Truewit and Clerimont endure Dauphine's scathing rebukes at different points during
the play; Morose is the constant target of abuse; Epicoene is ordered
about, poked, and prodded by both Dauphine and Morose. And
Dauphine makes a fool of everyone, including his bosom friends, in
stripping Epicoene of his disguise. The play's audience of readers
and viewers must necessarily be as stunned as any of the onstage
characters at this final development. Jonson's plot resolution, depending as it does on exploding the male-only performance conventions of the Renaissance commercial stage, would be impossible to
anticipate. By defying the playwriting tradition stipulating a privi-

leged position of knowledge for a theater audience, Jonson in *Epi-coene* asserts his absolute authority over the response of that audience. Any efforts at second-guessing or passing judgment on his work must be completely reevaluated at the very end. Only retro-spectively, with knowledge of Dauphine's machinations, can an audi-ence fully comprehend what the play has been "about." And yet, paradoxically, by keeping his readers and viewers ignorant of Epi-coene's "real" identity, Jonson has also made it impossible for them as they are watching or reading the play to be the vaunted "under-standers," the deeply discerning audience he spends his career claim-ing to cultivate—usually in the same breath as he excoriates the actual audiences of his commercial theater plays.

The anxieties that shape Jonson's well-known invective are also registered, although with greater reticence, in his recurrent need to characterize his elite audience in the texts of his masques. The *Masque of Queens* once again provides interesting evidence. In a descriptive passage following the entrance of the hags' Dame (a pas-sage not spoken in performance), Jonson touts his dramaturgical skill in arranging for exposition of motive and situation to be done in the course of the upcoming dialogue: "For to have made . . . [the hags] their owne decipherers, and each one to have told, upon their en-trance, *what they were, and whether they would,* had bene a most piteous hearing, and utterly unworthy any quality of a *Poeme.*" But Jonson doesn't stop with this assertion of literary standards. He continues by describing the kind of audience that makes such stand-ards both possible and necessary: "a *Writer* should alwayes trust somewhat to the capacity of the *Spectator,* especially at these *Specta-cles;* Where Men, beside inquiring eyes, are understood to bring quick eares, and not those sluggish ones of Porters and Mechanicks, that must be bor'd through, at every act, with Narrations" (101–10). Note that Jonson's language here stops short of an actual assertion: he doesn't say that court audiences *do* bring inquiring eyes or quick ears, but only that they are understood to do so.

Whether or not Jonson intended his syntax to be so permeable, the record of responses to his masques in fact suggests an audience no more—and no less—astute than the "porters and mechanics" and their fellow ticket buyers for commercial theater events. The newsletter writers and diplomats responsible for the bulk of informa-tion we have about the actual reception of Jonson's court entertain-ments describe the splendor of the costumes, the cost of the jewels, and the disputes over precedence. With rare exceptions, Jonson's rigorous intellectual program goes unremarked.[19] It is certainly true that the purpose behind most of this documentation—retailing court

gossip and regulating international affairs—is not especially compatible with disquisitions on Jonsonian Neoplatonism. But even under
circumstances more conducive to engaging with Jonson's aims, key
elements of his audience remained untouched. Indeed, the responses
of King James, Jonson's most important audience member for most
of his career, were evidently far from profound. In Herford and
Simpson's concise summing up, James, "who was erudite even to
pedantry, was certainly capable of understanding the 'remou'd *mysteries*' [of Jonson's conceits], but the only record we have of his
behavior at a masque is a display of vulgarity and an utter lack of
appreciation." The reference is to the king's tantrum at the first
performance of *Pleasure Reconciled to Vertue* (1618), during which
he was heard to shout at the flagging masquers, "Why don't they
dance? What did you make me come here for? Devil take all of you,
dance!"[20] The implication is that, despite his enormous intellectual
vanity—and very real scholarly accomplishments—James came to
these entertainments primarily for the athletic display of legs.

Several weeks after its initial performance, *Pleasure Reconciled to
Vertue* was presented again, substantially revised. Renamed *For the
Honour of Wales*, the new version eliminated the ambitious iconography of the antimasque, which had featured Comus, Hercules, and
Antaeus. In its place, Jonson substituted a drawn-out comedy routine
by ersatz Welshmen—a sustained vignette of the type I discussed
earlier. This version was apparently more pleasing to the king; proof,
perhaps, of the essential vulgarity of James and his court. But it is
also possible that *For the Honour of Wales* was deemed "better"
because it was easier to understand. In the initial version, Jonson had
overindulged his penchant for devising brief episodes by stringing
together too many of them. As replacements for an ostensibly dis-
jointed set of events held together by Jonson's dense allegorical
schema, the Welshmen make for far less demanding enjoyment.[21]

Pleasure Reconciled to Vertue/For the Honour of Wales is a unique
case of revision, but (and this is where I think *Epicoene* is useful in
counterpoint) this case raises questions about the comprehensibility
of Jonson's masques in general. No matter how adept court audiences
may have been, decoding the language of emblems and mythology
necessary to follow the "plots" of his entertainments must have been
difficult. The annotation with which Jonson surrounded a number
of his early masque texts indicates the multivalent associations required of his *real* "understanders." It is hard, though, to imagine the
marginalia in those texts actually illuminating—rather than intimidating—their readers. As with the final plot twist of *Epicoene*, the net

result would be to impress an audience with its intellectual inferiority to the master poet.

And yet, while an audience can excuse—even embrace—*Epicoene*'s obscurities of plot because of their thematic relevance, Jonson's demanding masque "inventions" could be assimilated for a different reason. However convoluted the masque iconography got, these entertainments were always comprehensible at a basic level of intention: they were "understood" to be written in praise of England's sovereign. Whatever kinds of criticism or advice may have been intended, a single message always overrode whatever subtleties an audience did or didn't follow. In Jonson's masques, any obscurities of action or allusion would not interfere significantly with an audience's grasp of the spectacle's essential meaning: the king is good, long live the king.

4

By placing this discussion of *Epicoene* in relation to other plays and masques, my goal has been to illuminate certain tendencies evident in all of Jonson's dramatic writing. The lapses of interest in coherent characterizations, stage mechanics, and plot transitions apparent in *Epicoene* are characteristic of many of Jonson's efforts. In the works that are traditionally considered his best (aside from *Epicoene*) Jonson compensated by choosing settings that, to a great extent, dictate, manage, and justify the flow of characters across the stage. In his court masques, such dramaturgical difficulties generally became formal virtues; his creative predilections as a commercial-theater playwright thus had a uniquely serendipitous relationship to his work in the court masque form. In collaboration with Inigo Jones, Jonson developed the masque to capitalize on limited, disposable characterizations, sudden and surprising shifts of place and dramatis personae, and plots that—however labyrinthine and intellectually freighted— were, as exercises in compliment and affirmation, always already familiar to their audiences.

Notes

1. By combining the public and private theaters for which Jonson wrote under the rubric "commercial" stage, I do not mean to ignore significant differences in the actors, audience members, and physical circumstances of performance that usually characterized the entertainments offered in these two kinds of theaters. However, the importance of preserving these distinctions is less germane to my argument than

the need to come up with terms that reflect the historically and critically understood division between Jonson's work for ticket-buying customers and for private patrons. Similarly, I am aware that not all of the entertainments which early seventeenth-century authors and audiences called "masques" fit my definition of "court masque." The term does, however, seem the most efficient one available for designating the other type of work—in contradistinction to commercial theater plays—that I will be discussing.

2. Donaldson, *The World Upside-down* (Oxford: Clarendon Press, 1970), 37–39; Riggs, *Ben Jonson* (Cambridge: Harvard University Press, 1989), 154. The wedding masques to which Riggs refers are *Hymenaei* (1606) and *The Haddington Masque* (1608), which forced Jonson to serve as King James's apologist for two scandalously unpopular court-sponsored marriages; the *Masque of Beauty* (1608) and the *Masque of Queens* (1609) starred the Queen and her ladies.

3. I directed *Epicoene* for Use Makes Perfectness Productions under the auspices of the Department of English at the University of California, Berkeley, in April 1992. I am indebted to the inspired work of all those involved for many of the insights that have shaped this essay.

4. Unless otherwise stated, Jonson's works are quoted from *Ben Jonson*, ed. C. H. Herford and Percy and Evelyn Simpson (Oxford: Clarendon Press, 1925–52), with "i," "j," "u," "v," and the spelling of Truewit's name modernized. For *Epicoene*, Herford and Simpson follow the 1616 folio version since no quarto for the play has survived. See W. W. Greg, "Was There a 1612 Quarto of *Epicoene*?" in *Collected Papers*, ed. J. C. Maxwell (Oxford: Clarendon Press, 1966), 314–21, for a discussion of the "phantom" 1612 quarto.

5. I am not making an argument about Jonson's *conception* of his characters, many of whom are associated with a "humour" that confers a kind of behavioral consistency. Rather, I am talking about how Jonson *deploys* his characters: how he uses them in various situations; how he moves them in and out of his plays.

6. *Epicoene* in fact has two prologues; the second was apparently written in response to charges that the play contained some kind of libelous personal references. See Greg, "1612 Quarto," for the likely historical circumstances behind the two prologues.

7. See James E. Hirsh, "The 'To be or not to be' Scene and the Conventions of Shakespearean Drama," *Modern Language Quarterly* 42, no. 2 (1981): 115–36, for a discussion of this stage convention and Shakespeare's use of it.

8. Thomas Becon, *The Sicke Man's Salve* in *Prayers and Other Pieces* (Cambridge: The University Press, 1844), 87.

9. Haughty's preemptive mention of the Becon and Greene pamphlet titles is one reason for disqualifying them as the punchline Trusty was meant to deliver. A brief inquiry into the content and history of the tracts suggests additional reasons why their comic value—and therefore the comic value of Trusty's naming them—would have been, at best, quite limited. Becon's tract is, to be sure, an easy and obvious target for Jonson's lampoon of city manners and moralizing—but that ease and obviousness as surely deprive the joke of any real snap. Greene seems a more equivocal choice. The maudlin hysteria with which Greene details the "rules" of his "repentance" in the pamphlet's final pages would certainly attract Jonson's contempt. And Greene's penultimate exhortation "To those Gentlemen . . . that spend their wits in making plaies" to find new occupations could also be a reason for savaging the pamphlet—except that Greene's own sense of the commercial stage milieu as demeaning to men of genuine talent closely parallels Jonson's own antitheatricalism (*Greenes Groats-worth of witte*, ed. G. B. Harrison [London: The Bodley

Head Ltd, 1923], 43). In fact, the two men would seem to have quite a lot in common: the *Groat's-worth of Wit*, with its story of inheritance, cozenage, and counter-cozenage, depicts the same venal, materialistic world that Jonson's own comedies so brilliantly animate.

Moreover, Becon and Greene were not new objects of ridicule for Jonson by the time he wrote *Epicoene*. The *Sicke-mans salve*, originally published in 1561 and reissued a number of times thereafter, is mentioned in 5.2 of *Eastward Ho* (1605) to signify the newfound humility of Quicksilver, formerly a wild and dishonest apprentice. The reference can be seen as gently satiric; but, oddly enough, *Eastward Ho* goes on to reach its happy ending when Quicksilver and another character sing songs of confession and repentance and are forgiven by the man they have maligned. The combination of penitence and sentimentality in these confessions is part of Jonson's apparent satire on quackery (and credulity) in the Trusty passage of *Epicoene*. Jonson was only one of three authors involved in *Eastward Ho*'s composition, and it is perfectly possible that the allusion to Becon was the work of either Chapman or Marston. Nevertheless, the relation of the tract to *Eastward Ho*'s structure gives a peculiar twist to Jonson's unambiguous mockery of Becon in *Epicoene*.

Jonson had taken aim at Greene, whose *Groat's-worth of Wit* had been available since 1592, as early as *Every Man Out of his Humour* (1599). In 2.3 of that play it is suggested that a character can "steale" witticisms "with more security" (228) from Greene than from Sidney's *Arcadia*, implying the obscurity of the former compared with the raging popularity of the latter. If Greene was unknown, of course, Jonson would not have needed to jeer at his readership then, or ten years later in *Epicoene*. Fletcher's prefatory verses to the 1611 quarto of *Catiline* lists the "dear Groatsworth" with other screeds preferred by an ignorant public over Jonson's classical endeavor (*Catiline his Conspiracy*, [London: Walter Burre, 1611]). Perhaps Jonson's resentment of Greene's enduring popularity is behind *Epicoene*'s ridicule of the long-dead author.

10. Nano, Castrone, and Androgyno in *Volpone* provide a counterpoint to the "uneven consequences" I've described in *Cynthia's Revels* and *The Magnetick Lady*. *Volpone*'s dwarf, eunuch, and fool are more closely woven into the events of the play proper than are the Children of *Cynthia's Revels* or the commentators of *The Magnetick Lady*. Not confined to *Volpone*'s structural peripheries—its Induction or entre-acts—these three characters, described by Volpone as his children, are crucial in establishing Volpone's simultaneously repulsive and compelling spirit. The "sport" they enact for him in 1.2 has many of the attributes of Jonson's antimasques: the presentation by grotesque figures of an erudite puzzle, presumably accompanied with energetic movement. And yet, although they receive considerable stage time at the beginning of *Volpone*, Nano, Castrone, and Androgyno are quite literally expelled from the play by Mosca in 5.5—told to "Goe, recreate your selues, abroad" (11)—in an act of dispossession that previews Volpone's own loss of wealth, social status, and personal freedom. Here again, Jonson has created a vivid set of characters, made dwindling use of them in the course of the action, and turned them out of the play before its end. Jonson has not, however, merely abandoned them. Instead, he has found (in Mosca's dismissal) a moment and a means with sufficient thematic coherence to excise these characters from his play.

11. *Neptune's Triumph* provides evidence that Jonson himself thought of his writing for masques and the public stage as commutative: after the court entertainment, scheduled for 1624, was cancelled, Jonson recycled the exchange between the Poet and the Cook into 4.2 of *The Staple of News* (1626).

12. See *Epicoene or The Silent Woman*, ed. L. A. Beaurline (Lincoln: University

of Nebraska Press, 1973), and *Epicoene,* ed. R. V. Holdsworth (London: Ernest Benn Limited, 1979).

13. Oddly enough, Jonson abdicates responsibility for an easier logistical problem (easier because no lines are involved) later in the play by not indicating when the Collegiates enter to observe the humiliation of Daw and LaFoole in 4.5: the marginalia at the start of the next scene simply announce that the ladies are now present, "Having discovered part of the past scene, above."

14. *The Silent Woman,* in vol. 3 of *The Works of Ben Jonson,* ed. William Gifford (London: W. Bulmer and Co., 1816).

15. Jewkes, *Act Division in Elizabethan and Jacobean Plays 1583–1616* (Hamden: The Shoe String Press, 1958), 247; Wright, "Jonson's Revision of the Stage Directions for the 1616 Folio *Workes,*" *Medieval & Renaissance Drama in England* 5 (1991): 257–85. See also Herford and Simpson, *Ben Jonson,* 9:46–47 for a discussion of Jonson's notation of acts, scenes, entrances and exits.

16. "Expostulation with Inigo Jones," line 39, in *Ben Jonson.*

17. Jonas Barish's "Jonson and the Loathed Stage" in *A Celebration of Ben Jonson* (Toronto: University of Toronto Press, 1973), 27–53, is the most important work on Jonson and his audience. Richard Finkelstein's "The Roman Background of Ben Jonson's Audience," *Iowa State Journal of Research* 60, no. 3 (1986): 385–94, is also valuable in documenting classical models for this tumultuous relationship. George E. Rowe Jr. sets the relationship in the context of changing Renaissance ideas about the method and purpose of interpreting literary works in his article "Ben Jonson's Quarrel with Audience and its Renaissance Context," *Studies in Philology* 81, no. 4 (1984): 438–60; Rowe is among those critics who assert that Jonson esteemed his masque audiences (see p. 447).

18. The groundlessness of these motives has affected critics differently over the years. Some commentators, Dryden among them, have taken the gulls' gullibility and the Wits' meager provocation as signs that the play is a lighthearted comic fantasy ("Examen of the *Silent Woman,*" *Essays on Dramatic Poesy* in *Dramatic Poesy and Other Essays* [London: J. M. Dent & Sons Ltd., 1912], 42–59). More recently, commentators have seen the Wits' cruelties—and Jonson's comic vision— in a more sinister light; for examples of this darker view, see Michael Flachmann's "*Epicoene:* A Comic Hell for a Comic Sinner," *Medieval & Renaissance Drama in England* 1 (1984): 131–42, and Helen Ostovich, "'Jeered by Confederacy': Group Aggression in Jonson's Comedies," *Medieval & Renaissance Drama in England* 3 (1986): 115–28. The range of responses that the play provokes, and the intellectual and emotional discomfort each audience member must undergo in deciding how to respond, are among Jonson's striking achievements (intentional or otherwise) in *Epicoene.*

19. Examples of those exceptions—letters in which the "conceit" of one of Jonson's masques is scrupulously recorded—are reproduced in Herford and Simpson, *Ben Jonson,* 10:457, 459. These conceits were, to be sure, much in demand by intellectuals, esthetes, and those who wished to keep up-to-date on affairs at court. Nevertheless, most of the surviving correspondence describes masques in terms of their surface glamor, not the ideas that Jonson considered to be their primary content.

20. Hertford and Simpson, *Ben Jonson,* 10:405; King James's outburst is quoted in Stephen Orgel and Roy Strong, *Inigo Jones: the Theatre of the Stuart Court* (London: Sotheby Parke Bernet Publications Limited, 1973), 1: 283.

21. Stephen Orgel has made a powerful argument for understanding *Pleasure Reconciled to Virtue* as a high point in Jonson's fusion and resolution of the disparate

masque ingredients he inherited. Nevertheless, Orgel himself admits that *Pleasure Reconciled to Virtue* is not "the ideal masque-as-poem," noting, among other flaws, that its structure is conceived in "discrete" sections and that it is "rather more diffuse than we, as readers, could wish" (*The Jonsonian Masque* [Cambridge: Harvard University Press, 1965], 189). I am arguing that the masque's original viewers— not just current readers—would also have been bothered by this discreteness and diffuseness. A surviving eyewitness account of *Pleasure Reconciled to Virtue* by Orazio Busino, a member of the Venetian ambassador's household, seems to suggest exactly these difficulties with the masque's first version. Even allowing for the foreign observer's bad eyesight and his less-than-perfect understanding of English, the impression Busino gives of a disconnected series of specialty acts cannot be dismissed altogether. Busino's description appears both in Italian and in an English translation in Orgel and Strong, *Inigo Jones,* 1:279–84.

Pleasure Reconcild to Vertue in Historical Context

CAROL P. MARSH-LOCKETT

THE composition and staging of Ben Jonson's *Pleasure Reconcild to Vertue* for the court of James I offers the twentieth-century reader insight into complex historical dynamics in England between 1612 and 1625. In the context of Jacobean court politics and power relations, European exploration and expansion into the New World, the slave trade, and the politics and poetics of literary patronage, *Pleasure Reconcild to Vertue* is an exploration into the relationship between gender and power in the court of James I. Although influenced by the tensions and limitations of his position as poet laureate, Jonson, nonetheless, draws us into a Eurocentric, masculine world that situates its power in maleness, thus upholding patriarchy while he simultaneously forces the reader to acknowledge the weaknesses of extreme patriarchal assumptions. It is also a world which, according to historical evidence, indicates political tensions generated by James's decisions and preferences that are consistent with the tension between Pleasure and Vertue enacted in the masque.

Such tension or polarity between the tangible and the intangible, between immediate and deferred gratification, is significant not only in the implications for English national interest but also, even more immediately in court circles, in the earlier split in 1611 between Jonson and the popular stage architect Inigo Jones. After this split, the masque in Jonson's hands moved steadily in a literary and dramatic direction, thus becoming more of a text of intellectual appeal than a spectacle of sensory appeal. However, while the Jonsonian masque matures into a form that resembles a play, the reduced iconography continues to interact with the verbal element to generate a consistent text that not only offers insight into the age but also, as Stephen Orgel's work on the court masque indicates, underscores the discrepancy between the ideal enacted in the masque and the real enacted in history. The problem here is the degree to which history, colored as it is by memory, vested interest, and power constructs,

154

is in fact fiction, a problem which, in turn, blurs acute definitions of "real" and "ideal." I submit, however, that because of the nature of the masque as a genre which, as Orgel has indicated in the introduction to the Yale edition of the masques, involves the audience directly and not vicariously,[1] the enactment of the masque—the transformation of the entire environment—creates a fiction powerful enough to perceive itself as fact which can become history simply because it does not have to contend with the dichotomy between self and other.

In spite of the psychological phenomena at work in the Stuart court, however, events in England in the last half of James's rule influenced the text of the court masque. This period witnessed continuing turmoil and was characterized largely by what S. Reid Brett appropriately termed "The Rule of Favorites" as well as an ongoing tug-of-war between king and parliament.[2] In fact, during this entire period, there were only three brief parliamentary sessions. Close reading of the court masques of this period demonstrates Jonson's delicate negotiation of his own aesthetic and his position at court. The works also, however, while generating fictions that obviously affirmed the court psyche, simultaneously exposed the dichotomy between pleasure and virtue and the ensuing conflict between the loyalties of the monarch and the well-being of the nation.

Robert Ashton cites the Venetian ambassador who, as early as 1607, had observed James's indolence, his devotion to recreation, his neglect of kingly duties, and his distance from his subjects. A statement to this effect appears in the *Venetian State Papers* (1603–1607):

> He does not caress the people nor make them that good cheer the late Queen did, whereby she won their loves. . . . The result is he is despised and almost hated. In fact his Majesty is more inclined to live with eight or ten of his favorites openly.[3]

Antonia Fraser and Brett in their discussions of James I expand upon the observations of the Venetian ambassador. Both historians argue that James's hedonism led to politically unsound alliances. Fraser holds that James was extravagant and lazy. Between 1607 and 1611, she adds, £75,000 was spent on entertainments.[4] Brett notes further that after the death of the Earl of Salisbury, James also bungled the administration of the treasury. Shortly thereafter Parliament refused to release funds to James except upon its own terms, which were that James should cease monopolies and exclusive privileges that were tantamount to monopolies.

The antagonism between James and Parliament further underscores the potential threat posed by James's irrational penchant for favorites. Fraser and others interpret this penchant as homosexuality. That this would be problematic is implied by Sir Anthony Weldon's suggestion of James's effeminacy:

> he was ever best when furthest from his queene . . . he naturally loved not the sight of a soldier or any valiant man.[5]

Fraser writes that the first political consequence of James's homosexuality was the power he gave to Robert Carr, his Scottish favorite. Carr had experienced a rapid rise in power from his knighthood in 1607 to his position as James's confidant, after the death of Salisbury in 1612. While Fraser has given attention to James's homosexuality and his empowerment of favorites, I have found James's sexual identity a less significant issue than his privileging of gender and the negative implications of such privileging for the welfare of the nation. James's sexual relations undermined social and political stability. Fraser also views the conduct of Carr and later that of George Villiers, Duke of Buckingham, as essentially exploitive.[6] Both men, she adds, "saw the crown as a sort of old established and utterly secure Cornucopia from which benefits for themselves and their families would flow in a happy and endless stream" (124). James, we know, made decisions affecting foreign policy and affairs of state based on their counsel.

Such, then, were the social and political constructs that characterized and contextualized the performance of *Pleasure Reconcild to Vertue* on Twelfth Night, 1619. Implicit in this masque, too, are reflections of the constructs of power and gender in James's reign that manifest themselves in pleasure that must be reconciled or, in the seventeenth-century sense of the word, be put in submission to virtue in order for the ideal to be celebrated. It is significant, however, that in the masque while Pleasure and Vertue are each referred to by the female subject pronoun, they are represented by male personae, Comus and Hercules. The masque, then, can present Renaissance notions of masculinity without incurring the risk of feminization. At the same time, however, it can also caution against the excesses of masculine privilege. By watching Hercules learn the proper relation of virtue to vice, therefore, the Stuart court could be reminded of that relationship and of the task of maintaining the supremacy of virtue. In this sense, then, we can read the masque as a didactic exercise couched in a larger Jacobean fiction—Jonson's text depending for its full significance on the extratextual reality.[7]

The plot of *Pleasure Reconcild* is simple. The masque opens with the real as opposed to the ideal. Immediately confronted with the iconography of pleasure and excess, we see "ye god of cheere, or ye belly, riding in triumph, his head crownd with roses, & other flowers; his hair curld" (lines 16–18).[8] He approaches the scene to the tune of "wild musique of *cimbals Flutes* & *Tabers*" (5–6). There is, then, chaos which results from the supremacy of vice—in this instance gluttony—which is initially celebrated in song by Comus himself:

> Roome, roome, make roome for ye bouncing belly,
> first father of Sauce, & Deuiser of gelly
> Prime master of arts, & ye giuer of wit,
> yt found out ye excellent ingine, ye spit.
>
> (13–16)

The song continues with an enumeration of the belly's contributions—an enumeration which amounts to a contrived glorification of gluttony—and ends with a description of the disordered society at hand:

> All wch haue now made thee, so wide i' ye waste
> as scarce wch no pudding thou art to be lac'd:
> but eating & drinking, vntill thou dost nod
> thou break'st all thy girdles, & breakst forth a god.
>
> (33–36)

At this point, the bearer of Hercules's drinking bowl continues the scene with a prose speech which denigrates Comus:

> Now you sing of Comus here, the *Belly-god.*
> I say it is well, & I say it is not well: it
> is well, as it is a Ballad, and 'twer forty yards
> of ballad, more: as much Ballad as tripe:
> But when ye Belly is not edified by it, it is not
> well: for where did you ever read, or heare,
> that the Belly had any eares? Come neuer pump
> for an answeare, for you are defeated.
>
> (44–51)

The irony, here, is that the lines address the very lack of insight into its own weakness that characterized the Stuart court. As the speech continues, however, it soon becomes clear that Hercules's drunken bowl bearer is integral to the action of the masque when he summons up the antimasque (70–79). This speech is followed by the first antimasque, performed, as the Venetian eyewitness Orazio Busino tells us, by "twelve extravagant masquers, one of whom was in a barrel, all but his extremities, his companions being cased in huge wicker flasks, very well made."[9] Their dance of antics takes place to the tune of cornets and trumpets, we are also told by Busino.[10] The characters of the antimasque celebrate the chaos that ensues from excessive indulging in pleasure.

Because the masque must present the ideal, however, the scene must change. Therefore, Hercules, the embodiment of the Renaissance concept of virtue, by his appearance, facilitates the change. His presence provides the necessary model of virtue for the noble company at Whitehall. The quality of poetry he utters manifests his nobility and reinforces the court's notion of itself as an ordered environment.

Hercules, direct from the slaying of Antaeus, initially expresses anger at the disorder that the antimasquers represent (87–98). In the same angry spirit, he banishes the antimasquers (105–14), and the world is momentarily restored to order. The scene then becomes pastoral:

> the whole *Groue* vanisheth, and the
> whole *Musique* is discouered, sitting at
> ye foote of ye Mountaine, wth *Pleasure*
> & *Vertue* seated aboue yem.
>
> (115–18)

Having thus restored order, Hercules can now be rewarded with rest and be acknowledged as the envoy of virtue:

> giue thy troubled spirits peace,
> whilst Vertue, for whose sake
> thou dost this godlike trauaile take,
> may of ye choicest herbage, make,
> vpon this Mountaine bred,
>   a Crowne, a Crowne
> for thy imortall head.
>
> (124–30)

As soon as the hero is rewarded, however, the second antimasque, this one of pygmies, appears. Attempting to avenge the death of Antaeus, they threaten to disrupt the order by destroying Hercules. This threat is articulated by the first pygmy:

> pray Anger there be any,
> whereon to feed my iust revenge, and soone,
> how shall I kill him? hurle him 'gainst ye Moone,
> & break him in small portions Give to *Greece*
> his braine & Euery trait of earth a peece?
>
> (140–44)

But their efforts are thwarted. Indeed, they must be if the court (particularly in this era of expansion into the new world and the slave trade) is to retain its Eurocentric, male identity and a notion of England as a separate, special, and virtuous place. Virtue cannot be overcome, and in the Whitehall setting, the company must see that virtue survives chaos. The pygmies, therefore, in their role as moral and physical inferiors, do not initiate an open confrontation with Hercules and choose flight over fair and honest conflict.

At this critical moment in the masque, the power of Hercules, the power of virtue, is then heralded in song (160–64). At this point, Hercules can be duly rewarded; and Mercury, recounting the feats of Hercules, "the active frend of Vertue," presents him with a crown of poplar. This crucial moment of reward links Jonson's use of the myth of Hercules, the meaning of the myth for the court, and the meaning of the text as it is influenced by the myth for the reader. Jonson's erudition is now evident in the light of Mercury's speech. The scene, according to Jonson's early stage directions, is Mount Atlas: "His top ending in ye figure of an old man, his head and beard all hoary & frost: as if his shoulders were covered wth snow, ye rest wood & rock: a groue of Ivy at his feet" (1–4). Jonson's use of Atlas bears many implications for the Stuart court. The viewers would have recognized Jonson's use of Ovid, where we are told how Atlas became a mountain. This myth would have been available to Jonson, according to Richard Peterson, in Natalis Comes's *Mythologia* where it appears with Virgil's description of Atlas in *The Aeneid* (128). According to Ovid, Atlas refused Perseus entry into the garden when the latter was returning from having slain Medusa. In Virgil's account Mercury (Jove's messenger) stopped at Mount Atlas before traveling to Carthage to tell Aeneas his duties. Jonson had represented James as Aeneas in *The Haddington Masque* (1606) and in so doing had fostered conventional expectations held of the monarchy. When Mercury reached Carthage, however, he found Aeneas torn between his love for Dido and his higher calling, and it was Mercury's duty to remind Aeneas of his purpose. Atlas, therefore, becomes for James and the Stuart court a reminder of the necessity of virtue which is manifested in duty.

That virtue is not easily maintained is reinforced in the image of the hill. As the Oxford editors note, the concept of the hill of virtue dates back as far as Hesiod's *Works and Days.* Indeed, vice (or pleasure) is easy to follow, but virtue poses special difficulties. Such was the case for Hercules, the role model for the Whitehall audience. The presentation of Atlas as a mountain, then, becomes an expression of the difficult virtue that James in his privileging of favorites had abandoned. In addition, as the Oxford editors also note, the scene is laid in Africa, a detail that has special significance for the Stuart court and the meaning of the masque. The African motif was not a new convention in the Jonsonian court masque. Ann Kelly has noted, in her extensive discussion of Jonson's use of light and water motifs in *The Masque of Blacknesse* (1605), that Jonson used the African motif to link the court with the cradle of civilization and life. Jonson, she shows, had managed to "praise the epitomes of a white culture in a dramatic setting centered on blackness."[11] In *Pleasure Reconcild* there is also a powerful use of blackness which draws attention to white culture. In this case, however, the use of blackness conforms more closely to Eurocentric expectations and works in conjunction with the image of the hill in facilitating the didactic function of the masque.[12] Atlas, the mountain, therefore, functions on two levels; and we find that at the core of the nation's life, that is, the court, there is a need for virtue. This virtue, however, is not to be achieved without a struggle. Hence, Comus appears as the envoy of vice. While he is easily banished by Hercules, the environment is not yet rid of its ills. Therefore, the pygmies, icons of disorder, pose a special threat.

In the light of the history of the period, then, the allegory of *Pleasure Reconcild*—the struggle between virtue or order and pleasure or disorder—becomes clear. As Peterson has noted, the literal seventeenth-century meaning of "reconciliation" (i.e., "submission") is also operant in the masque (138). Mercury recounts Hercules's feats (168–86) and reports that according to the promises of Atlas (prior to his becoming a mountain), there should be "a cessation of all iars / 'twixt Vertue, & her noted opposite, / Pleasure" (189–91).

The implications of the masque for the Stuart court are initially expressed in Mercury's speech when he states that the reconciliation will occur in the sight of Hesperus, the Evening Star, here representing King James. As a source of light, the Evening Star was a symbol of wisdom. James is further described in terms of praise which, as has been established in scholarship on the masque, convey to the monarch what he should be:

> ye glory of ye West
> the brightest star, yt from his burning Crest
> lights all on this side ye *Atlantick seas*
> as far as to thy Pillars Hercules.
> Se where He shines: *Justice* & *Wisdom* plac'd
> about his *Throne* & those wth *Honor* grac'd.
> *Beautie* & *Loue.*
>
> (192–98)

These attributes, according to Mercury, allow Hesperus (James) to rule his world, in contrast to Atlas, who bears his. The irony here is abundantly clear. In reality James cannot be said to have ruled his England effectively, for we are continuously aware of the machinations of Somerset and Buckingham. In addition, according to Brett, the Spanish ambassador Gondomar was attempting to manipulate James's foreign and domestic policies with the prospect of a marriage alliance between the two countries through the marriage of Charles and the Spanish princess (41–51). Moreover, it was precisely because of the absence of "*Justice* & *Wisdom* plac'd / about his throne" that James's relationship with Parliament continued to be fraught with tension and that seeds of unrest continued to be planted in England.

Nevertheless, in spite of the realities of affairs within or beyond Whitehall, the court must now celebrate and share the reward of the triumph of virtue achieved within the masque. Thus, the masquers, led by Prince Charles, are to perform the revels. Pleasure, then, has been redefined. It now means the celebration of virtue. We soon find, however, that even in the revels there is irony expressed in the song which suggests that the person whose embodiment of virtue is ostensibly being celebrated falls short of what he should be:

> Ope, aged atlas, open thy lap
> and from thy beamy bosom, strike a light
> yt men may read in thy mysterious map
>   all lignes
>   and signes
> of roial education and the right
>
> (218–23)

We find in these lines perhaps the most direct link between the masque and its context. The significance of the lines, as Orgel notes, is especially illuminated by the *OED*, which indicates that in a seventeenth-century reading, "map" meant "a detailed representation in epitome; a circumstantial account of the state of things."[13]

The link continues in the three songs of Daedalus which accompany the revels. Daedalus was one of the archetypal craftsmen. His presence in the masque as coordinator of the revels bespeaks the function of art: to impart knowledge and to render more fulfilling the knowledge of those who possess it. Art also, however, generates fictions that undergird power. In this instance, the medium is dance. It has already been widely established that dancing in the masque is a visual manifestation of the degree of order in the environment. This was evident in *The Masque of Queenes* (1609) where the dance of hags indicates a world gone awry. The revels in *Pleasure Reconcild* represent the celebration of order and the establishment of a proper hierarchy of values in the world of the masque.

In the process of affirming the court, therefore, the dance physically demonstrates the theme of the masque: that the pursuit of virtue is difficult. Daedalus makes this point in the instructions to the masquers, in which he continues the reference to the myth of Hercules on which the masque is built:

> Come on, come on; and where you goe
>   so enter—weaue the curious knot
> as eu'en th'observer scarce may know
>   wch lines are Pleasures, and wch not.
> First, figure out ye doubtfull way
>   at wch, a while all youth should stay
> where she and Vertue did contend
>   wch should haue Hercules to frend.
>
>   (253–60)

Here again, Jonson's erudition is evident. A similar reference to Hercules can be found in Whitney's emblem *Bivium Virtutis et Vitii*, in which Hercules (like James) is solicited by both Pleasure and Virtue.

The revels, moreover, are to portray a labyrinth ("the curious knot") like that constructed by Daedalus in Crete. The masque, then, appeals to the skill of the spectators who are to perceive the theme of the masque in the dance:

> Then, as all actions of mankind
>   are but a Laborinth, or maze
> so let your Daunces be entwin'd
>   yet not perplex men, unto gaze,
> But measur'd, and so numerous too,
>   as men may read each act you doo.

> And when they see ye Graces meet,
>   admire the wisdom of your feet
> For Dauncing is an exercise
>   not only shews ye mouers wit,
> But maketh ye beholders wise,
>   as he hath powre to rise to it.

(261–72)

In these lines we find Jonson's aesthetic as outlined in the preface to *Hymenaei* (1605). The dance, according to Daedalus, is so designed that there is a link between the physical act and the intellectual sharpness of the viewers. The link is expressed in such phrases as "read each act you doo"; "wisdom of your feet"; "maketh the beholder wise." All these phrases reflect Jonson's notion of what a masque should be: an educative and intellectual exercise.

The tensions external to the masque are reinforced when we realize that the skill to which Daedalus refers can come about only after the court has been exposed to the lesson of Hercules and can appreciate the true meaning of virtue. Only then can the court perceive pleasure in its true form: not as adherence to vice but as the discovery of beauty and love which are conveyed in the labyrinthine formations of the first and second dances.

In spite of the revels, however, the message of the masque is not complete. The text goes further to suggest that all is not well in England. In Mercury's comment to Hercules, we find a statement of the monarch's obligation:

> You must returne vnto ye Hill
>   and there aduance
> wth labour, and inherit still
>   that height, and crowne,
> from whence you euer may looke downe
>   vpon triumphed Chaunce.
>
> .   .   .   .
>
>   There, there is Vertues seat
> Striue to keepe hir your owne,
>   'tis only she, can make you great,
> though place, here, make you knowne.

(333–38; 345–48)

The instructional element and the subtext of these lines are obvious, for there is a clear link between what Hercules must do and the expectations held of the crown just as there is a clear link between the subtext and the state of England. As the history of the period indicates, however, James appreciated the masque only on a superficial level, and the tensions between Vertue and Pleasure in the Stuart court continued.

Notes

1. *Ben Jonson: The Complete Masques* (New Haven: Yale University Press, 1969), 1.
2. *The Stuart Century: 1603—1614* (London: George Harrap, 1961)
3. Quoted in Robert Ashton, *James I by His Contemporaries* (London: Hutchison, 1969), 101.
4. *King James VI of Scotland; I of England* (London: Wiedenfeld & Nicholson, 1974), 123.
5. Quoted in Ashton, *James I,* 13–14.
6. In the first chapter of *Homosexuality in Shakespeare's England* (Chicago: University of Chicago Press, 1991), Bruce Smith cites correspondence between James and Buckingham and James and Carr in his discussion of homosexual discourse. The context and content of the letters suggest possible homoerotic alliances.
7. Earlier criticism has made much of the iconography of this masque. Richard Peterson provides an extensive exploration of Jonson's sources in his article "The Iconography of Jonson's *Pleasure Reconciled to Virtue*" in which he examines Jonson's use of the writings of Philostratus, Diodorus Siculus, Comes, Catari, Ovid, and Virgil, in addition to ancient sculptures as well as paintings by Rubens. All of these Peterson terms the sources of the "moral ideas and compelling visual images" of the masque (*Journal of Medieval and Renaissance Studies* 5, 1975, 123–51).
8. Ben Jonson, "Pleasure Reconciled to Vertue," in *Ben Jonson,* ed. C. H. Herford and Percy and Evelyn Simpson (Oxford: The Clarendon Press, 1941) 7 :479–91. All quotations are cited in the text.
9. Quoted in Stephen Orgel, *The Jonsonian Masque* (Cambridge, Mass.: Harvard University Press, 1965), 160.
10. Ibid.
11. "The Challenge of the Impossible: Ben Jonson's *Masque of Blacknesse,*" *CLA Journal* 20, no. 3 (1977): 352.
12. The banishing of the pygmies is significant beyond the world of the masque and the court. In *Black Britannia: A History of Blacks in Britain* (Chicago: Jonson Publishing Company Inc., 1972), Edward Scobie dates the increasing number of Africans in England from 1554 when John Lok, a London trader, returned to England with a cargo of five African slaves. According to the Acts of Privy Council (11 August 1596), Queen Elizabeth voiced concern about the increasing numbers of Blacks and indicated that they should be "sent forth of the land" (8).
13. Orgel, *The Jonsonian Masque,* 176.

The Mythical Failures of Jonson

FRANCES TEAGUE

NARRATIVE rides on the backs of its characters. Thus when we make narratives about literary history, we need to give thought to who the characters are that help shape our story.[1] When scholars write a narrative of English drama, Shakespeare is the protagonist, but an important secondary character, Shakespeare's foil as it were, is Ben Jonson. Indeed, Jonson's reputation has suffered mightily because he provides such a convenient contrast within any narrative that centers on Shakespeare. As E. B. Partridge summarizes the reputation of Jonson, the dramatist is an unfortunate man:

> Could even Jonson have fashioned a more ironic fate than the one he found himself in—or, more precisely, the one we find him in? To write plays—when Shakespeare did? To write occasional poems for a circle that Donne moved in and wrote for? To be a critic—just after Sidney? To conceive of the heroic life—in the shadow of Spenser? To be concerned with the "advancement of Letters"—when there was a high government official who could write *The Advancement of Learning* and a *Novum Organum?*[2]

In this narrative, Jonson plays the role of perennial also-ran to a series of greater figures. To use Partridge's phrase, "we find him" not as literary lion, poet laureate, and royal favorite, but instead as a writer ironically destined to dwell in the shadow of others. Ben Jonson is a victim of bad timing.

Other narratives have preferred to cast Jonson as villain, rather than as foil. The eighteenth century, for example, brought forth literary forgeries specifically intended to defame Jonson, as well as gross misrepresentations of his life and relationship to Shakespeare. Inevitably, such narratives cast Jonson as the envious antagonist. Antipathy toward Jonson did not die in later centuries, of course. While some twentieth-century scholars deprecate what Samuel Schoenbaum calls "Jonson-baiting,"[3] others argue that Jonson is rightly perceived as a hostile, even envious character. Thus, T. J. B. Spencer is not the first to argue that Jonson's elegy for Shakespeare is marked not only by a "lack of sympathy," but also by overt "antipathy."[4] Robert Watson thinks Jonson's plays show his resentment of other playwrights' popularity,[5] and Robert Evans devotes chapter 5 of his book to "Jonson's dealings with antagonists and competitors."[6] Such analyses as these construct Ben Jonson's character as aggressive, hostile (particularly to Shakespeare), and envious of the success that others enjoy.[7]

Twentieth-century discussions do not, however, falsify the events of Jonson's life, as eighteenth-century writers sometimes did. The desire for a narrative in which Jonson is an enemy to Shakespeare led Thomas Davies, Edmond Malone, Robert Shiells, Charles Macklin, and William Henry Ireland to provide, even to forge, distorted evidence of Jonson's villainy. Documents that showed Jonson as an invidious cheat or a blowhard bully were manufactured by Macklin, Shiells, and Ireland; Davies added a scene to *Henry IV, Part Two*, that attacked Jonson; Malone debunked the forgeries but argued that they were true to Jonson's real nature.[8] In the forgeries, Jonson repeatedly attacked Shakespeare, while Jonson's authentic comments on literature were misread as slurs aimed specifically at Shakespeare. Even Jonson's death was reconstructed so that he died in a fit of pique. Discussing such phenomena, Jonas Barish rewrites the narrative to explain the remarkable twists and turns that the history of Jonson's reputation has taken:

> What has happened—to transpose the matter into terms which the editors in question would neither have understood nor approved—is that they have come to see in Shakespeare a Christ figure, and in Jonson both the Judas and the mob demanding blood. Jonson's "slights" and "malignances," his "sneers," "contempts," and "invectives," constitute his direct persecution, his scourging and buffeting, of Shakespeare. The Judas kiss is his famous dedicatory epistle to the 1623 Folio, in which he addresses Shakespeare as "beloved master" and exalts him above Sophocles—for had not Dryden himself pronounced these verses "sparing" and "invidious"?
> . . . To the extent to which they articulated their own motives, the critics aimed to deify Shakespeare, to show that in the precise degree to which Jonson was raucous, hostile, and vindictive, Shakespeare was gentle, mild, and forbearing. The hidden analogy with Christ insured that every act of aggression on Jonson's part would redound to Shakespeare's greater glory. But this ostensible purpose, however perverse in itself, concealed, one suspects, a deeper one: the desire to find a suitable victim to maul and mangle.[9]

Barish's construction creates a second version of Jonson as victim. Unlike Partridge's Jonson, who is a victim of ironic bad timing,

Barish's Jonson serves as a sacrificial victim "to maul and mangle" for "Shakespeare's greater glory." Yet a narrative that casts Jonson in the role of victim—whether beleaguered and reviled or ironically second to his betters—has its own set of problems.

Criticism of Jonson that follows either victim narrative often insists that Jonson is a self-conscious failure. Partridge distinguishes between the place in literary history where Jonson found himself and that place where we find him. If one is to construct Jonson as feeling anxiety or envy, those places merge: one must assume that he shared the current judgment that he was equalled, even surpassed by others. He thought himself a failure. Whether blaming or pitying him, such critics have found that in his own lifetime Jonson suffered as the victim of ignorant audiences, royal hostility, and his own intractable personality. Thus, such accounts focus on both his theatrical failures and his troubled relationship with his audience.

Jonson's rivalry with other writers is easily established, so I do not challenge it. I shall, however, question how much is actually known about Jonson's various failures. Indeed, if the information about such failures appears scant or contradictory, one might even question the Jonson-as-victim narrative altogether. Accounts of Jonson's victimization used to begin with the early events in his career: contemporaries sneered at his attempts to write serious comedy until Shakespeare, as the story went, helped the young man to success by urging production of *Every Man in His Humour*. Yet this narrative has now passed out of fashion. As David Kay has remarked,

> Literary historians have traditionally depicted Ben Jonson's career as a narrative which is itself fully dramatic—a sequence of events marked both by meteoric success and by resounding failure, by plays which met with public indifference or hostility and by those which decisively altered the mode of comedy dominant in his age.[10]

To demonstrate the power (and the fictionality) of the narrative, Kay reassesses four of the early plays, showing that they were more successful than stage historians have realized and that *Every Man Out*, not *Every Man In* "established Jonson as the leading humour satirist."[11] Kay's article has had an effect on such recent biographical critics as Rosalind Miles, Anne Barton, and David Riggs, all of whom cite Kay in their discussions of Jonson's early career, although they continue to suggest that the failures he encountered with the late plays resulted in a bitter and unhappy close to his life.[12]

What, then, of Jonson's last plays, the notorious "dotages" as Dryden called them?[13] Scholars may have misread the history of the early comedies, but few have argued that Jonson's late plays were successful. Received opinion holds that Jonson's popular success in the theater ended with the 1611 production of *Catiline*. To quote a recent biography,

> *Catiline* proved to be a watershed in Jonson's dramatic career. Never again was he to enjoy a success equivalent to that of *Volpone* or *The Alchemist*. Indeed he had no further popular success of any kind, since virtually all his later plays were given their one introductory performance only. What the Globe audience had brought about [in their condemnation of *Catiline*] was not merely the dismissal of one play but the demolition of Jonson's career as a popular dramatist.[14]

Statements like this one are commonplace in accounts of Jonson's life and work. What I want to do is re-examine this claim that Jonson's theatrical success ended in 1611 and dismantle at least part of it. I shall discuss the plays in chronological order.[15]

Catiline was first performed in 1611. The title page to the play in the 1616 folio says "This Tragoedie was *first* Acted . . ." (my emphasis), phrasing that might suggest subsequent performances between 1611 and 1616. A later edition (1635) reports on the play as "now Acted by his Maiesties Servants with great Applause," so *Catiline* remained in the company's repertoire nearly twenty years later. John Downes included it in "A Catalogue of part of His Ma^tes Servants Plays as they were formerly acted at the Blackfryers & now allowed of to his Ma^tes Servants at ye New Theatre," a listing that suggests it was performed before 1663. (The "New" playhouse is the Theatre Royal.) Later Restoration revivals enjoyed considerable success in the 1660s.

Why, then, should anyone consider the play a devastating failure? Several contemporary documents may suggest that the play was disliked. In a preliminary epistle Jonson states that the first audience had given the play "crude and ayry reports," praising the first two acts, but disliking Cicero's fourth act oration. Commendatory verses by Beaumont and Field "hint delicately at the failure" according to Herford and the Simpsons[16]; in fact, these verses suggest only that the first performance had an unsympathetic audience. In a poem about Shakespeare's excellence (1640), Leonard Digges commented that *Catiline*, unlike *Julius Caesar*, had been "tedious (though well laboured)."[17] This record hardly suggests a disastrous failure. The initial audience was unenthusiastic, but later spectators seem to have liked the play well enough that the company still played it twenty years later; the company was unlikely to produce a play that they expected to fail. By the same token, a Restoration company was unlikely to exhume a complete failure, so *Catiline* may have had some record of success.

I have discussed *Bartholomew Fair* (1614) elsewhere at some length: I would argue that it enjoyed success both at the Hope Theatre and at court when first produced, was revived on occasion before the closing of the theaters, and may have formed the basis for an illicit droll.[18] Its speedy revival in the Restoration may be attributed either to its earlier success on the Jacobean or Caroline stage or simply to the Restoration audience's pleasure in the satire on Puritans. No evidence exists to suggest that *Bartholomew Fair* failed, nor is it customarily included as one of Ben Jonson's dotages.

No contemporary comments about the success or failure of *The Devil Is an Ass* (1616) survive. The second folio simply records that it was "Acted in the yeere, 1616," phrasing that may suggest the play had only one production. Downes included *The Devil Is an Ass* on his list, however, and his mention may mean other performances occurred before 1663. The record suggests that whatever success (or failure) the play had, it was not sufficient for Jonson and his contemporaries to comment on.

Evidently *The Staple of News* (1626) had both public and court performances since Jonson wrote a prologue for each; presumably the invitation to perform at court means the play enjoyed some success. Because of its topicality, the play made enemies for Jonson, particularly of Nathaniel Butter, whose newspaper he mocked. When Jonson decided to print the play in 1631, he was quarrelling with Inigo Jones and did not want the public to think he had been too savage in his satire on Butter five years before. Accordingly, before act 3 he inserted an epistle to his readers to assure them that his dramatic portrait of the newspaper office was not to be taken as having any sinister implication. Bentley comments that this epistle indicates "that *The Staple of News,* in spite of its court performance, was not a success in the theatre,"[19] but I can see no reason to assume the play was anything except a success. Certainly Jonson engaged in quarrels with Butter and Jones, but bad temper need not be congruent with bad box office.

With *The New Inn* (1628/29), we finally come to a Jonson play that was unquestionably a failure. Although he had suffered a stroke the year before the play's production, Jonson did not blame himself for the play's reception. Instead he complained of the actors and vowed to leave the stage as a result of their failure. In addition to Jonson's own commentary, records show that the play's court performance was cancelled. Furthermore, several contemporaries remarked on the play's failure. Yet even this instance of failure is suggestive. The commentary on this play raises questions about the supposed failures of Jonson's preceding works. One might ask why a playwright who had already experienced nearly two decades of theatrical failure would wait so long to react to rejection and then react so angrily. If the other plays had failed, moreover, why would his contemporaries have suddenly begun commenting on his failure with this one?

The last of the so-called dotages is *The Magnetic Lady* (1632). Alexander Gill wrote some satirical verses against the play and said its failure had pleased Inigo Jones and Nathaniel Butter. No one seems to have questioned Gill's claim that these two attended the opening of a play by Jonson, whom they detested. Gill says the comedy was played only three times; he provides the principal (indeed the only direct) evidence that the play failed, but his verses are undated so he may have written before any revival. Yet there is some indication of a successful revival when one looks for it. The play has an epilogue to the king, suggesting a court performance. Sir Henry Herbert investigated certain oaths that the actors had inserted; he seems to have heard this complaint about the play a year after the first production, a delay that implies the play was revived in the 1633 season. Finally, the play was included on Downes's list of plays performed early in the Restoration. Gill's gloating verses may suggest that the play initially had a mixed reception, but other evidence suggests success, at least in revival.

In summary, the idea that Jonson's late plays (i. e., every play he wrote from 1611 on) were failures in the playhouse is unfounded. Indeed one might even argue that several of his late plays enjoyed fair success. But the idea of theatrical failure is very convenient to the Jonson-as-victim narrators, allowing discussion of the playwright's brooding and anger, his futile attempts to win back audiences with experiments, his stoic endurance of his fate, and so on. Such a narrative falsifies the history of the plays and of the life, for the critic must also overlook Jonson's achievements as a writer of masques, an occupation that kept him busy and successful in the 1620s. Furthermore, the issue of Jonson's rivalries with other writers is grossly simplified if Jonson always fails. He becomes a stock figure, like Wile E. Coyote, always bound for disaster. The effect of the victim narrative is to reduce the artist's stature.

The power of this narrative to distort one's understanding of Jonson's canon may be gauged if one tries to transpose it to Shakespeare's career. Were scholars to approach Shakespeare as they have approached Jonson, they would study a very different playwright. Let me give my imagination free rein. Surely our account of the

Shakespearean canon would adjust to take in the dreadful psychic wounds that Shakespeare must have suffered when *Troilus and Cressida* failed and *Timon of Athens* went unproduced. I might imagine using the *Troilus and Cressida* epistle to read across the entire Shakespeare canon: Shakespeare's plays become mere commodities and humiliating pleas, aimed at an audience that sullies them with smoky breath, stales (urinates on) them, and—at the very best—clapper claws them vulgarly.[20] The playwright yearns for death as an escape, fantasizing that "when he is gone, and his Commedies out of stale, you will scramble for them, and set vp a new English Inquisition." (Presumably in death he will be beyond the tortures of such an Inquisition.)

To construct Shakespeare's narrative in such a fashion would produce a very different figure from the one we now study, and few of us would welcome the difference. The narrative that we have constructed about Ben Jonson might benefit from revision. It would help us recognize his plays' strengths if we credit the playwright with strengths as well; and a new narrative will inevitably have an effect on our version of Shakespeare. The heyday of bardolatry demanded a villain and bully who could heighten Shakespeare's grace. The triumph of Shakespeare demanded both a victim, whom Shakespeare could help, and a failure, to whom Shakespeare could be compared. A successful Jonson narrative (i.e., a version of Jonson's success that is itself successful in supplanting the current narrative) will not only allow scholars to see Jonson's work anew, but also give a fresh perspective on Shakespeare.

Notes

I began work on the ideas of this essay for a theater history seminar at the 1989 meeting of the Shakespeare Association of America. That session was chaired by Professor Roslyn Knutson; the comments she and other members of the seminar made have helped me.

1. My discussion of this process—constructing the author's character—shows a clear debt to the ideas set forth by Michel Foucault in "What Is an Author?" in *Language, Counter-Memory, Practices: Selected Essays by Michel Foucault* (Ithaca: Cornell University Press, 1977), 117–38. The research that Gary Taylor has done on how Shakespeare was constructed in various periods in *Reinventing Shakespeare: A Cultural History from the Restoration to the Present* (New York: Oxford University Press, 1989) is also suggestive.

2. E. B. Partridge, "Jonson's Large and Unique View of Life," *Elizabethan Theatre* 4 (1972): 147–48.

3. Samuel Schoenbaum, "Shakespeare and Jonson: Fact and Myth," *Elizabethan Theatre* 2 (1970): 13.

4. T. J. B. Spencer, "Ben Jonson on his beloved, The Author William Shake-speare," *Elizabethan Theatre* 4 (1972): 39–40.

5. Robert Watson, *Ben Jonson's Parodic Strategy* (Cambridge, Mass.: Harvard, 1987), 8, 30.

6. Robert Evans, *Ben Jonson and the Poetics of Patronage* (Lewisburg, Penn.: Bucknell University Press, 1989). James Shapiro in *Rival Playwrights: Marlowe, Jonson, Shakespeare* (New York: Columbia, 1991), and David Riggs in *Ben Jonson: A Life* (Cambridge, Mass.: Harvard, 1989) follow this line of thought as well. I am not suggesting that this type of analysis is "Jonson-baiting" or that Jonson's relationships with his contemporaries were tranquil. I am simply pointing out that such analysis has its own history to which scholars must attend.

7. Michael McCanles sees an even wider range of roles than I do. In *Jonsonian Discriminations: The Humanist Poet and the Praise of True Nobility* (Toronto: University of Toronto Press, 1992), he comments: "the current Jonson literature has produced several versions of 'Ben Jonson': the plain-style Jonson; the stoic Jonson; the psychologist's Jonson fixated on authority figures; the misogynist Jonson; and most recently the new historicist's Jonson as just the sort of figure he most abhorred, an envious and resentful sycophant" (vii).

8. D. H. Craig discusses these interesting libels on Jonson's career and character in the introduction to *Ben Jonson: The Critical Heritage 1599–1798* (London: Routledge, 1990); see esp. 29–32. I discuss the fiction about Jonson's deathbed in my article, "Ben Jonson's Poverty" *Biography* 2 (1979): 260–65.

9. Jonas Barish, "Introduction," in *Ben Jonson: Twentieth-Century Views* (Englewood Cliffs, N.J.: Prentice-Hall, 1960), 4–5.

10. David W. Kay, "The Shaping of Ben Jonson's Career: A Re-examination of Facts and Problems," *Modern Philology* 67 (1970): 224.

11. Ibid., 225.

12. Rosalind Miles, *Ben Jonson: His Life and Work* (London: Routledge & Kegan Paul, 1986); Anne Barton, *Ben Jonson, Dramatist* (Cambridge: Cambridge University Press, 1984); Riggs, *Ben Jonson: A Life.*

13. Dryden used the term "dotages" in a parenthesis:

> As for *Johnson*, to whose Character I am now arriv'd, if we look upon him while he was himself, (for his last Playes were but his dotages) I think him the most learned and judicious Writer which any Theatre ever had.

From Craig, *Ben Jonson: The Critical Heritage*, 253. Later critics took up the term, expanded it to include potentially any play following *The Alchemist*, and often emphasized the notion that Jonson suffered from a "waning of the author's physical and intellectual vigor," as Larry Champion argues in *Ben Jonson's 'Dotages': A Reconsideration of the Late Plays* (Lexington: University of Kentucky Press, 1967), 3.

14. Miles, *Ben Jonson: His Life and Work*, 144.

15. In the discussion that follows I take information from the standard sources: Chambers, *The Elizabethan Stage*, 4 vols. (Oxford: Clarendon Press, 1923); G. E. Bentley, *The Jacobean and Caroline Stage*, 7 vols. (Oxford: Clarendon Press, 1941–68); C. H. Herford and Percy and Evelyn Simpsons' discussions of performance in *Ben Jonson*, 11 vols. (Oxford: Clarendon Press, 1925–52); and, of course, Robert Noyes, *Ben Jonson on the English Stage 1660–1776* (1935; reprint, New York: Benjamin Blom, 1966).

16. Herford and the Simpsons, *Ben Jonson*, 9:240.

17. Ibid.

18. Frances Teague, *The Curious History of "Bartholomew Fair"* (Lewisburg, Penn.: Bucknell University Press, 1985), chapter three.

19. Bentley, *The Jacobean and Caroline Stage* 4:632.

20. Since I am speculating so freely, I see no reason to let the play's textual problems stop me; nonetheless, the authority of the *Troilus and Cressida* epistle has been questioned. I quote from G. Blakemore Evans, *The Riverside Shakespeare* (Boston: Houghton Mifflin, 1974).

The Ordure of Things: Ben Jonson, Sir John Harington, and the Culture of Excrement in Early Modern England

Bruce Thomas Boehrer

In 1596 Sir John Harington published his *Metamorphosis of Ajax*, thereby filling a much-needed gap in the history of English letters.[1] The book's declared purpose is to introduce the flush toilet to England, and when Harington finally—after much preamble and general silliness—gets around to describing his invention, he contrasts it with the modes of waste disposal generally favored in sixteenth-century English houses:

> The first and the ancientest, is to make a close vault in the ground, widest in the bottome, and narrower upward, and to floor the same with lime and tarris . . . : for if it be so close as no aire can come in, it doth as it were smother the savour . . . Another way, is either upon close or open vaults, so to place the sieges or seats as behind them may rise tunnes of chimneys, to draw all the ill aires upwards: of which kind I may be bold to say, that our house of Lincolnes Inne, putteth downe all that have bene made afore it.[2]

Neither of these arrangements is adequate, in Harington's opinion, for neither one genuinely moves the offending matter through and out of the living space in question. Instead, both aim primarily to deposit the contents of human bowels into the more capacious bowels of the buildings those human beings inhabit. Hence the mock-epideictic reference to Lincoln's Inn, guaranteed to make any senior-bencher wince; one of the grand institutions of English law would appear, saving your reverence, to have been built upon a vast and ever-expanding midden.

Harington exploits this insight gently, but with a certain glee; among his objections to the old ways of handling dung, he notes explicitly that "in a Princes house [as well as, we may assume, in public edifices like Lincoln's Inn] where so many mouthes be fed, a close vault will fil quickly" (162). Indeed, early modern commenta-

174

tors suggest that once the privy vaults of such buildings were filled to overflowing, the denizens tended to load every rift with ore; as one country adage of the day observed, "A great housekeeper is sure of nothinge for his good cheare save a great Turd at his gate."[3] The trick, for Harington, is to liberate such buildings from an economy of waste retention and connect them to an economy of waste expulsion instead, and his primary instrument for doing so is the sublimatory medium of the written word. Thus Harington's project rapidly acquires not just a visceral, but also a rhetorical character. As the author's metamorphosed jakes seeks "to convey away both the ordure & other noisome things, as also the raine water that falles into the courts" of great houses (160), so his prose describes—and in describing, helps to constitute—a process of excremental circulation from, to, and among the various texts of classical antiquity and European modernity. As the author's fecal matter is to mingle with the local rainwater, so his book is to celebrate a pisspot with a classical name, derived from "the ancient house of AJAX" (69), and celebrated previously by Rabelais (68), Ovid (71), Martial (97), Saint Augustine (71), Sir Thomas More (101), John Heywood (102–03), and even holy writ itself (86–87).

In his day, Harington was as noted for his epigrammatic wit as for his exploits in the field of sanitary engineering; he was more or less equally renowned, that is, for circulating filth on both the alimentary and the rhetorical levels. The latter measure of his fame descended, in turn, to the other great epigrammatist of the English Renaissance, Ben Jonson, and therefore it is perhaps fitting that Jonson should conclude his only book of epigrams with the feculent mock-epic "On the Famous Voyage"—a poem that itself concludes with a brief homage to "hi[m], that sung A-IAX" (196). The present essay regards this work as marking a point of juncture between the scatological concerns of Harington and those of Jonson; as a result, I shall argue, Jonson's epigram invites readers to reexamine the much-vexed issue of its author's anality, and to supplement the psychoanalytic embedment of that issue with information drawn from social history. In effect, I want to propose a revised notion of Jonson as an anal poet. Counter to Edmund Wilson's famous vision of him as a "constipated writer well primed with sack,"[4] given over wholly to "the hoarding and withholding instinct,"[5] I would suggest that the poet's anality—like Harington's before him—takes form in large part as a sustained exploration of alternative strategies for the treatment and disposal of excrement. This effort enlists the author's rhetorical capacities simultaneously as a supplement to, an alternative for, and a symbolic conduit for the ordure it represents. Furthermore, the scatology of "On the Famous Voyage" parallels a historical return to processes of waste management characteristic of Jonson's beloved antiquity.[6] Finally, the poem helps reshape Jonson's own reputation as an early neoclassicist, for whom—to borrow a phrase from Roland Barthes—"language . . . was transparent, . . . flowed and left no deposit."[7] The resultant version of Jonson extends Joseph Loewenstein's claim that the poet "has allowed his very body to leave an imprint on his creativity,"[8] for the poet's body emerges as self-consciously constituted through the ambient processes whereby it and its products are integrated into society as a whole.

1

A Chinese proverb maintains that "waste is treasure,"[9] thereby rendering explicit an equation long taken for granted by anus psychology. Freud, and Sandor Ferenczi following Freud, and Ernest Jones following both, have traced this correspondence in detail through a series of conversions and equivalencies that they consider fundamental to the constitution of the adult ego[10]; on this view children grow out of an initial, jealous fascination with their own dung by a combined process of sublimation and repression, gradually replacing the feces themselves with such substitutes as mud, marbles, buttons, and coins. Mainstream Freudian analysis views this sequence of displacements as a primary instance of the principle that "the mind evolves from the body and . . . the body and its functions continue throughout life to influence how we feel and how we think"[11]; if therefore, as Loewenstein has argued, Jonson's body has left an imprint upon his creativity, that imprint may at least partly be explained through Freudian models of anal substitution.

Such explanations have been proposed and debated more or less continuously ever since Wilson's original identification of anal motifs in the Jonson corpus. The present essay seeks to contribute to this process by coordinating an analysis of the author's work with a consideration of the anal development of Elizabethan and Jacobean social practice in general. In other words, I want to return to Freud's original claim that psychic ontogeny recapitulates phylogeny, for this claim, properly considered, must exert some influence upon any assessment of the development of individual writers. If, as Freud argued, anal erotism falls victim in individual cases to "the sexual repression which advances along with civilization,"[12] it is at least worth considering the precise forms this advance has taken before we dismiss a writer like Jonson as an anal neurotic. Moreover, in the case of early modern England, one encounters records of a society virtually consumed by tropes of anal retention and aggression. Jonson's anality, such as it is, deserves to be considered in the context of these records at least as much as it deserves to be evaluated from the standpoint of twentieth-century psychoanalytic theory.

David Riggs has pointed the way toward such a consideration in his distinguished recent biography of Jonson. Noting that the poet's childhood home in Hartshorn Lane abutted "one of the major sewage canals in the greater London area,"[13] Riggs has identified the waste-is-treasure equation as a point of contact between the formal preoccupations of Jonson's work and the historical circumstances of his upbringing as a bricklayer's stepson. For Riggs, a Jonsonian character like the treasure-burying Jacques de Prie, of *The Case Is Altered*, offers a dramatic instance both of the poet's oedipal aggression and of his fascination with the products of the alimentary tract. When, for instance, de Prie hides his wealth within a pile of excrement (3.5), Riggs sees him as assuming the role of a "wicked stepfather—the villain of an archetypal family romance" who, "carrying his scuttle full of horse dung, . . . resembles nothing so much as a bricklayer bearing a load of malodorous mortar."[14] Thus, within the compass of *The Case Is Altered*, de Prie can serve as an outlet for Jonson's primal animosity: a fantasy substitute for "the man who married [Jonson's] mother and tried to make a bricklayer out of him."[15]

This suggestive analysis only invites correction through its emphasis upon the idiosyncratic aspect of Jonson's anality. If the poet was preoccupied with what we might call the social significance of the anus, he was not alone in that respect; nor should his interest in matters excremental be regarded merely as an outgrowth of his family circumstances. Sir John Harington, for one, produces his own version of Jacques de Prie early in the *Metamorphosis of Ajax:*

an Hermit being carried in an evening, by the conduct of an Angell, through a great citie, to contemplate the great wickednesse daily and hourly wrought therein; met in the street a gongfarmer with his cart full laden, no man envying his full measure. (85)

The course of this tale is predictable. The hermit "stopt his nosthrils, & betooke him to the other side of the street," whereas "the Angell kept on his way, seeming no whit offended with the savour"; yet soon thereafter, "a woman gorgeously attyred, well perfumed, well attended with coaches" passed by, causing the angel to cringe and "hasten . . . him selfe away"; and thus the story concludes that "this fine courtesan laden with sinne, was a more stinking savour afore God & his holy Angels, then that beastly cart, laden with excrements" (85).

In effect, Harington's dung farmer can serve as a distraction for hermits and angels precisely because he is a distraction for Harington's readers in general. Occupying a necessary position in the social order, he exists outside that order at the same time, as the distinct point at which tropes of civilized waste disposal metamorphose into patterns of "beastly" waste retention. (Indeed, the London dung farmer tended to traffic more or less indiscriminately in both human and animal excrements, thereby further undermining his own status within culture.) Circumscribed by rituals of physical avoidance and required by law to do his work at night,[16] he toils his way forward with a "full measure" that arouses no one's envy, in large part because everyone has had a role in producing it. As a result, the dung farmer comes to stand metonymically for the ordure it is his job to collect; the very process of conveying away our accumulated filth returns it to us in his new and altogether more animate form.

This excremental return of the repressed seems to have taken various shapes in early modern English towns and cities. Thus, for instance, the large institutions of the land—great houses, universities, ecclesiastical and legal buildings, and so on—constructed "vaults," closed or open, to hold the filthy treasure of their respective inhabitants, and as these receptacles filled, their contents were typically exhumed and conveyed away by dung farmers like the hapless fellow of Harington's anecdote. In other words, such latrines never really did the work they were designed for; rather than hiding away the users' excrement once and for all, they simply held it for later withdrawal, rather as a bank holds its own peculiar deposits. As for the withdrawal itself, it was scarcely a welcome sight, and was therefore relegated by statute to those hours of the evening when it could be most concertedly ignored; yet nonetheless, the excremental holdings of Renaissance great houses tended to accrue interest in the form of a pervasive stench. Again and again, Harington complains about the odors of Renaissance latrines. He alludes to the "stately stinking privy in the Inner Temple" (173); he objects to the "infection or annoyance" of old-fashioned toilets on the ground that "Sensus non fallitur in proprio obiecto" ["Sensation is not deceived in an object that is near to it" (163)]; and in an elegant combination of euphuistic prose and Aristotelian categories, he remarks that "Ajax was alwayes so strong a man, that this strength being an inseparable accident to him, doth now onely remain in his breath" (78). To this extent, The Metamorphosis of Ajax develops out of a system of waste management in which anal retention and anal expulsion remain at constant and frustrating loggerheads.

Beyond the privileged confines of great houses, the social mechanisms of anal retention assumed a much more aggressive form in early modern England. Recent historical research on the "relatively urban and compact" Lancashire town of Prescot has traced out regular patterns of dung accumulation that would have been typical of many English towns and villages in the sixteenth and seventeenth centuries.[17] From 1580 on, the inhabitants of Prescot enjoyed the statutory right "to pile solid waste products in the street near their doors for up to a week"; moreover, citizens regularly left their middens on the street for much greater lengths of time, and could apparently secure the right to do so by paying "a fee, sometimes called a 'tax,' that went for street repairs"; and in any event citizens who wished to maintain a permanent (or semipermanent) dunghill on their property could "avoid the fee by piling dung on the back side of their residence."[18] These middens may have been composed primarily of animal, as opposed to human, refuse; early modern agricultural manuals make mention of both, but primarily of the former. In any case, however, the distinction between animal excrement and human sewage tended to erode steadily as urbanization took its course.

Indeed, the fact that citizens were willing to pay a fee for the privilege of accumulating shit points, in turn, to the pervasive presence of the waste-is-treasure motif in modes of early English household and city management. The fee was worth paying because the shit was worth keeping. And kept it was; contrary to the popular view of early modern streets—a view encouraged by "Mac Flecknoe" and Swift's "Description of a City Shower"—as clogged with discarded waste matter, such streets seem often to have been clogged with *non*discarded waste matter. Even William Shakespeare's father was fined a shilling in 1552 "for making a dungheap (*sterquinarium*) before his house in Henley Street," Stratford-upon-Avon,[19] and while John Shakespeare does not seem to have regarded this midden as part of his overall estate, it was nonetheless clearly his. Similar stories abound—among them the case of William Conygrave of Southwark, haled into court in 1605 because he slaughtered hogs on his property, "and wth the filth & excrements Comminge of the said hoggs [did] much annoye & hurt all his neighbours . . . by raysing of great stinks & stenches."[20] Likewise, turning again to Stuart Prescot, we find that when the innkeeper Thomas Parr died in 1680 he held assorted turds in the value of £3 13s. 4d., or "four percent of his total worth"; furthermore, "another eleven inventories of inhabitants of Stuart Prescot mentioned between 6d. and 20s. in dung and muck."[21] The township itself reserved the right to confiscate and sell dung that was unclaimed or illegally piled.[22] In the nearby village of Ormskirk a "carter"—a professional relative of the "gongfarmer" in Harington's *Metamorphosis*—"was paid 5s. annually to carry away for his own use each Monday whatever 'small heaps and Cobbs of Dung' he found in the streets."[23] In short, "dung was a valuable commodity in pre-industrial society for improving soil fertility,"[24] and for other functions as well. As Trinh Minh-ha has remarked, "Wet dung remains an environmental potential. In many societies it serves to plaster earthen walls, protecting them from the weather";[25] nor was this practice alien to early modern England, where plaster was regularly concocted out of a mixture of lime, sand, straw, and animal dung. In addition, there is at least some evidence to suggest that laystalls were occasionally used as landfills for marshland reclamation.[26]

However, the patterns of agrarian waste retention typical of England's farming communities do not necessarily apply to the increasingly urban landscape of seventeenth-century London and Westminster. Indeed, if the townspeople of Prescot tended to treat their dung differently than did the inhabitants of great houses—hoarding it openly for agricultural use whereas the latter hoarded it privily for eventual removal—we may expect the exigencies of London life to generate a different accommodation between the imperatives of retention and excretion. Even the documents of Stuart Prescot indicate that local authorities had begun to react to population increases in the late seventeenth century by assuming a "less tolerant attitude" toward public health issues,[27] and the question of how to handle large accumulations of fecal matter must have begun to trouble Londoners at a much earlier date. Records show that "even as far back as Edward I, the Fleet river was a nuisance" to Londoners[28]; Stow's *Survey of London* could note in the reign of Elizabeth I that the suburbs between the Tower and Wapping had recently developed into "a continuall streete, or filthy straight passage, with Alleyes of small tenements or Cottages"[29]; in the reign of Henry VIII, moreover, the city's "main streets had been paved for the first time . . . with runnels to permit sewage to escape more rapidly to the Fleet River and to the Thames"[30]; and the relatively few buildings lucky enough to border one of the local rivers simply placed their privies directly athwart the water itself.

One obvious result of these arrangements was that different sorts of waste matter tended to commingle indiscriminately. Whereas rural communities seem to have made an effort to distinguish between different varieties of animal droppings (which were of particular nutritional value for different crops), as well as between animal droppings and human waste, no such distinction was worth pursuing in an urban environment. Human sewage, animal droppings, animal offal, and every sort of garbage thus tended to collect together in kennels and laystalls. A further consequence of such arrangements was the rapid pollution of the local waterways, particularly the Fleet, which had become a vast open privy by the end of the eighteenth century; indeed, "in Charles Dickens's time it was still reasonable to describe the Thames itself as an enormous sewer that ebbed and flowed."[31] Moreover, the pollution of the Fleet and related waterways had reached a crucial stage by the reign of James I; within a few years of the publication of "On the Famous Voyage," James's Parliaments enacted a series of laws expanding previous provisions for cleansing of the city. The initial such statute, 3 James I, cap. 14, reaffirms, in more or less *pro forma* fashion, an old Henrician law establishing a local commission of sewers; but then follows a series of other acts without any precedent. A later statute, 3 James I, cap. 18, seeks to divert waters from outside the London area into the city itself and entrusts this job to the commission of sewers; 4 James I, cap. 12 stipulates that the said waters be conveyed by closed vault rather than by open ditch; and 7 James I, cap. 9 provides that a closed waterway be built from Hackney marsh and the river Lea to "the King's College at Chelsey."[32] These laws, in turn, find an echo in the "nine Proclamations against spending the legal-term holidays in London . . . issued by King James between 1614 and 1627 [sic] . . . to curb the inordinate growth of the metropolis."[33] Taken as a whole, such legislation suggests a dawning awareness that London could not continue indefinitely to transact infrastructural business as usual.

In sum, Tudor and Stuart London, with its rapid population growth and concomitant municipal works, tended to rely upon the waste disposal systems of the great houses, supplemented by the capacities of the local rivers. As the city's accumulated waste increased in mass, its agrarian value tended to diminish, and city dwellers reacted by depositing enormous quantities of it into chamber pots and privy vaults, then into sewer conduits, then into the local waterways—where it remained, stinking and congealing, until the nineteenth century. By then, the disadvantages of this system of waste management were manifest. The Fleet, whose vapors had long since taken on a life of their own, was roofed over in the mid-1700s (Edmund Wilson mistakenly believed this had been done in Jonson's time)[34]; a series of cholera epidemics culminated in the Great Stink of 1858, when the odors of the Thames forced Parliament into recess; and as a result the London Metropolitan Board of Works began excavating an ambitious series of new sewer lines which would eventually divert the city's waste far downstream, to Beckton and Crossness. Likewise, in 1775, the Londoner Alexander Cummings took out a patent upon Harington's old invention of the valve toilet, which grew steadily more common and came to be indisseverably associated, in popular memory, with the risible name of Thomas Crapper.[35] After three centuries of stench and neglect and concerted fecal retention, Ajax had finally achieved his long-awaited metamorphosis.

Thus we can trace a broad pattern, from English great houses to farming villages to London itself, of vacillation over how best to address the business of sewage disposal: whether by retention and sublimation, by expulsion and reaction-formation, or by some uneasy amalgam of these processes. In general, the tendency to retain and recycle seems to have done best in rural communities, whereas the impulse to expel and sublimate gained greater vigor as London and other urban areas grew in size and importance. Still further, however, individuals seem to have explored at least one other model of how to do things with turds; the men and women of Renaissance England occasionally used the fruit of their bodies, in more or less deliberate ways, to counteract the imperatives of civilization, discipline, and politicosocial restraint. Or to be more blunt, people used their sewage for a kind of rebellious fun, often at the expense of others. This extension of Bakhtinian carnival, with distinguished literary antecedents that include the work of Aristophanes and Hipponax and the latrine poems of the Greek Anthology,[36] appears repeatedly in English legal records of the early modern period. Jonson himself alludes to the "grave fart . . . let in Parliament" in 1607 to object to a proposal from the House of Lords (the utterer of the fart in question was Sir Henry Ludlow, and his eloquence seems to have elicited some admiration).[37] Keith Thomas likewise recalls the 1598 case of a Cambridge man who allegedly disrupted church services with his "most loathsome farting, striking, and scoffing speeches."[38] Then there is the case of John Kibbitt, a servant in Leighe, Essex, who was charged on 2 October 1630, "for that in prophane manner in tyme of the sermon upon a Sundaye, in the afternoon he did——in the church into the hat of one that sate by him."[39] For a late medieval instance of similar behavior, one wonders what could have been in the minds of Joan de Armenters and William de Thorneye when they "removed the privy-wall (claustram) and roof" from their tenement's single house of easement, "so that the extremities of those sitting upon the seats [could] be seen, a thing which is abominable and altogether intolerable."[40]

Such behavior may constitute a special instance of the tendency to retain waste. However, to my mind, the impulse to make one's sewage part of the family estate is categorically distinct from the desire to rub one's neighbors' noses in filth. If that is indeed the case, then any reading of Jonson's "On the Famous Voyage" should identify, as an important part of the poem's historical context, at least three different, interrelated, and popular strategies for the cultural disposition of offal: the urge to retain and transform, the desire to expel and ignore, and the impulse toward carnivalesque *enmerdement*. The remainder of this essay will argue, first, that Jonson's work explores all three of these strategies to one degree or another; second, that in doing so it presages an exceptionally fertile notion of the cultural instrumentality of anal behavior; and third, that commentators on Jonson have on occasion sought to narrow this fecundity in ways that fail to do justice to the poet's achievement as a whole.

2

The events of Jonson's "On the Famous Voyage" occur precisely in the heart of London's old-style sewage system, in the Fleet Ditch itself. The poem's two mock-heroes, Thomas Shelton and Sir Christopher Heydon,[41] undertake to sail a small boat up the Ditch from its confluence with the Thames at Bridewell to its northern limit at Holborn Bridge. This itinerary traverses the full length of the Fleet itself; above Holborn, it took on various different names, and arguably a different epistemological status as well. In its more rural reaches it was known as "the Hole-bourne, or stream in the hollow," referring to the deep valley of the lower part of its course,"[42] and it was also called "the River of Wells, from the many wells or springs that fed it."[43] Near Holborn, on the other hand, "it was called Turnmill Brook, from the mills on its banks."[44] Finally, running parallel to and immediately beyond the old western walls of London, the north-to-south stretch of the Ditch itself was defined by its contiguity to the city rather than by its relation to its source. Thus if, as Nicholas Barton has observed, "the history of the Fleet River has been described as a decline from a river to a brook, from a brook to a ditch, and from a ditch to a drain,"[45] in Jonson's day this decline was apparent not as a temporal so much as a spatial phenomenon. The Ditch becomes for Jonson a geographical counterpart to the dung farmer of Harington's *Metamorphosis:* a liminal manifestation of the city that excludes it, and a space in which the city's accumulated, ignored filth may therefore reappear in new, disturbing forms.

As for those forms themselves, they are characterized by a grim, seriocomic tenacity, confounding all efforts at civilized repression even while demonstrating the manifest importance of keeping one's waste unseen. The Fleet Ditch functions almost as a repository of the city's collective unconscious; it is a place where nothing gets lost, and where things that one would like to lose have a habit of turning up again and again. Turds "languish . . . stucke vpon the wall" of the ditch (136), or, having been "precipitated downe the jakes," they nonetheless survive to swim "abroad in ample flakes" (137–38), or again they simply lie "heap'd like an vsurers masse" in the accumulated sludge—neither liquid nor precisely solid—of the ditch itself (139). These unsavory products of the alimentary tract, in turn, meet in the Ditch an image of their former selves:

> Cats there lay diuers had beene flead, and rosted,
> And, after mouldie growne, again were tosted,
> Then, selling not, a dish was tane to mince 'hem,
> But still, it seem'd, the ranknesse did conuince [i.e.,
>   betray] 'hem.
>
> (149–53)

As the cats go through their various culinary incarnations and are consigned to the Ditch, eaten or uneaten, so too the gaseous byproduct of digestion finds its way to the same spot:

> Here, seu'rall ghosts did flit
> About the shore, of farts, but late departed,
> White, black, blew, greene, and in more formes out-started,
> Than all those *Atomi* ridiculous,
> Whereof old DEMOCRITE, and HILL NICHOLAS,
> One said, the other swore, the world consists.
>
> (124–29)

The metamorphic variety of the Ditch is that of the world itself, in an alienated and repressed valence. Within the compass of the Fleet, dung meets meat meets flatulence, and the base elements of Democritean science are perpetually regenerated in the process.

Hence the mock-heroic character of Jonson's poem. Shelton and Heydon acquire a debased epic stature ("right able / To haue beene stiled of King ARTHVRS table" [23–24]) because the Ditch itself is a congeries of figures and situations from Graeco-Roman myth. A recrudescence of the classical underworld, populated by "ghosts . . .

of farts," a Scylla-figure "Ycleped *Mud*" (62), and sundry other literary atavisms, the landscape of "On the Famous Voyage" stands in
relation to its enveloping cultural matrix as the Fleet Ditch stands in
relation to the city of London; it is composed from pieces of floating
pagan debris that keep popping up incongruously amidst a thousand
years of Christian repression. The Ditch's counterpart to "bold BRI-
AREUS" (81), for instance, turns out to be an offal-laden barge,
which in turn does double duty, on festival days, as "the Lord *Maiors*
foist" (120); monsters from classical myth thus melt into the quotidian business of London waste disposal, which itself survives as a
ghost (of farts?) in the Lord Mayor's pageant machine. Likewise,
the spirit of "MERCVRY" rains down "*ab excelsis*" upon the voyag-
ing heroes (96), having himself been transformed into "potions, /
Suppositories, cataplasmes, and lotions" for the treatment of venereal
disease (101–2). Just as the Fleet Ditch harbors the cast-off elements
of Democritean natural philosophy, so, too, it preserves those of
Pythagorean metaphysics:

> But 'mongst these *Tiberts* [the discarded carcasses of
>   uneaten cats], who d'you thinke there was?
> Old BANKES the iuggler, our PYTHAGORAS,
> Graue tutor to the learned horse. Both which,
> Being, beyond sea, burned for one witch:
> Their spirits transmigrated to a cat.
>
>   (155–59)

Like the Lord Mayor's pageant barge and the messenger of the Roman gods, even the ghosts of a(n un)dead[46] mountebank and his
performing horse get reprocessed by the retentive capacities of the
Ditch. Nothing there, or anywhere, goes to waste.

Indeed, this tendency to rediscover and preserve discarded waste
matter not only characterizes individual lines of Jonson's epigram;
it reappears as the structural principle of the poem's overall narrative.
Just as (contrary to the adage that "this too shall pass") the filth in
the Fleet refuses to go away, so, too, the heroes of the famous voyage
itself end up precisely where they started. Jonson's narrative supplies
an appearance of purposeful motion, as the heroes embark from
Bridewell Dock and head northward, moving through three major
challenges on their way to Holborn; however, the challenges themselves are never resolved, and the poem's ending, as James Riddell
has observed, "is both obvious and otiose."[47] Indeed, as Shelton
and Heyden move from one obstacle to another—from the "vgly
monster, / Ycleped *Mud*" (61–62) to a dung-barge "So huge, it
seem'd, they could by no meanes quite her" (86), and finally to

their culminating vision of "Old BANKES the iuggler" (156)—the wording of the verse carefully suggests that their progress is illusory. The mud refuses to go away, and in fact it is described in grosser detail at the end of the poem than at the beginning; the rubbish-lighter not only seems, but is, too big to evade, for it will certainly reappear at the appropriate city pageant; and Bankes, who is both metempsychosal and inconveniently alive when Jonson describes him as dead, obviously presents problems for any notion of straightforward passing. As for the conclusion of the heroes' exploit, it simply sends them "back, without protraction" to the spot from which their journey began (192). The memorial Shelton and Heydon earn for themselves by thus traversing an endless river of sewage is itself clearly redundant, for "In memorie of [their] most liquid deed, / The citie hath since rais'd a Pyramide" (193–94). That pyramid, correlative to the "vsurers masse" of ordure in the Fleet Ditch, was arguably there all along—only perhaps a bit less lofty and fetid. Moreover, this fecal monument constitutes yet another piece of re-processed and transfigured classical refuse; in recalling the Horatian "Exegi monumentum aere perennius / regalique situ pyramidum altius" ["I have completed a monument more lasting than brass, / And higher than the fabric of royal pyramids"], the celebratory pyramid elides Jonson's verse with the very filth it describes and celebrates. We are left with a moment of almost Yeatsian transcendence, in which one cannot tell the dancer from the dance, or the song from the sump.

At least since the time of Swinburne, critics have deplored "On the Famous Voyage" as "a hideous and unsavoury burlesque,"[48] as "the plunge of a Parisian diver into the cesspool,"[49] and as a "morceau repugnant [de la] grossierete rabelaisienne."[50] More recently, scholars like Wesley Trimpi, Peter Medine, and Bruce Smith have argued that Jonson's scatological epigram functions as a more or less broad-based condemnation of Jacobean London, its citizens, and various of its literary and sanitary practices.[51] (Indeed, for Smith the poem's final lines become a thinly veiled attack on Harington, and in this one respect—although not in most others—I must disagree with Smith's findings.) Both of these views strike me as largely justifiable, but their most particular interest derives from the fact that, despite their apparent incompatibility, they can nonetheless occupy the same literary space. Jonson's work can be characterized both as a Rabelaisian hog-wallow and as an effort at neoclassical purification, and criticism should be able to account for this duality as something other than mere paradox. Likewise for Edmund Wilson's notion of Jonsonian anality in general: the most concerted recent rejoinder to Wilson has pointed out that while "an inordinate number of Jonson's characters" are indeed "uncompromisingly anal," still

> Wilson's version of Ben Jonson is neither a complete nor a fecund truth. If the retentive character is defined by stinginess, to what do we attribute the extraordinary abundance . . . of Jonson's creativity? And what accounts for a play like *Bartholomew Fair* [or a poem like "On the Famous Voyage"], which not only celebrates the anus, but is a paean to every orifice, every bodily fluid, every quiddity of man's [sic] animal nature . . . To argue that such bounty is nothing but a transformation of miserliness leads to a nightmarish world, where nothing is but what is not.[52]

On this view, the tensions that structure critical response to "On the Famous Voyage," when writ large, structure response to Jonson's career as a whole.

As Peter Stallybrass and Allon White have summarized matters,

> Jonson emphasized the notion of the "gathered self," which . . . presents such a closed face to the world that it is invulnerable to invasion and always remains "untouch'd." Yet within his writings Jonson also projected a self quite antithetical to this, the man "of prodigious waste," "laden with bellie," who knew "the fury of men's gullets."[53]

"On the Famous Voyage" develops out of a geographical space that itself embodies this antithesis; testimony to "the fury of men's gullets," the Fleet Ditch likewise exemplifies the dramatic urbanization and concomitant repression that subtend the development of modern civilization in the West. The duality of Jonson's verse arguably arises from this fact, rather than from any unique predisposition to anal neurosis on the part of the poet himself. To put this case as simply as possible: Jonson writes the epic of a society trying to come to terms with its own sewage. If he cannot quite decide what to do with it all, if his thought oscillates between the opposed, coextensive, and equally unsatisfactory poles of sublimation and reaction-formation, at least he is not alone.

3

Indeed, in "On the Famous Voyage" sublimation tends to enable reaction-formation, and vice versa. Jonson's reformation of the abuses of Jacobean society depends not only upon the existence of such abuses, but upon his capacity to represent them in print; likewise, such representation justifies itself as a means of reprocessing actual filth through modes of literary substitution. Harington clearly understood this interdependence, and he made it the subject of a long introductory section to his *Metamorphosis*. Worried that readers might consider his work obscene, Harington insists repeatedly that it is in fact a means of combatting obscenity, and that "He that would scorne a Physition, because for our infirmities sake, he refuseth not sometime the noisome view of our lothsomest excrements, were worthy to have no helpe by Physicke" (83); yet by the same token, Thomas Nashe could speculate of Harington's work, "What shold moue him to [publish] it I know not, except he [m]eant to bid a turd in all gentle readers teeth."[54] Likewise, Jonson's scatological writing displays a pervasive awareness of the extent to which efforts at civilized—and civilizing—repression must founder upon "the anal priority of human beings."[55]

This observation, in turn, may help explain the poem's placement at the end of the 1616 *Epigrammes*—which Jonson himself, with perhaps an unintended fecal resonance, called "*the ripest of my studies*" (8:25). After all, one governing concern of the epigrams is, in George Rowe's words, to establish "hierarchy and order out of . . . confusion,"[56] or, as Richard Helgerson has remarked, to demonstrate "the power of exclusion" by "heroically drawing the line" between virtue and vice, excellence and mediocrity.[57] To this extent, the epigrams are an exceptionally repressive literary instrument; they exist for the purpose of tidying things up, sorting the acceptable from the unacceptable, the clean from the unclean. Yet this sustained effort culminates in a poem that manifestly challenges any such activity; as Bruce Smith has observed, "On the Famous Voyage" can scarcely even be called an epigram,[58] and while it may lend itself to various modes of interpretation and categorization, it is manifestly unconfined by criteria of linguistic decorum or organizational clarity. Awaiting the reader at the promised end of Jonson's meticulous epideictic and satirical discriminations, this last poem sits like a pile of untreated garbage, and, like the garbage it describes, it refuses to go away. It constitutes the external limit of Jonsonian classicism, both negating and enabling all that has preceded it.

That Jonson should take pains to include this negation within the body of his work would suggest, at least, that he was sensitive to its status as the starting point for his own creativity. Various models of critical activity—including psychoanalytic, Bakhtinian, poststructuralist, and feminist theories—have focused upon the irreducible alterity of signification, and Jonson's paean to the Fleet Ditch would seem, among other things, to be a self-conscious acceptance of the extent to which the poet's work is always already determined by the Other it must and yet cannot exclude. In characterizing this relationship, Trinh Minh-ha has recently used the language of Zen, in which "The One is the All and the All is the One; and yet the One remains the One and the All the All. Not two, not One either."[59] Bakhtin's work on Rabelais, which no study of Jonson should ignore, makes much the same point. Discussing the presence of excremental images in late-medieval billingsgate, Bakhtin remarks that

> each image is subject to the meaning of the whole; each reflects a single concept of a contradictory world of becoming, even though the image may be separately presented. Through its participation in the whole, each of these images is deeply ambivalent, being intimately related to life-death-birth. This is why such images are devoid of cynicism and coarseness in our sense of the words. But these things, such as the tossing of excrement and drenching in urine, become coarse and cynical if they are seen from the point of view of another ideology.[60]

The standard myth of Jonson as an anal neurotic fails in large part because it represents an unwarranted narrowing of this vision—a narrowing that is unjust both to Jonson and to psychoanalytic theory. In 1908, when first introducing his views on anal erotism, Freud concentrated upon defining the characteristics of what we now term the anal-retentive personality. These qualities—orderliness, parsimony, and obstinacy—exist, Freud argues, "as the first and most constant results of the sublimation of anal erotism."[61] Yet even in this earliest brief study of the subject, Freud observes that sublimation is not the only way of dealing with the erotogenicity of the anal canal, out of which adult character traits may develop either as "unchanged prolongations of original instincts, or sublimations of those instincts, or reaction-formations against them."[62] To be sure, Freud's terminology is itself untidy—and perhaps wisely so, for subsequent efforts, such as those of Ernest Jones,[63] to distinguish completely between the psychic mechanisms of sublimation and reaction-formation are not entirely satisfactory. Thus, although Freud groups orderliness, parsimony, and obstinacy together as instances of anal sublimation, in his very next paragraph he redefines orderliness as "a reaction-formation against an interest in what is unclean and disturbing and should not be part of the body"[64]; moreover, his focus upon the unstably exclusive categories of sublimation and reaction-formation leads him away from the question of what constitutes an "original instinct" and/or its "unchanged prolongation." Yet even so, this earliest work on the subject of anality suggests sublimation to be only one of several interrelated, coextensive psychic mechanisms. When

Freud returns to the subject five years later, his linkage of anal eroto-genicity with sadism complicates matters further.[65]

As Sandor Ferenczi observed after Freud, "A part of anal-erotism is not sublimated at all, but remains in its original form. Even the most cultivated normal being displays an interest in his [sic] evacuation functions which stands in a curious contradiction to the abhorrence and disgust that he manifests when he sees or hears anything of the kind in regard to other people."[66] Indeed, Ernest Jones's "Anal-Erotic Character Traits" describes a whole panoply of disparate and sometimes exclusive behavioral mechanisms as typical of anal erotism; they include (but are not limited to) all forms of collecting,[67] "giving-out,"[68] cleaning,[69] staining and contaminating,[70] "sculpture, architecture, wood-carving, photography, etc.,"[71] and even grafitti writing.[72] Given this impressive and incomplete catalogue, one could reasonably ask what kind of behavior is *not* implicated in anal-erotism. Traditional notions of Ben Jonson as a "negative and recessive" personality,[73] "impoverished emotionally" by his excremental fixations,[74] effect a narrowing of psychoanalytic theory in which anality becomes synonymous with neurosis, and in which anal-erotic impulses find their satisfaction only via a kind of niggardly retention. It need hardly be added that such a reading of psychoanalysis is itself both grudging and retentive, leading to the construction of Ben Jonson as one of the two great anal basket cases of English literary history. (Swift deserves mention as the other.) But Jonson himself knew better than to accept such an impoverished vision.

4

So far, this essay has argued that the culture of excrement in early modern England displays concurrent and contradictory tendencies toward retention and expulsion—or, in Freudian terminology, sublimation and reaction-formation; that "On the Famous Voyage," like its precursor in the work of Harington, exploits both of these tendencies; that in the process it demonstrates an awareness of the ways in which such contradictory tendencies enable and depend upon one another; and that therefore Jonson's poem helps us to revise, rather than simply to discard, traditional notions of Jonson himself as an anal poet. In the event, one is left with a Jonson whose fascination for the workings of the anus is neither impoverished nor unhealthy nor unique. If anything, it is marked by an extraordinary richness of range and capacity, encompassing the extremes of reaction-formation through the poet's famous rage for order; of sublimation through his voluminous literary output as well as his notoriously bad temper; and of an unrepressed and unabashed interest in shit for shit's sake.

Indeed, one could go a step further in revising Jonson's reputation, for the poet's credentials as an anal neurotic are seriously affected by any effort to consider him within a wide range of competing personalities. The early modern period offers a rich variety of historical figures whose attitudes toward excrement were at least as pronounced as—and arguably more imbalanced than—Jonson's own, and who therefore stand in marked contrast to Jonson in terms of individual temperament and cultural significance. If one wants the anality of reaction-formation, after all, there is always Elizabeth I, whose stinginess, meager diet, distrust of doctors, wicked temper, and inclination to micromanage the affairs of her courtiers were all legendary, even in her own day. For sublimation, one need only bury oneself in the logarithmically expanding piles of theological discourse that flowed from the pens of Luther, his detractors, and his followers. For the fecal obsession in all its unrepressed glory, one may turn to Jonson's own prince and patron, James I, who earned an early reputation both for revelling in toilet humor and for fouling his hose under stress. Given this context, one can only admire the range and robustness of Jonson's commitment to exploring the various strategies his culture had articulated for the material and psychic disposal of human waste.

If the present analysis is correct, Jonson's fascination with the products of the alimentary tract cannot simply be deplored as a symptom of emotional morbidity, nor can it be dismissed as irrelevant to the poet's overall literary achievement. On the contrary, it constitutes a sustained inquiry into the conditions that make his achievement possible in the first place. Jonson's scatology may be viewed as robust or perverse, naive or satirical, but its outstanding quality is its capacity to remain within and outside of all these categories at once. Like the waste it represents, Jonson's excremental verse refuses to be disposed of once and for all; it keeps coming back in different shapes that cannot be entirely ignored or dismissed, sublimated or repressed.

Indeed, if one wants a graphic historical instance of the failure of such sublimations and repressions, one need not turn to the English Renaissance at all. One might be tempted, for instance, to draw attention to Peru's recent cholera outbreak—an epidemic linked, like those of nineteenth-century London, to problems of public sanitation; but in the event there is more resonant matter at hand. The dung barge of Jonson's final epigram, or a vessel very like it, reappeared on the international scene in 1987, laden with more than three thousand tons of garbage from New York City and Long Island, and plying its way south through the Atlantic in search of a safe place to deposit its cargo. Ironically, the barge itself—the *Mobro*—and its attendant tugboat—the *Break of Dawn*—had set out in one more failed attempt to reconcile the imperatives of anal expulsion with those of retention and recycling; the vessels were initially engaged by Alabama businessman Lowell Harrelson, and they were to bear their cargo to North Carolina, "where, after ripening for a time, it would give off methane gas, which could be sold at a tidy profit."[75]

The sequel to this venture is now matter of near-legend. Six states and three nations rebelled at the prospect of being gongfarmers to the city of New York, and the *Mobro* eventually returned to Long Island in disrepute. As it was shunted away from one prospective dumping ground after another, newscasts followed its daily progress, symbolically repatriating America's trash in America's living rooms, and demonstrating to all who wished to notice that the contents of Fleet Ditch cannot be ignored, buried, carted away, channeled downstream, or dumped in Third World nations. In fact, even the rhetoric of the event held its ironies. Johnny Carson, who had made predictable capital out of the garbage barge in his comedy monologues, was eventually informed by reporters that a good bit of the *Mobro*'s trash had come from a film studio—the Kaufman Astoria—of which he himself was part owner. Putting the best possible face on matters, a Carson spokesperson responded by quoting Ecclesiastes: "Cast thy bread upon the waters: for thou shalt find it after many days."[76] As Sir John Harington understood, Lincoln's Inn was built on this trash. Jonson knew it, too.[77]

Notes

1. The research and writing of this essay were substantially finished in May 1993. Since then, I have become aware of the work done, on similar lines, in Gail Paster's *The Body Embarrassed: Drama and the Disciplines of Shame in Early Modern England* (Ithaca: Cornell University Press, 1993). Paster does not deal with Jonson's "On the Famous Voyage," and her discussion of anality tends to focus upon the processes of repression documented by Norbert Elias. But her work (esp. pp. 112–62) is of great importance as a more generalized treatment of the matters that this essay surveys with respect to a particular Jonsonian poem.

2. Sir John Harington, *The Metamorphosis of Ajax*, ed. Elizabeth Story Donno (New York: Columbia University Press, 1962), 161–63. Further references are to this edition.

3. Quoted in Lawrence Stone, *The Crisis of the Aristocracy* (Oxford: Clarendon Press, 1965), 562.

4. Edmund Wilson, *The Triple Thinkers: Twelve Essays on Literary Subjects* (New York: Oxford University Press, 1948), 226.

5. Ibid., 218.

6. It is of at least incidental interest that Harington's new jakes was apparently a re-invention of technology used by the Minoans (Roy Palmer, *The Water Closet: A New History* [Newton Abbott: David & Charles, 1973], 14). Neither Jonson nor Harington could have known this particular fact; however, both authors were distinctly interested in classical civilizations which made more than an incidental investment in matters of civil engineering.

7. Roland Barthes, *Writing Degree Zero*, trans. Annette Lavers and Colin Smith (New York: Farrar, Straus & Giroux, 1968), 3. In the most influential description of Jonson as a stylistic neoclassicist, Wesley Trimpi relates the Jonsonian plain style to a Ciceronian rhetoric whose "language will be pure . . . , plain and clear" (*Ben Jonson's Poems: A Study of the Plain Style* [Stanford: Stanford University Press, 1962], 60). Similarly, Judith Gardiner notes that "Jonson's 'plain style' throughout the epigrams is fairly consistent, with its frequent use of abstract diction, unobtrusive imagery, functional figures of sound and rhythm, simple rhetorical structures, and highly articulated syntax" (*Craftsmanship in Context: The Development of Ben Jonson's Poetry* [The Hague: Mouton, 1975], 52). Richard Flantz credits Jonson with "helping to establish in England . . . a plain-style genre modeled on Latinate forms" ("The Authority of Truth: Jonson's Mastery of Measure and the Founding of the Modern Plain-Style Lyric," in Claude J. Summers and Ted-Larry Pebworth, eds., *Classic and Cavalier: Essays on Jonson and the Sons of Ben* [Pittsburgh: University of Pittsburgh Press, 1982], 59).

8. Joseph Loewenstein, "The Jonsonian Corpulence, or The Poet as Mouthpiece," *ELH* 53.3 (Fall 1986): 508.

9. Quoted in Martin Pops, "The Metamorphosis of Shit," *Salmagundi* 56 (Spring 1982): 50.

10. See Freud, "Character and Anal Erotism" and "The Disposition to Obsessional Neurosis" (1908 and 1913 respectively; all references to Freud are to *The Complete Psychological Works of Sigmund Freud*, ed. James Strachey [London: Hogarth Press, 1952–1964]); Ferenczi, "The Ontogenesis of the Interest in Money" (1914; collected in *Sex in Psycho-Analysis*, trans. Ernest Jones [New York: n.p., 1950]); and Jones, "Anal-Erotic Character Traits" (1918; in *Papers on Psycho-Analysis* [Baltimore: Williams & Wilkins, 1949]).

11. Leonard Shengold, *Halo in the Sky: Observations on Anality and Defense* (New York: Guilford Press, 1988), 12.

12. Freud, *Civilization and Its Discontents*, in *The Complete Psychological Works*, 21:106.

13. David Riggs, *Ben Jonson: A Biography* (Cambridge, Mass.: Harvard University Press, 1989), 10.

14. Ibid., 30.

15. Ibid., 31.

16. Ernest Sabine, writing in "Latrines and Cesspools of Mediaeval London" (*Speculum* 9 [1934], 317) mistakenly claimed this ordinance to be of Restoration origin; however, Anthony Munday's enlargement of Stow's *Survey of London*, published in 1633, lists among the "Statutes of the Streets of this City" the provision that "No Goungfermour shall carry any Ordure till after nine of the clocke in the night" (John Stow, *The Survey of London: Conteyning The Originall, Increase, Moderne Estate, and Government of that City . . . inlarged by . . . A[nthony] M[unday]* (London, 1633), sig. 3L2v).

17. Walter King, "How High Is Too High? Disposing of Dung in Seventeenth-Century Prescot," *Sixteenth Century Journal* 23, no. 3 (Fall 1992): 444.

18. Ibid.

19. Samuel Schoenbaum, *Shakespeare's Lives* (Oxford: Clarendon Press, 1991), 7.

20. London Public Record Office Assize 35, 47/5, m. 40.

21. King, "How High," 447.

22. Ibid., 444.

23. Ibid., 447.

24. Ibid., 447.

25. Trinh Minh-ha, *Woman, Native, Other: Writing Postcoloniality and Feminism* (Bloomington: Indiana University Press, 1989), 54.

26. Stow notes, for instance, that by his time Finsbury Fields had been drained and "made main and hard ground, . . . since the which time, also the further grounds beyond Fensbury Court have been so overheightened with Laystalls of dung, that now three windmills are thereon set" (John Stow, *A Survey of London*, ed. Charles Lethbridge Kingsfield [Oxford: Clarendon Press, 1908], 2:71; further references to Stow are to this edition). Stow further notes that Moorditch had become "a verie narrow, and the same a filthie channell, or altogither stopped up for Gardens planted, and houses builded thereon" (1:19). A handwritten archivist's note in the London Guildhall Record Office copy of Geoffrey Cumberledge's *The Corporation of London: Its Origin, Constitution, Powers and Duties* ([Oxford: Oxford University Press, 1950], 129) adds that even into the early 1900s refuse was removed from London to "marshland at Rainham, 130 acres having been purchased in 1903 of John Abbott for £23,411."

27. King, "How High," 454.

28. John Ashton, *The Fleet: Its River, Prison, and Marriages* (London: T. Fisher Unwin, 1889), 26.

29. Stow, *Survey of London*, 2:71.

30. Christopher Trent, *Greater London: Its Growth and Development Through Two Thousand Years* (London: Phoenix House, 1965), 83.

31. Ibid., 139.

32. *Statutes at Large* (London: King's Printer, 1767–1866), vol. 6.

33. Stone, *Crisis*, 397.

34. Wilson, *Triple Thinkers*, 228.

35. Palmer, *Water Closet*, 22, 106.

36. Jeffrey Henderson's *The Maculate Muse: Obscene Language in Attic Comedy* (New York: Oxford University Press, 1991) naturally pays close attention to Aristophanes, who, according to Henderson, uses scatology "primarily in slapstick routines," as "a way to degrade a character" (54), and in the construction of "scatophagous insults" (192). George Rowe, in turn, has argued convincingly that Jonson is indebted to Aristophanes for a vocabulary of competition and aggression—the very vocabulary of which Aristophanes's scatology was an integral part (*Distinguishing Jonson: Imitation, Rivalry, and the Direction of a Literary Career* [Lincoln: University of Nebraska Press, 1988], 105–12).

37. Ben Jonson, "On the Famous Voyage," 108, in *Ben Jonson*, ed. C. H. Herford and Percy and Evelyn Simpson (Oxford: Clarendon Press, 1925–1952), vol. 8. Further references to Jonson's work are to this edition.

38. Keith Thomas, *Religion and the Decline of Magic* (Harmondsworth: Penguin, 1978), 192.

39. J. S. Cockburn, ed., *Calendar of Assize Records, Essex Indictments, Charles I* (London: Her Majesty's Stationery Office, 1982), 252.

40. Helena Chew and William Kellaway, eds., *London Assize of Nuisance 1301–1341: A Calendar* (Chatham: W. and J. Mackay, 1973), 79.

41. Peter Medine, "Object and Intent in Jonson's 'Famous Voyage'," *Studies in English Literature* 15 (Winter 1975): 100–103.

42. Nicholas Barton, *The Lost Rivers of London* (London: Leicester University Press, 1962), 29.

43. Edward H. Sugden, *A Topographical Dictionary to the Works of Shakespeare and his Fellow Dramatists* (Manchester: Manchester University Press, 1925), 194.

44. Ibid., 194.

45. Barton, *Lost Rivers*, 29.

46. Herford and Simpson note that Jonson refers to Bankes in *Every Man Out* (4.6.60) as well as the present poem, that records indicate Bankes was still alive in 1625, and that he became a vintner in Cheapside (11:32).

47. James Riddell, "The Arrangement of Ben Jonson's *Epigrammes*," *Studies in English Literature* 27 (1987), 54.

48. Herford and Simpson, *Ben Jonson*, 2:341.

49. Algernon Charles Swinburne, *A Study of Ben Jonson* (London: Chatto & Windus, 1889), 95.

50. Maurice Castelain, *Ben Jonson, l'homme et l'oeuvre* (Paris: Hachette, 1907), 765 n.

51. Trimpi, *Ben Jonson's Poems*, 97–98; Medine, "Object and Intent," 105–10; Bruce Smith, "Ben Jonson's *Epigrammes*: Portrait-Gallery, Theater, Commonwealth," *Studies in English Literature* 14 (Winter 1974): 109.

52. E. Pearlman, "Ben Jonson: An Anatomy," *English Literary Renaissance* 9 (1979): 366.

53. Peter Stallybrass and Allon White, *The Politics and Poetics of Transgression* (Ithaca: Cornell University Press, 1986), 78.

54. Thomas Nashe, *The Works of Thomas Nashe*, ed. R. B. McKerrow (Oxford: Basil Blackwell, 1958), 5:195.

55. Pops, "Metamorphosis of Shit," 27.

56. Rowe, *Distinguishing Jonson*, 21.

57. Richard Helgerson, *Self-Crowned Laureates: Spenser, Jonson, Milton, and the Literary System* (Berkeley: University of California Press, 1983), 171.

58. Smith, "Ben Jonson's *Epigrammes*," 109.

59. Trinh, *Woman, Native, Other*, 39.

60. Mikhail Bakhtin, *Rabelais and His World*, trans. Helene Iswolsky (Bloomington: Indiana University Press, 1984), 149–50.

61. Freud, "Character and Anal Erotism," in *The Complete Psychological Works*, 9:171.

62. Freud, "Character," 9:175.

63. Jones, "Anal-Erotic Character Traits," 436.

64. Freud, "Character," 9:172.

65. Freud, "The Disposition to Obsessional Neurosis," in *The Complete Psychological Works*, 12:320–21.

66. Ferenczi, "Ontogenesis," 328.

67. Jones, "Anal-Erotic Character Traits," 430.

68. Ibid., 432.

69. Ibid., 431.

70. Ibid., 432.

71. Ibid., 433.

72. Ibid., 432.

73. Wilson, *Triple Thinkers*, 221.

74. Pearlman, "An Anatomy," 366.

75. Andy Logan, "Around City Hall: Everything that Rises," *The New Yorker* 63 (15 June 1987): 88.

76. Ibid., 89–90.

77. I am grateful to Ralph Berry, Barbara DeMent, David Lee Miller, Arthur Searle, and Jerome Stern for various kinds of help with this work. I am also indebted to Florida State University for a Developing Scholar Award that enabled me to complete the research for this study.

"Not of an Age": Jonson, Shakespeare, and the Verdicts of Posterity

Ian Donaldson

1

"He was not of an age, but for all time!" declared Ben Jonson in his poem "To the Memory of My Beloved, The Author, Mr William Shakespeare, and What He Hath Left Us," that stands at the head of Shakespeare's 1623 first folio.[1] These were brave words in 1623: no one until then had so positively asserted the perennial and enduring nature of Shakespeare's genius, hailing him so boldly as a writer *for all time.* By the late eighteenth century Jonson's phrase had changed from a lively prediction to an uncontested truism. Shakespeare had by then self-evidently stood the test of time and appeared to belong to more ages than one. In the late twentieth century the tribute has become debatable: Shakespeare is no longer viewed as a timeless and transhistorical genius, but as a textual phenomenon that is constantly reconstructed, constantly reinvented, constantly reinterpreted by every age according to its needs, priorities, and preconceptions. At the end of his memorial poem, Jonson figures Shakespeare as a fixed star, shining chidingly and cheeringly from the heavens throughout all time. For Gary Taylor, Shakespeare is no longer a star but a black hole, an insatiable vortex, "spinning, sucking, growing," a source and center of massive critical turbulence.[2] In this new and sharply relativist vision, Shakespeare has become, as Derek Longhurst puts it in the title of a recent revisionist essay, "*Not for all time, but for an Age.*"[3]

The variations in Ben Jonson's own literary reputation, as I wish to show, have been similarly linked to changing historicist assumptions, his writings having been at various times valued and devalued on account of their supposed relationship to the age in which Ben Jonson lived—and of the supposed relationship of *that* age to the historical present. The author who vowed to show "an Image of the times," to "oppose a mirrour" to the audiences that viewed his plays, who was hailed in turn at his death as the "Mirror of our *Age!*", was judged by the late seventeenth century and early eighteenth century to have reflected all too faithfully the manners and mores of his bygone times.[4] Historicized (so to speak) out of existence, Jonson was to be seen as an author fit chiefly for antiquarian study; a poet of his age, perhaps, but scarcely *for all time.*

The shape of this story is in part chiasmic, with Jonson's star sinking as Shakespeare's climbs ever higher in the skies. Nothing so exciting or voracious as a black hole, Jonson was to move quietly into a part of the literary heavens where, for years to come, he would not be much admired or even much observed. The story is also circular: for the age which Jonson and Shakespeare were thought (variously) to have represented and transcended was largely an imaginary construct, fabricated out of the very writings of the authors themselves. The story thus concerns the conjunction of "history" and "literature," and the use (and misuse) of literary texts as historical evidence.

2

> Soule of the Age!
> The applause! delight! the wonder of our Stage!
> My *Shakespeare*, rise. . . .

(17–19)

When Ben Jonson's great poem of tribute was published in 1623, Shakespeare had been dead for seven years. A minor Oxfordshire poet named William Basse had already written some memorial verses celebrating Shakespeare as a kind of distinguished literary corpse, worthy to be squeezed by some means or other into the great bed of fame. In Basse's rhapsodic vision, the bed seems already uncomfortably crowded.

> Renowned Spenser, lye a thought more nye
> To learned Chaucer, and rare Beaumont, lye
> A little neerer Spenser to make roome
> ffor Shakespeare in your threefold, fowerfold Tombe.[5]

Jonson chooses to see Shakespeare not as a corpse to be bedded down, but as a living spirit to be summoned up: "My *Shakespeare*, rise."

> I will not lodge thee by
> *Chaucer,* or *Spenser,* or bid *Beaumont* lye
> A little further, to make thee a roome:
> Thou art a Moniment, withoute a tombe,
> And art alive still, while thy Booke doth live,
> And we have wits to read, and praise to give.
>
> (19–24)

The age of which Shakespeare is the soul is the present age, as well as that in which he literally lived. The word "Soule" is carefully chosen. Jonson uses the word elsewhere quite precisely in relation to literary texts. In the 1606 quarto of *Hymenaei* he distinguishes the text of that masque, which will survive to posterity, from its spectacular and scenic elements, devised by Inigo Jones, which are transitory and ephemeral.

> It is a noble and just advantage, that the things subjected to *understanding* have of those which are objected to *sense,* that the one sort are but momentarie, and meerely taking, the other impressing, and lasting: Else the glorie of all these *solemnities* had perish'd like a blaze, and gone out in the beholders eyes. So short-lived are the *bodies* of all things, in comparison of their *soules.* And though *bodies* oft-times have the ill luck to be sensually preferr'd, they find afterwards, the good fortune (when *soules* live) to be utterly forgotten. (1–10)

Shakespeare is the *soul* of his age, then, in the sense that he represents that element which will endure and carry to posterity. There is consequently a faint air of paradox but no actual contradiction when Jonson moves to his supreme tribute to Shakespeare, to the phrase that is now carved in stone on the exterior of the Folger Shakespeare Library: "*He was not of an age, but for all time!*" (43). Shakespeare is the soul of the age, but is not of an age: the double truth is nicely poised.[6]

By the Restoration, the age of Shakespeare and of Jonson already seemed remote; those placid, far-off days before the Civil War were now "the last age," "the age before the flood."[7] With the growing sense of temporal distance came a new sense of cultural progressivism. Dryden in his epilogue to the second part of *The Conquest of Granada*[8] in 1672 measures the advance of English manners and English dramatic writing since the final years of Queen Elizabeth and the early years of King James, "When men were dull, and conversation low" (4). To the more cultivated audiences of the Restoration, the comedy of Jonson seemed dated, labored, gross.

Then, Comedy was faultless, but 'twas course:
Cobbs Tankard was a jest, and *Otter*'s horse

. . . .

Wit's now arriv'd to a more high degree;
Our native Language more refin'd and free.
Our Ladies and our men now speak more wit
In conversation, than those Poets writ.

(5–6, 23–26)

Dryden's own good fortune is now "To please an Age more Gallant than the last" (34).

It is tempting to regard this epilogue as itself no more than an act of strategic gallantry toward those audiences whose gallantry it ingratiatingly salutes. Dryden's compliment rests upon the premise that dramatists are of necessity the products and mirrors of the societies for which they collusively and mimetically write. Whether, and how, a writer such as Shakespeare may transcend his age is a question that is never seriously addressed; indeed, it is a necessary part of Dryden's strategy in the epilogue to keep the very name of Shakespeare, which might threaten the cogency of his proposition, safely out of sight. Instead he concentrates his attention upon Jonson, firmly relegating him to the dull mechanic age for which he conformingly wrote. There is nonetheless a noticeable ambivalence about the way in which Dryden seems at once to concede and to deny the supremacy of his dramatic predecessors. That ambivalence is more clearly evident in Dryden's essay written in defense of the epilogue later in the same year, "On the Dramatic Poetry of the Last Age."[9] In this more measured and generous, yet still determinedly progressivist account, Dryden acknowledges the greatness of Jonson and Shakespeare, but attempts to demonstrate in a more detailed way how deeply their work is flawed by the cultural backwardnesss of the age in which they lived. Many of his examples may seem, to modern eyes, somewhat unpersuasive. Both writers, we are told, resorted on occasions to puns and wordplay; Jonson at times finished a sentence with a preposition, and was known occasionally to use a Latinism at the expense of a common English word; both Shakespeare and Jonson used the double comparative from time to time; some of Shakespeare's plots seem nowadays ridiculous and incoherent. Neither writer had the benefit of listening to polite conversation at the court of Charles II, and their dramatic dialogue suffered accordingly.

What is remarkable about this account is the way in which it attempts to substantiate a general view of an entire historical period—one might almost say, a general view of the processes of history—

from a handful of literary texts; indeed, from certain aspects of those texts which to readers in another age might seem of very slight significance. Small changes in linguistic and grammatical usage that have occurred between the age of Shakespeare and the age of Dryden are taken as evidence of a larger process of cultural refinement. The late Elizabethan/early Jacobean period is historically constructed as a culturally primitive age which nevertheless produced, by a process of inexplicable paradox, the greatest dramatists the English stage has ever known.

G. E. Bentley has argued that, up until the time of Dryden, it was Jonson and not Shakespeare who was widely regarded as England's "arch poet," her supreme literary genius; and that when Shakespeare's reputation began at last to move ahead of Jonson's in the 1690s, this was largely owing to the testimony of Dryden himself.[10] The next century was to witness the rapid and spectacular rise of Shakespeare's reputation and a corresponding plummeting in the fortunes of Ben Jonson.[11] These two phenomena are intimately and complicatedly related: the greatness of Shakespeare being often explained throughout the eighteenth century by contrastive reference to the supposed weaknesses of Jonson, which are in turn regularly highlighted by reference to the seemingly opposite practice of Shakespeare. I want to concentrate here upon one aspect of this complex realignment of literary reputations by looking at the way in which the promotion of Shakespeare's reputation necessitated his being detached more and more from the supposedly primitive age in which he lived, idealized to a transcendental role, seen as belonging to *no age;* while the subordination of Jonson necessitated, conversely, that he be increasingly associated with and relegated to the age in which he lived, seen as its product, its chronicler, and ultimately its victim.

This process begins with the routine explanation that such faults as Shakespeare possessed could be attributed to the times in which he lived, and that he himself in his own person somehow stood free of guilt. Initially this indulgence was granted to three major writers, Shakespeare, Jonson, and Fletcher; progressively it was to be reduced. "Their Slips were more the Age's Fault than theirs," wrote Robert Gould in his poem *The Play-House: A Satyr* in 1695:

> Where *Fletcher's* loose, 'twas Writ to serve the *Stage,*
> And *Shakespeare* play'd with Words to please a Quibbling
> Age.[12]

Much was to be said about this quibbling age in the years to come. "As for his Jingling sometimes, and playing upon Words, it was the common Vice of the Age he liv'd in," wrote Nicholas Rowe in his edition of the works of Shakespeare in 1709 (viciously completing his sentence with a preposition).[13] Charles Gildon the following year agreed with Rowe: Shakespeare's faults were to be ascribed to "the Ignorance of the Age he liv'd in."[14] Elijah Fenton expressed his opinion in couplets in 1711:

> *Shakespeare* the Genius of our Isle, whose Mind—
> The universal Mirror of Mankind—
> Express'd all Images, enrich'd the Stage
> But stoop'd too low to please a barb'rous Age.
> When his Immortal Bays began to grow
> Rude was the Language, and the Humour Low.[15]

The processes of bardolatry and transcendentalism are here already visible. Shakespeare is now not merely "the Genius of our Isle," but "the universal Mirror of Mankind." Yet it would seem Shakespeare also mirrored the language and humor of the barbarous age in which he lived. His genius appears to have survived despite this regrettable contact; it is not seen in any sense to have been nourished by the age. "The Faults of Shakespeare, which are rather those of the Age in which he liv'd," pronounced John Dennis in 1719, "are his perpetual Rambles, and his apparent Duplicity (in some of his Plays) or Triplicity of Action, and the frequent breaking the Continuity of the Scenes."[16] As for "the poor witticisms and conceits" of Shakespeare, Sir Thomas Hanmer explained in his edition of Shakespeare in 1744, "it is to be remember'd that he wrote for the Stage, rude and unpolished as it then was; and the vicious taste of the age must stand condemn'd for them."[17] Shakespeare's *"jingles, puns,* and *quibbles,"* judged Zachary Grey a few years later, "were certainly owing to the false taste of the times in which he lived."[18]

In all these examples it is clear that two things are happening. First, an agreed historical view of the late Tudor and early Stuart age is being consolidated from literary evidence: the evidence of puns, double plots, indecorous witticisms, which, taken together, are thought sufficient to stamp the age as vicious and barbarous. No other literary, cultural, or social factors are brought under consideration; how the age produced so many distinguished writers and artists is allowed to remain a mystery. Second, a rescue operation is being mounted on behalf of Shakespeare, who is gradually prized away from the age in which he unhappily lived, and "universalized" in such a way as to accommodate his work to eighteenth-century tastes and dispositions. Elizabeth Montagu in 1769 perfectly demonstrates these two coordinated rhetorical strategies:

> Shakespeare wrote at a time when learning was tinctured with pedantry, wit was unpolished and mirth ill-bred. The court of Elizabeth spoke a scientific jargon, and a certain obscurity of style was universally affected. James brought an addition of pedantry, accompanied by indecent and indelicate manners and language. By contagion, or from complaisance to the taste of the public, Shakespeare falls sometimes into the fashionable mode of writing. But this is only by fits, for many parts of all his plays are written with the most noble, elegant, and uncorrupted simplicity. Such is his merit that the more just and refined the taste of the nation has become the more he has encreased in reputation. He was approved by his own age, admired by the next, and is revered, and almost adored by the present.[19]

Dr. Johnson by a more strenuous process of argumentation arrived at a similar position. His editing of the works of Shakespeare is premised on the belief that, with the passage of time, Shakespeare's language, his allusions, his very systems of belief have become in many ways obscure, demanding editorial explication. "In order to make a true estimate of the abilities and merit of a Writer," he declares in his *Miscellaneous Observations on the Tragedy of "Macbeth"*, "it is always necessary to examine the genius of his age, and the opinions of his contemporaries."[20] Thus to understand *Macbeth* one must attempt to understand what Shakespeare and his contemporaries may have felt on the subject of witchcraft.[21] Johnson speaks frankly of the "barbarity" of Shakespeare's age. Yet Shakespeare's chief distinction, in Samuel Johnson's view, is that he ultimately transcends that age:

> Shakespeare is above all writers, at least above all modern writers, the poet of nature; the poet that holds up to his readers a faithful mirrour of manners and of life. His characters are not modified by the customs of particular places, unpractised by the rest of the world; by the peculiarities of studies or professions, which can operate but upon small numbers; or by the accidents of transient fashions or temporary opinions: they are the genuine progeny of common humanity, such as the world will always supply, and observation will always find. His persons act and speak by the influence of those general passions and principles by which all minds are agitated, and the whole system of life is continued in motion. In the writings of other poets a character is too often an individual; in those of Shakespeare it is commonly a species.[22]

Shakespeare in Samuel Johnson's analysis is presented as the poet of nature, not of a particular society; his work is seen to belong not merely to his age but to "common humanity," to exemplify what Johnson roundly calls "the whole system of life."

It remained for Coleridge to take the universalizing process one step further, dehistoricizing Shakespeare in a way that Dr. Johnson had not. "Shakespeare," wrote Coleridge in 1834,

> is of no age—nor, I may add, of any religion, or party, or profession. The body and substance of his works came out of the unfathomable depths of his own oceanic mind: his observation and reading, which was considerable, supplied him with the drapery of his figures.[23]

And again:

> Least of all poets colored in any particulars by the spirit or customs of his age, [so] that the spirit of all that it had pronounced intrinsically and permanently good concentrated and perfected itself in his mind. Thus we have neither the chivalry of the North, nothing indeed in any peculiar sense of the word, and as little of the genii and winged griffins of the East; in an age of religious and political heat nothing sectarian in religion or politics; in an age of misers so flagrant in all the dramas of his contemporaries and successors, no miser characters; in an age of witchcraft and astrology, no witches (for we must [not] be deluded by stage directions); but the female character, the craving for presight (Macbeth), all that must ever be elements of the social state, etc.[24]

The difference between Johnson's position and that of Coleridge is nicely indicated by that passing comment on the delusive nature of stage directions. For Johnson, it was necessary to remember that while Shakespeare spoke to modern sensibilities he also lived in an age in which people believed quite literally in the existence of witches. For Coleridge, the weird sisters of *Macbeth* are not witches but transhistorical beings, manifestations of "the female character," equally comprehensible, equally mysterious in any age, the recurrent products of human society.

3

While Shakespeare was being thus abstracted, generalized, and decontextualized, Ben Jonson was undergoing a contrary course of treatment. By the 1690s other critics were echoing Dryden's complaint that Jonson's plays seemed products of a bygone age. His characters were based on well-known types and personalities of that age, and yet, said one commentator,

> Such Representations are like Painters taking a Picture after the Life in the Apparel then Worn, which becomes Ungraceful or Ridiculous in the next Age, when the Fashion is out.[25]

Jonson was seen as having opportunistically exploited such fashions for satirical purposes within his plays. The character of Volpone, wrote one critic in the 1730s, was no doubt based upon some figure of the day, but the allusion, like others, is now lost on modern audiences.

> 'Tis highly probable that this Method of *Ben*'s might be of great Service, as to the immediate Fortune of his Plays, tho' at this Day it doubtless leaves us in the Dark, as to many Particulars which, if we had an exact Character of him against whom the Satyr is pointed, would become Beauties instead of being thought Defects; . . . such is the Variety of Characters presented in the Space of a few Years on the publick Theatre of Life, that in a short time the most striking grow antiquated, and the Publick by gazing continually on what passes in their own Times, lose all Ideas of what passed before. Hence it follows that not only *Johnson's* Plays, but all the Tribe of Writers who followed him, fail of moving a Modern Audience upon the Stage, or of entertaining them in their Closets.[26]

Having witnessed a revival of Jonson's comedy *The Silent Woman* in 1752, the theater historian Thomas Davies regretted that "the frequent allusions to forgotten customs and characters render it impossible to be ever revived with any probability of success. To understand Jonson's comedies perfectly," he went on, "we should have before us a satirical history of the age in which he lived."[27] History must now be brought to the service and understanding of dramatic literature. The difference between Shakespeare and Jonson, declared B. Walwyn in 1782, is that "the portraits of Shakespeare are made to last till Doomsday; while the lustring and fashionable shadows of the day drawn by Ben Jonson grow obsolete in the wearing of them."[28] It remained for Nathan Drake in 1817 to put the final nail in Jonson's coffin, by recalling and reversing the famous tribute which Jonson had once paid affectionately to Shakespeare:

> When Jonson, in his noble and generous eulogium on Shakespeare, tells us, that
> "He was not of an age, but for all time,"

he seized on a characteristic of which the reverse, in some degree, applies to himself; for had he paid less attention to the minutiae of his own age, and dedicated himself more to universal habits and feelings, his popularity would have nearly equalled that of the poet whom he loved and praised.[29]

There are several ironies in this developing contrast between the generalized, universalized, eternalized Shakespeare and the particularized, ephemeral, transitory Ben Jonson. For one thing, Jonson himself in his own lifetime had placed great faith in the judgment of posterity; however spurned or neglected his works might be in his own age, he never ceased to believe that their true value would be recognized in the years to come. When his Roman tragedy *Catiline* was hissed from the stage in 1611, Jonson defiantly published the text of the play, commending it to William Herbert, Earl of Pembroke, with a characteristic dedication:

> In so thick, and darke an ignorance, as now almost covers the age, I crave leave to stand near your light: and, by that, to bee read. Posteritie may pay your benefit the honor, & thanks: when it shall know, that you dare, in these Jig-given times, to countenance a legitimate Poeme. (1–6)

It was a strategic necessity in the eighteenth-century rescue of Shakespeare to insist that Shakespeare had done all that he could to reform the evil theatrical and linguistic practices of his day, and distance himself from them. "While the stage was thus over-run with ignorance, impertinence, and the lowest quibble, our immortal Shakespeare arose," wrote William Guthrie in 1747. "But supposing him to have produced a commission from that heaven whence he derived his genius, for the reformation of the stage, what could he do in the circumstances he was under? He did all that man and more than any man but himself could do."[30] The truth is, however, that Shakespeare did not see it as his divine mission to berate and reform the age or the stage, while Jonson undeniably did. It is Jonson who speaks of these jig-given times, of darkness and ignorance covering the age; it is Jonson who asserts, in the epistle dedicatory to *Volpone*, that the manners and natures of the writers of these days are inverted, that the age is one "wherein *Poetrie*, and the Professors of it heare so ill, on all sides, there will a reason bee look'd for in the subject" (11–12); it is Jonson who roundly declares, in his "Ode to Himself" written after the failure of *The New Inn*, "Come, leave the lothed stage, / And the more lothsome age." The first line of this ode has attracted more attention than the second; but how, one may ask, does Jonson, in this remarkable phrase, expect to leave the loathsome age, other than by death? The answer is: through his verse, which Jonson vows will "hit the starres" (58). It is as a star that Jonson finally pictures Shakespeare in the poem to his memory, through his rage or influence chiding or cheering the dropping stage. Jonson, too, aspired to an elevated position, somewhere remotely above "our Daintie age": "high and aloofe, / Safe from the wolves black jaw, and the dull Asses hoofe."[31]

"*Good men* are the Stars, the Planets of the Ages wherein they live, and illustrate the times," wrote Jonson in his commonplace book, *Discoveries* (1100–01). "These, sensuall men thought mad, because they would not be partakers, or practisers of their madnesse. But they, plac'd high on the top of all vertue, look'd downe on the Stage of the world, and contemned the Play of *Fortune*" (1104–08). The stars, the great figures who illustrate the age—illuminate it, make it illustrious—are paradoxically detached from it, placed high above like divine spectators of the play of human folly. It is as a star that Jonson depicts those great figures of his age whom he most admires: Lucy, Countess of Bedford; Elizabeth, Countess of Rutland; Henry, Lord La Warr; and the dead Sir Henry Morison, who

> leap'd the present age,
> Possest with holy rage,
> To see that bright eternall Day:
> Of which we *Priests*, and *Poets* say
> Such truths, as we expect for happy men
> And there he lives with memory; and *Ben*
>
> *Jonson*, who sung this of him, e're he went
> Himselfe to rest . . . [32]

In this remarkable figure, Jonson pictures himself, too, as having "leap'd the present age," already living mentally "*there*," in the elevated, priestlike region above his society where the dead Morison will find him.

Jonson returned repeatedly in his writings to the question of poetic survival. "The common Rymers powre forth Verses, such as they are, (*ex tempore*) but there never comes from them one Sense, worth the life of a Day," Jonson wrote in *Discoveries* (2445–48); "They had their humme; and, no more. Indeed, things, wrote with labour, deserve so to be read, and will last their Age" (2464–66). Jonson's tribute to Shakespeare, "He was not of an age, but for all time!", encapsulated his own most powerful ambitions: to live beyond his age, to be matched against the great writers of the past, to be admired by the unknown readers of the future. For Jonson, great poets lived

in effect out of time, or equally in all times, Horace and Virgil and
Homer inhabiting the present as though they were contemporaries.
As Oscar Wilde aptly remarked of Jonson, "He made the poets of
Greece and Rome terribly modern."[33]

4

Jonson was taught by one of the great historians of his day (William
Camden), admired and befriended others (Selden, Savile, Bacon, Ra-
leigh), and was deeply interested in the function and methodologies
of history.[34] But what kind of "historian" was Jonson himself? What
kind of "mirror" do his imaginative writings hold to the age; what
sort of "image of the times" do they present? Does Jonson deserve
the reputation which overtook him so disablingly in the eighteenth
century and which lingers in some form to the present day: the
reputation of a faithful chronicler whose work is locked irretrievably
within the confines of the age in which he lived and about which he
wrote; a writer routinely contrasted with the free-floating Shakespeare, whom Jan Kott a quarter of a century ago styled "our
contemporary"?

These are questions which can be addressed here only in the most
preliminary and partial way. To approach them, I want to look at
one form of historical representation which Jonson practiced and
examine the way in which he chose to describe a celebrated contemporary: his patron William Herbert, third Earl of Pembroke. This
case study isn't chosen entirely at random, for Jonson's account of
Pembroke has been thought by one scholar, Dick Taylor, Jr., to
be historically more trustworthy than the description of Pembroke
offered by the Earl of Clarendon in his *History of the Rebellion*,
constituting a characteristically dependable, characteristically Jonsonian "image of the times."[35] Yet it seems worth asking what kind
of mirror Jonson holds up to Pembroke, and how truly he depicts
both the man and the age in which he lived.

Clarendon's account of Pembroke in *The History of the Rebellion*
begins eulogistically. Pembroke, he declares, was well bred, learned,
witty, affable, generous, magnificent, pious, patriotic, just, and
courtly. As if to give credibility to this warmly admiring account,
Clarendon then adds a few more stringent words about the man:

> Yet his memory must not be so flattered that his virtues and good inclina-
> tions may be believed without some allay of vice, and without being
> clouded with great infirmities, which he had in too exorbitant a propor-

tion. He indulged to himself the pleasures of all kinds, almost in all excesses. Whether out of his natural constitution, or for want of his domestic content and delight, (for which he was most unhappy, for he paid much too dear for his wife's fortune by taking her person into the bargain) he was immoderately given up to women. But therein he likewise retained such a power and jurisdiction over his very appetite, that he was not so much transported with beauty and outward allurements, as with those advantages of the mind as manifested an extraordinary wit and spirit and knowledge, and administered great pleasure in the conversation. To these he sacrificed himself, his precious time, and much of his fortune.[36]

This part of Clarendon's account, as Taylor points out, was later seized upon by scholars keen to establish Pembroke as the young man celebrated in Shakespeare's sonnets. But how reliable a witness, Taylor asks, was Clarendon, and is his testimony really to be believed? Taylor notes that Clarendon was only twenty-three when Pembroke died in 1630, and that he had never been closely associated with Pembroke either socially or politically, nor with any of his colleagues. His account was (moreover) put together forty years after Pembroke's death. It is possible, Taylor suggests, that at this distance of time Clarendon may have confused William Herbert with his less admirable brother Philip.

As a better witness to the nature of Pembroke's character, Taylor summons Ben Jonson, who (he points out) was a close acquaintance of Pembroke and his family, had visited their various houses, associated with their friends, and would have been alert to court gossip and scandal. Jonson, Taylor adds, was a man of "sturdy integrity" who would not be likely to suppress the truth. The testimony that Taylor chooses to examine is Jonson's popular masque *The Gypsies Metamorphosed* that was performed before King James on three separate occasions in 1621. Pembroke is, in fact, addressed only briefly in this long, skittish, and lively masque, but the Jackman's speech of salutation is the evidence on which Taylor chooses to rest his case:

> Though you, Sir, be Chamberlaine, I have a key
> To open your fortune a little by the way:
>   You are a good Man,
>   Denie it that can;
>   And faithfull you are,
>   Denie it that dare.
> You knowe how to use your sword and your pen,
> And you love not alone the Arts, but the Men.
> The Graces and Muses everie where followe

You, as you were theire second *Apollo*.
Onelie your hand here tells you to your face,
  You have wanted one grace
To performe what hath beene a right of your place,
ffor by this line, which is *Mars* his trenche,
You never yet help'd your Master to a wench.
  'Tis well for your honor, hee's pious and chaste,
  Or you had most certainlie beene displac't.

(681–97)

How does one interpret these lines? There is, to begin with, the problem of tone. The masquing occasions are festive, and the Jackman's lines are in some sense bantering. As James wasn't best known for his chastity—or, for that matter, his love of wenches—the final couplet is more lighthearted than Taylor appears to recognize. Yet the speech is uttered in the king's presence, and in Pembroke's, and some caution is needed in the midst of merriment. In such circumstances, Jonson's silence concerning the alleged weaknesses of Pembroke's character can't really be taken as evidence that these weaknesses didn't exist. Jonson cannot have been ignorant, for example, of the fact that Pembroke had fathered the two illegitimate children of Sir Robert Sidney's daughter, Lady Mary Wroth, whom Jonson also celebrates repeatedly as a lady of exemplary virtue.[37]

To test Jonson's reliability as a witness, to understand the manner in which he chooses to depict his patron and his age, it would be necessary to think more carefully about the kind of relationship that probably subsisted between the two men. Jonson had known Pembroke since the early years of the century, and was beholden to him for many acts of protection and patronage. His 1605 letter of appeal to Pembroke from prison where Jonson had been confined for making fun of King James in the comedy *Eastward Ho* already suggests the existence of past favors.[38] Later Jonson was to tell William Drummond that Pembroke paid him twenty pounds every New Year's Day to buy books: a vital commodity for the impoverished poet.[39] It was to the protection of Pembroke that Jonson committed his tragedy *Catiline* after its disastrous performance in 1611, and it was to Pembroke (recently appointed Lord Chamberlain) that Jonson in 1616 strategically dedicated his *Epigrams*, "the ripest of my studies," which carried "danger in the sound" (4, 5). It was Pembroke who in 1619 recommended Jonson for an honorary degree at the University of Oxford, of which he was now Chancellor.[40] By the time Jonson came to write *The Gypsies Metamorphosed*, then, a complex relationship had developed between the two men; a relationship of patronage, on the one side, and dependency on the other. It's a relationship which places Jonson's "sturdy integrity" in a particular light, by which both his utterances and his silences need to be read.

If one were searching through Ben Jonson's writings for a more positive tribute to Pembroke's character, the obvious text to examine would be the one that Taylor oddly ignores: *Epigram* 102, "To William, Earl of Pembroke," published in Jonson's folio in 1616. Jonson's rehearsal of Pembroke's virtues in this poem, as it happens, closely resembles and endorses Clarendon's account. That Jonson says nothing here about Pembroke's amorous adventures is scarcely surprising in a poem addressed directly to Pembroke in a collection that is also dedicated to him. What Jonson offers in this poem is not a balanced assessment of moral character of the kind favored by Clarendon, but a starkly simplified and generalized vision of the age:

> I doe but name thee, PEMBROKE, and I find
>   It is an *Epigramme*, on all man-kind;
> Against the bad, but of, and to the good:
>   Both which are ask'd, to have thee understood.
> Nor could the age have mist thee, in this strife
>   Of vice and vertue; wherein all great life
> Almost, is exercis'd: and scarse one knowes
>   To which, yet, of the sides himselfe he owes.
> They follow vertue, for reward, to day;
>   To morrow vice, if shee give better pay
> And are so good, and bad, just at a price,
>   As nothing else discernes the vertue' or vice.
>
> (1–12)

"Bad," "good," "vice," "virtue": the moral "strife" which Jonson describes here is as sharply and clearly divided as the worlds of court masque and antimasque. Though struggle and doubt are mentioned, Pembroke himself is depicted in an unwavering stance, pitted "Against the bad, but of, and to the good." Though Pembroke is *named* in the poem's opening line, though his character is generally invoked, it is never particularly described; and the poem concludes with an appeal to examine a life that is lived, so to speak, outside the poem's rhetorical limits: "and they, that hope to see / The commonwealth still safe, must studie thee" (19–20).

One might almost say that this poem is scarcely about Pembroke at all, sketching instead a timeless and generalized figure of virtue, a type equally familiar to the poets of antiquity as to those of the seventeenth century; a type to which the real life William Herbert, by various rhetorical maneuvers, is brought to conform. The age referred to in this poem is not uniquely and specifically the age of

King James. It is a perennial and recurrent state, the times whose condition Cicero deplored, and which, like the poor, are always with us.[41] Jonson effortlessly reworks various passages from Seneca in order to construct a vision of the age in which he too happened to live.[42] Jonson's laments on the present age frequently derive in this way from classical sources, which in turn frequently posit the notion of an earlier age, when manners and morals were exemplary. The very ease with which this trope was deployed is indicative of Jonson's view of history, which he perceived not as a succession of entirely individual and unrepeatable experiences, events, personalities, and dilemmas, but as a recurrent and in part predictable process, presenting similar terrors, similar declines from innocence, similar threats to public order, similar exemplars of public virtue, over and over again.

The methods of modern historical scholarship illuminate the work of Ben Jonson only to a certain point. Turn the light higher, peer more closely, and what you find are not, after all, local and topical quiddities and particularities, the grainy texture of actual characters and events, but something more closely akin to what Samuel Johnson believed he had found in the works of Shakespeare: "those general passions and principles by which all minds are agitated, and the whole system of life is continued in motion"; the portrait not of an age, but of "common humanity."[43]

Notes

1. *Ungathered Verse*, 26.43. Throughout the essay, Jonson's works are cited from *Ben Jonson*, ed. C. H. Herford, Percy Simpson, and Evelyn Simpson, 11 vols. (Oxford: Clarendon, 1925–52). I/j and u/v spellings have been regularized.

2. Gary Taylor, *Reinventing Shakespeare* (London: Vintage, 1991), 410–11.

3. Derek Longhurst, "'Not for all time, but for an Age': An Approach to Shakespeare Studies," *Re-Reading English*, ed. Peter Widdowson (London: Methuen, 1982), 150–63.

4. *Every Man in his Humour*, prologue, 23; *Every Man out of his Humour*, Induction, 118 (cf. 3.6.202–7); Edmund Waller, "Upon Ben Johnson," *Ben Jonson*, 11:447.

5. William Basse, in *Poems* by Shakespeare (London, 1640).

6. The most helpful account of Jonson's poem is that of T. J. B. Spencer in "Ben Jonson on his beloved, The Author, Mr William Shakespeare," *The Elizabethan Theatre* 4 (1974): 22–40. Anthony Miller has pointed to Ciceronian borrowings in the poem and suggested that in the phrase "not of an age, but for all time!" Jonson may be recalling and outgoing Cicero's praise of each of the ancient poets and orators he hails as *princeps temporibus illis* ("Jonson's Praise of Shakespeare and Cicero's *De Oratore* III.vii," *Notes and Queries* 236 ns 38 [March 1991]).

7. See, for example, "To my Dear Friend Mr Congreve, on his COMEDY, call'd The Double Dealer" (*The Poems of John Dryden*, ed. James Kinsley, 4 vols. [Oxford: Oxford University Press, 1958], 2: 852–54).

8. *Poems of John Dryden* 1:134–35.

9. John Dryden, *Of Dramatic Poesy and Other Critical Essays*, ed. George Watson, 2 vols. (London: Dent, 1962), 1:169–83.

10. G. E. Bentley, *Shakespeare and Jonson: Their Reputations in the Seventeenth Century Compared*, 2 vols. (Chicago: University of Chicago Press, 1945). Bentley's methodology has been challenged, most notably by David L. Frost in *The School of Shakespeare* (Cambridge: Cambridge University Press, 1968). Details of Bentley's thesis certainly need correction, but the broad picture he gives of Jonson's commanding reputation throughout the seventeenth century seems indisputable.

11. Indispensable documentation is provided in Brian Vickers, *Shakespeare: The Critical Heritage*, 6 vols. (London: Routledge, 1974–81), and in D. H. Craig, *Ben Jonson: The Critical Heritage, 1599–1798* (London: Routledge, 1990). The secondary literature on this realignment is extensive. See R. G. Noyes, *Ben Jonson on the English Stage, 1660–1776* (Cambridge, Mass.: Harvard University Press, 1935); R. W. Babcock, *The Genesis of Shakespeare Idolatry, 1766–1799* (Chapel Hill: University of North Carolina Press, 1931); Stuart Tave, *The Amiable Humorist* (Chicago: University of Chicago Press, 1960); Jonathan Bate, *Shakespearean Constitutions* (Oxford: Clarendon, 1989); Margreta de Grazia, *Shakespeare Verbatim* (Oxford: Clarendon, 1991); and especially Howard Felperin, *The Uses of the Canon* (Oxford: Clarendon, 1990), chap. 1.

12. Robert Gould, *Works* (1709), quoted in Vickers, *Shakespeare*, 1:416.

13. Nicholas Rowe, ed. *Shakespeare* (1709); Vickers, *Shakespeare*, 2:197.

14. Charles Gildon, *An Essay on the Art, Rise, and Progress of the Stage in Greece, Rome, and England*, Vickers, *Shakespeare*, 2:217–18.

15. Elijah Fenton, *An Epistle to Mr. Southerne, From Kent;* Vickers, *Shakespeare*, 2:265.

16. John Dennis, *Letter to Judas Iscariot, Esq: "On the Degeneracy of the Publick Taste";* Vickers, *Shakespeare*, 2:351; cf. 2:282.

17. Sir Thomas Hanmer, ed., *The Works of Shakespeare*, Vickers, *Shakespeare*, 3:119.

18. Zachary Grey, et al., *Preface to Critical, Historical, and Explanatory Notes on Shakespeare*, 2 vols. (1754); Vickers, *Shakespeare*, 4:148.

19. Elizabeth Montagu, *An Essay on the Writings and Genius of Shakespeare;* Vickers, *Shakespeare*, 3:329.

20. Samuel Johnson, *Johnson on Shakespeare*, ed. Arthur Sherbo, vols. 7–8 of the Yale Edition of the Works of Samuel Johnson (New Haven: Yale University Press, 1968), 7:3.

21. Ibid.

22. "Preface to Shakespeare" (1765); *Johnson on Shakespeare*, 7:62.

23. Samuel Taylor Coleridge, *Table Talk*, 15 March 1834, in *Table Talk From Ben Jonson to Leigh Hunt*, ed. James Thornton (London: Dent, 1934), 251–52.

24. Samuel Taylor Coleridge, *Shakespearean Criticism*, ed. T. M. Raysor, 2 vols. (London: Dent, 1960), 1:216–17.

25. The opinion of "Julio" in James Wright's *Country Conversations* (1694; quoted in Noyes, *Ben Jonson*, 29).

26. Anonymous, *Memoirs of the Life of Robert Wilks, Esq.* (1732), vii–viii (quoted in Noyes, *Ben Jonson*, 29).

27. Thomas Davies, *Dramatic Miscellanies*, 2 vols. (London, 1784), 2:101–02.

28. B. Walwyn, *An Essay on Comedy* (1782); Vickers, *Shakespeare*, 6:327.

29. Nathan Drake, *Shakespeare and his Times*, 2 vols. (London, 1817), 2:580. Commenting on Jonson's tribute to Shakespeare, "Horatio" had reached a similar

verdict: "Ben's reputation was partly confined to the age in which he lived, and that which immediately succeeded to it. He delighted to catch the Cynthia of the minute; to paint the follies of the times, which are as uncertain as the forms of court-address, and as changeable as the fashions of our cloaths." *The Gentleman's Magazine* 42 (1772): 522.

30. William Guthrie, *An Essay upon English Tragedy;* Vickers, *Shakespeare,* 3:193.

31. *The Underwood* 23, ll. 31, 35–36.

32. Lucy, Countess of Bedford in *Epigrams* 94; Elizabeth, Countess of Rutland in *The Forest* 12.65; Henry, Lord La Warr in *The Underwood* 60.14; and Sir Henry Morison in *Underwood* 70.79–86.

33. Oscar Wilde, *The Artist as Critic: Critical Writings of Oscar Wilde,* ed. Richard Ellmann (New York: Random House, 1969), 34–35.

34. Blair Worden, "Ben Jonson Among the Historians," *Culture and Politics in Early Stuart England,* ed. Kevin Sharpe and Peter Lake (Basingstoke: Macmillan, 1994), 67–89.

35. Dick Taylor, Jr., "Clarendon and Jonson as Witnesses for the Earl of Pembroke's Character," *Studies in the English Renaissance Drama,* ed. Josephine W. Bennett, Oscar Cargill, and Vernon Hall, Jr. (New York: New York University Press, 1959), 322–44. On Pembroke, see also Taylor's essay "The Third Earl of Pembroke as a Patron of Poetry," *Tulane Studies in English* 5 (1950): 41–67; and Margot Heinemann, *Puritanism and Theatre* (Cambridge: Cambridge University Press, 1980); Michael G. Brennan, *Literary Patronage in the English Renaissance: The Pembroke Family* (London: Routledge, 1988); Brian O'Farrell, *Politician, Patron, Poet: William Herbert, Third Earl of Pembroke, 1580–1630* (Ann Arbor: University Microfilms, 1966); David Riggs, *Ben Jonson: A Life* (Cambridge, Mass.: Harvard University Press, 1989); and Robert C. Evans, *Ben Jonson and the Poetics of Patronage* (Lewisburg: Bucknell University Press, 1989).

36. Edward Hyde, First Earl of Clarendon, *The History of the Rebellion,* ed. W. Dunn Macreay, 6 vols. (Oxford, 1888), 71–74.

37. Josephine A. Roberts, *The Poems of Lady Mary Wroth* (Baton Rouge: Louisiana State University Press, 1983), 24–25. See Jonson, *The Alchemist,* folio dedication; *Epigrams* 102, 105; *The Underwood* 28; *Conversations with Drummond,* 355–56.

38. *Ben Jonson,* 1:199–200.

39. *Conversations with Drummond,* 312–13.

40. According to a marginal note by George Chapman (see *The Poems of George Chapman,* ed. P. B. Bartlett [New York: Russell, 1962], 478).

41. Ian Donaldson, "Jonson and the Moralists," *Two Renaissance Mythmakers,* ed. Alvin B. Kernan (Baltimore: Johns Hopkins University Press, 1977), 146–64.

42. For example, see G. B. Jackson's annotation in regard to the Elder Knowell's complaint against the times in *Every Man in His Humour* (folio: 2.5.1ff), an annotation which traces sources in Juvenal, Ovid, Horace, and Quintilian (*Every Man in His Humour,* ed. G. B. Jackson [New Haven: Yale University Press, 1969], 196–98).

43. Analyzing Jonson's procedures in his Roman tragedies, Philip Ayres reaches a similar conclusion: "The truth . . . is that to the materials of history he has so carefully sifted and assembled Jonson brings not the subtly discriminating mind of a historian but that same critical, simplifying eye of the moralist that critics have detected in his handling of the central 'tragic' characters, especially Tiberius and Sejanus. His Roman plays may be 'archaeologically' unexceptionable, but in the final analysis they are not, by Roman or for that matter Elizabethan standards, good history" (Philip Ayres, ed., *Sejanus His Fall* [Manchester: Manchester University Press, 1990], 30).

Contributors

BRUCE BOEHRER is an Associate Professor of English Renaissance literature at Florida State University and is the author of *Monarchy and Incest in Renaissance England*. His work on Ben Jonson has appeared in *PMLA, Philological Quarterly*, and *English Studies*.

JENNIFER BRADY coedited *Ben Jonson's 1616 Folio* with W. H. Herendeen and *Literary Transmission and Authority: Dryden and Other Writers* with Earl Miner. She has published essays on Jonson and Dryden in *Studies in English Literature, Studies in Philology, The Dalhousie Review*, and *Modern Language Quarterly: A Journal of Literary History*. She is an Associate Professor of English at Rhodes College, where she is Charles R. Glover Chair of English Studies.

IAN DONALDSON, Regius Professor of Rhetoric and English Literature at the University of Edinburgh, has edited Ben Jonson's poetry and is currently completing a life of Jonson. His recent publications include *Shaping Lives: Reflections on Biography* and *Jonson's Walk to Scotland*.

ROBERT C. EVANS is Distinguished Research Professor at Auburn University at Montgomery. His work on Jonson includes *Ben Jonson and the Poetics of Patronage; Jonson, Lipsius, and the Politics of Renaissance Stoicism; Jonson and the Contexts of His Time;* and *Habits of Mind: Evidence and Impact of Ben Jonson's Reading*. He is a member of the editorial board of the *Ben Jonson Journal*. His most recent work has focused on Martha Moulsworth, a newly discovered Renaissance poet.

JAMES HIRSH, an Associate Professor of English at Georgia State University, is the author of *The Structure of Shakespearean Scenes* and of articles in *Modern Language Quarterly, Essays in Theatre, Studies in the Novel, Shakespeare Quarterly*, and elsewhere. He edited *English Renaissance Drama and Audience Response*, the spring 1993 issue of *Studies in the Literary Imagination*. He was a scholar-in-residence at the Oregon Shakespearean Festival in the summer of 1986.

ALEXANDER LEGGATT is Professor of English at University College, University of Toronto. His publications include *Shakespeare's Comedy of Love*, *Ben Jonson: His Vision and His Art*, *Shakespeare's Political Drama*, and *Jacobean Public Theatre*.

KATE D. LEVIN is Pforzheimer Professor of dramatic literature in the English department of the City College of New York. Her work on London's Lord Mayor's shows appears in *The Collected Works of Thomas Middleton*.

CAROL P. MARSH-LOCKETT is an Assistant Professor at Georgia State University where she teaches courses in seventeenth-century literature and African-American literature. She has previously published in the areas of seventeenth-century, African-American, and Caribbean literature.

GEORGE A. E. PARFITT was, until 1991, Reader in Modern English Literature at the University of Nottingham. He has written books on Jonson, Donne, and English poetry of the seventeenth century, as well as two on literature of the First World War. He has edited Jonson's collected and selected poems, *The Plays of Cyril Tourneur*, and an anthology of seventeenth-century verse; and coauthored a biographical dictionary of writing by British women, 1580–1720.

ANNE LAKE PRESCOTT, a Professor of English at Barnard College of Columbia University, is the author of *French Poets and the English Renaissance* and articles on Renaissance topics for such journals as *ELH*, *English Literary Renaissance*, *Spenser Studies*, and *Renaissance Quarterly*. She has recently coedited *Edmund Spenser's Poetry* and is completing a book on Rabelais and Renaissance England.

FRANCES TEAGUE, a Professor of English at the University of Georgia, has published *The Curious History of "Bartholomew Fair"* and a number of articles on Jonson; she has also edited (with John Velz) Joseph Crosby's letters on Shakespeare in *"One Touch of Shakespeare,"* written about *Shakespeare's Speaking Properties*, and edited a collection of essays about *Acting Funny* in Shakespeare's plays.

Index

217